POWERFUL GIRLS
Raising Strong, Just, and Compassionate Young Women

ANN MUNO

ROWMAN & LITTLEFIELD
Lanham • Boulder • New York • London

Published by Rowman & Littlefield
An imprint of The Rowman & Littlefield Publishing Group, Inc.
4501 Forbes Boulevard, Suite 200, Lanham, Maryland 20706
www.rowman.com

86–90 Paul Street, London EC2A 4NE, United Kingdom

Copyright © 2025 by Ann Muno

All rights reserved. No part of this book may be reproduced in any form or by any electronic or mechanical means, including information storage and retrieval systems, without written permission from the publisher, except by a reviewer who may quote passages in a review.

British Library Cataloguing in Publication Information Available

Library of Congress Cataloging-in-Publication Data Available

ISBN 9781538193242 (cloth) | ISBN 9781538193259 (electronic)

∞™ The paper used in this publication meets the minimum requirements of American National Standard for Information Sciences—Permanence of Paper for Printed Library Materials, ANSI/NISO Z39.48-1992.

For Kim
*If grief is "love with no place to go," my
love for you went into my work.*

Contents

Acknowledgments ix

Introduction xi

1: The Incomplete Revolution: Maintaining Momentum for Girls........................... 1
2: The Eight Powers and How to Catalyze Them........ 9
3: Creating Healthy Girl Culture 21
4: Shifting Conflict Norms among Girls 45
5: Developing Race Consciousness and Confronting Racism... 71
6: Using Choice, Not Chance 99
7: Trusting Her Instincts, Voicing Consent 125
8: Celebrating Identity, Not Image 147
9: Deciphering the Codes of Dominant Culture 179
10: Embracing Horizontal Leadership 209

Closing: Visioning a Better World 243

Notes 249

Bibliography 265

Index 277

About the Author 285

Acknowledgments

What it takes to create *Powerful Girls*, the book, is *a lot* like what it takes to support the development of a powerful girl. Immeasurable thanks to the team at Rowman & Littlefield for believing in both.

For the girls and instructors who gave of—and continue to give of—their love and grit to build the girl justice movement: you are the bones, heart, and soul of this book.

For those who "created healthy culture" and helped sort out the heart of the book—Rita Alcantara, Devon de Leña, Sarah Walczyk, Kathryn Robinson, Anne DePue, Isabel Tan, and Jody Rosentswieg—I thank you from the bottom of my heart.

For those who took the power of "shifting conflict" and "being race conscious and confronting racism" and guided me and the book toward a higher understanding of allyship and authenticity in girls' work—Morgain MacDonald, Jaya Duckworth, Chimaera, Hailey Gray, and Danielle Miller—I am deeply indebted.

For those who helped "trust my instincts" in my parenting over many years—my Libertyville High School, U of I, and Seattle community—you are dear, cherished friends, old and new.

For those who wrestled with me about "identity versus image" and shaped an authentic culture for girl justice work to happen in Washington state over many years—Julia Kagochi, Sarah Walker, Amanda Rodriguez, Sarah Veele, Gabriela Ramos, Sammie Alizadeh, Shonda Proby, Tristan Eddy, Kelli Parcher, Arina Gertseva, LeeAnn Delk, Chris Simons, and Wendy Heipt—your loving attention celebrated the work's identity.

Acknowledgments

For all my fellow alums of the Robert Wood Johnson Interdisciplinary Research Leadership Fellowship, thank you for exploring the real-world impacts of the "power of code-switching." The community we've created allowed me a much richer understanding of this power's complexity.

For those who held the book as we debated "the power of choice, not chance" and lived the experience of "horizontal leadership" from start to finish—Julie Edsforth, Laura Culberg, and Katrina Davis—I thank you for being a powerful and hilarious think tank.

For my daughters, Bella, Betelhem, Lena, and Adanech, supporting you in whatever ways you blossom and struggle will always be my greatest mission in life. There would be no *Powerful Girls* without the family we've built and sustained.

To Kevin, for raising *Powerful Girls* across her lifespan, and raising these four powerful girls whom we love so deeply. You are a gem.

And to my very dear mom, Shirl the Pearl; my dad; my tenacious surviving sisters Janice, Aileen, and Laura and their families; and my brother Mark, I say this: our powerful girl Kim, taken so brutally before her time, holds a legacy that *Powerful Girls* honors.

Introduction

In 1976, Libertyville, Illinois, offered little to fear for girls like me. I lived with my parents and five siblings in a split-level ranch in a new housing development, where we were actively involved in both church and neighborhood. My mother, a nurse, worked the swing shift at the local hospital, and my risk-averse father managed risks at a boat motor manufacturer. We ate most of our family dinners around a table purchased with S&H Green Stamps, which my mother diligently collected. On special nights, we'd go downstairs and eat in front of the color TV, careful not to drop food on the new orange shag rug.

My town represented many ideals of White middle-class American life of the 1970s. Local schools had high graduation rates, spirited sports teams, and strong arts programs. College or some type of postsecondary education was expected for most. Family businesses were passed down from one generation to the next. Kids who needed braces usually got them, even if their parents could only pay the lower end of the fee scale. Being out after dark was not something to which we gave a second thought. The town's architecture mirrored a turn-of-the-century movie set, complete with turreted buildings on Main Street's four corners. Libertyville felt like a safe haven where bad things didn't happen.

When I was ten, I was at a sleepover at my best friend's house when the phone rang. "Annie, you need to pack up your things right away," said my friend's mother. I quickly made my last move in our Monopoly game. "I'll leave all the pieces where they are," promised my friend.

INTRODUCTION

I walked the short distance home, wondering about the urgent call, the morning's peaceful silence broken only by the snow crunching beneath my boots. When I opened the front door, I saw my brother, three of my sisters, and my parents sitting in our living room. We never gathered there unless we had company. Sitting with them was a uniformed police officer, who held a coffee cup in his hand. "Your sister did not come home from work last night," said my mother, who was still in her cotton pajamas.

Kim had recently gotten her license and had a job as a salesclerk at the new mall. She was punctual and trustworthy and took her role as the oldest child seriously. Something was wrong. My mother knew it. We all knew it.

Soon many in our community fanned out in a frantic search, while other neighbors and friends brought food and sat in silence with us. Eternity was finally interrupted when the phone rang. My mother ran to answer. "Dead or alive?" we heard her ask. The phone hit the linoleum kitchen floor. Kim's lifeless body had been discovered by a snowmobiler on the banks of a frozen creek. The evidence revealed a gruesome truth—she had fallen victim to an attempted sexual assault and strangulation. Overnight, Kim, my beloved sister, became a murder statistic.

We learned that her murderer was a classmate who asked for a ride after she finished her shift at work. Of course, it's impossible to know how Kim felt about her assailant. Girls in her class came forward to acknowledge that this boy "creeped them out." I imagine that, on some level, her instincts told her the same. But she, like most of us girls in our community, had been socialized to ignore her gut instincts and be polite at all costs.

Back then, we did not understand how widespread gender-based violence was in all levels of society. Back then, in our town, Kim's death was so unusual that the "cheerleader murder" was local front-page newspaper fodder for weeks, eventually making it into the *Chicago Tribune*. Back then, this kind of thing just didn't happen, or so we thought.

Introduction

At her funeral, a brawny group of wrestlers with tear-stained cheeks carried Kim's wooden casket into St. Joseph's. The undertaker managed to hide the marks around her neck with makeup so the casket could remain open. The girl tucked inside was pallid and waxy-looking, an affront to Kim's wavy brown hair, her warm olive-shaped eyes, and her gymnast's sparkle. I alternated between staring straight ahead at the body in the casket and down at the hole in my brown tights. The pews of the church spilled into the aisles. The teen-fronted guitar band sang "Song for Judith," Kim's favorite, and "Raise Him Up," my mother's. The songs were oddly comforting, illuminating a life that I would never again know.

The funeral also marked the beginning of a steady stream of salacious unwanted attention. The trial would start later that spring. My mother and father could not afford to stop working, so my dad wasn't able to attend. My mom worked the hospital night shift. By day, she would sit in the courtroom by herself while the defense attorney implied that my sister was a slut or had "asked for" the assault.

There were some tender mercies that came with the small-town notoriety, enveloping us in subtle ways. The number of lasagnas in our fridge, along with the cases of soda deposited anonymously on our front porch. My mom's supervisor at the hospital purchased Kim's last library book for us—*Little Women*—so the library fines wouldn't stack up. The nearby Benedictine nuns hosted an intimate prayer breakfast, bestowing us with rosaries hand-hewn from the rose petals from Kim's funeral.

While many in our tight-knit community were outwardly comforting, many also—consciously or unconsciously—blamed Kim for what had happened. Even years later, at what would have been Kim's twenty-year high school reunion, one of her schoolgirl friends made a point of saying, "You know, Kim could be kind of a tease"—a not uncommon victim-blaming refrain heard across the country, not just in my community.

Introduction

Even I, mourning my sister, couldn't escape blaming her for the tragedy. I blamed her for leaving me. I blamed her for what happened to the bonds in our family. People felt sorry for us, which filled me with shame. In my floral-covered journal with the gold-plated lock I wrote things like, "Why did she let him get in the car? Why did she do this to our mom and dad?" "We'll work on back handsprings tomorrow," Kim had said as she left for that Saturday work shift at the mall. My journal was peppered with anger about broken promises, all directed at my sister.

At home, my family's once-promising sister culture had turned sour. We'd not only lost Kim as our role model, we'd lost our exemplar of healthy girl culture. If a conflict erupted over what television show to watch, Kim would have been the one to shut the knob off and help us agree on what to watch. She freely pushed boundaries in defining her clothing style and sharing her clothes with us. Everyone's voice, no matter your birth order, had a spot at the dining room table. Without Kim, there was less of that spirit of openness and generosity. It was never Kim's way or the highway. She listened to what we, her siblings, needed, and responded in kind. As we grew older, and in the aftermath of her absence, any time my sisters and I tried to regroup, we fell flat. Instead of nurturing each other, we nurtured the bonds of our trauma. We self-medicated. We sought solace either by having *no* relationships outside of family or by having *so many* outside relationships that we could avoid each other altogether.

As young women, we chose exile from one another as a way to cope with our loss. The fingerprints of grief left on each of us were unique. We had no language for simple conflicts, such as when clothes were borrowed without permission or when one half of the room was a mess when the sister who shared the room preferred order. Yet, anger was taboo. We slammed the door shut on one another—both literally and otherwise—and felt unsafe asking for what we needed from each other.

Introduction

Though Kim's murder marked me as different, I searched for normalcy in this changed landscape. One place I found guidance was at a girls' group offered at a neighborhood church. Each week, Claire, the group leader, in her knee-high patent-leather boots with an aura of beyond-the-suburbs cool, would introduce us to a different "survival skill": what to do when a friend drops you, how to get your grades up, how to make s'mores over a camp stove. We were an eclectic mix from different middle schools: popular girls and sidelined girls, athletic types and bookworms. Together, we dissected issues such as discomfort with our changing bodies, our looks, and the price of popularity.

Claire also spoke to us of the opportunities that went along with growing up in a newly anointed Title IX world, a trail she was blazing even in her early twenties. "I would have *killed* to play volleyball," she'd told us, "but I didn't have a choice. *You* do." So we got to ponder with her: Should we quit cheerleading to try out for gymnastics or softball? Why did we think there were only girls in home economics class? What did we think of the book *Blubber*? These were the kinds of topics we discussed as we sat on the carpeted floor of the church basement and ate popcorn. Claire listened to us, and we learned to listen to each other, a welcome respite from the rest of my life.

Claire's girls' group was a space where I could witness—even welcome—the profound anger I had confined to my diary. By self-policing my anger, I think I felt I could somehow show compassion for my parents, even protect them. Claire's group wasn't therapy, but it provided a space to navigate the confines of societal expectations. It was a place where a girl could explore who she was in relation to the limits of what the larger culture expected.

The group was where I began to define myself by the power *I* had as a girl. As I matured, through high school and into college, I realized that I had internalized an identity—"sister of a murdered girl"—without having been given the tools to make sense of it. Being in a girls' group had helped, but could not provide all the guidance I needed. I remember feeling displaced, angrily questioning my Catholic faith, and severing ties with what had been a spiritual source in my life. After all, what kind of God would allow something like this to happen? Why were people saying things like, "She's in a better place"?

I also unconsciously believed that, since violence against girls and women wasn't a larger issue in the world, it could *never* happen to me. I became too quick to trust boys and began freely experimenting with drugs. I walked home alone along the railroad tracks at night or across campus after evening football games.

It wasn't until my final semester of college, when I accidentally discovered Simone de Beauvoir's *The Second Sex*, that my shift in understanding of "how this could happen" to "why this happens" truly began. De Beauvoir shined a light on the issue of socially constructed gender identities and the internalization of powerlessness, shame, and self-blame that often accompanies this construction. The book marked my initial foray into understanding the broader challenge of violence against women in various contexts—relationships, families, communities, and workplaces. It was a revelation—one that fueled a strong desire for change.

Ten years later, I found myself in a makeshift tent in Beijing, surrounded by women from across the globe. Acting on the advice of a professor from my graduate school social work program, I had flown to China for the United Nations Fourth World Conference on Women. There, I shared cinder-block rooms, meals, and ideas with activists from grassroots organizations worldwide. I engaged with women facing daily struggles against poverty, sexual violence, and extremely limited access to education. On shoestring budgets and with immense courage, they confronted oppressively restrictive governments every day of their lives.

Any initial fear or ambivalence I had about joining the global girls' and women's movement vanished in the face of the political courage exhibited by the 40,000 women in attendance. After

Beijing, I began to ask myself, "Why not me?" Something within me, born in the aftermath of Kim's murder, took root in Claire's girls' empowerment group and flourished as I delved into the language and theory of power and powerlessness. I made a vow to establish something similar to what I had experienced: mentoring and empowerment for girls.

Creating Powerful Voices

I cofounded Powerful Voices in 1995 with two other recent graduates of the University of Washington master of social work program. Our mission was dedicated to creating programs and cultural spaces that foster a more just world for and with girls.[1] Naive yet full of moxie and fresh out of academia, Laura, Julie, and I set up in a converted garage in Seattle while we juggled other social work jobs.

In the halcyon days of the early 1990s, the study of adolescent girls gained widespread attention. Psychologists, journalists, and academics initiated a wave of studies, articles, and books, leading to the emergence of a new movement centered on girls' empowerment.[2] Most newsworthy was *Shortchanging Girls, Shortchanging America*,[3] a report focused on how gender bias hurts girls' self-esteem, school achievement, and career aspirations, while journalist Peggy Orenstein's runaway bestseller *Schoolgirls*[4] reported how Bay Area girls from vastly different communities had real-life experiences that matched the data in *Shortchanging Girls*. Psychologist Lyn Mikel Brown and Carol Gilligan found that many girls silenced their own needs to please others and fit these gender-based expectations,[5] while others examined how girls exert control over each other's health, sexual choices, and overall safety.[6]

Researchers studied aggression among girls and documented the emotional and social harm girls inflict on one another.[7] However, many studies, predominantly conducted by White women, suffered from serious flaws due to inadequate representation. Studies looked at too few Black, Indigenous, and people of color girls.[8] Examining the issues through a White feminist lens overlooked the glaring impact of structural racism on many girls' choices.

At Powerful Voices, we dedicated ourselves to understanding how the gaping holes in the research could be filled through an antiracist[9] understanding of the on-the-ground concepts that Ibram X. Kendi, years later, would describe in his book *How to Be an Antiracist*. In our organization's early days, circa the mid-1990s, having three cofounders like us—that is, White women—meant making mistakes that were fairly common for nonprofits led by people with our demographics at the time. Discussing racism was something we were particularly bad at doing. Becoming defensive when called out for actions that others experienced as racist was something we were particularly adept at doing.

However, in working at Powerful Voices I began to examine my internalized racism, first in the ways I interacted with staff of color. By 2000, I began to recognize where I failed to receive feedback that something I had done had a racist impact, where I expected staff of color to educate me about the burden of everyday racism they experienced, where I tried to shut down staff of color when they talked about their own racial perspectives, where I was reflexively agreeing with fellow Whites' racial perspective. We closely examined the organizational culture to see what aspects felt "top-down" and exclusionary. What was especially helpful was learning about what Kenneth Jones and Tema Okun call "the elements of white supremacy culture."[10] One element that showed up frequently was a continued "sense of urgency," which made it difficult to take time to be inclusive, encourage democratic and/or thoughtful decision-making, think long term, or consider consequences. Another was a perpetual fear of open conflict. We in power were scared of conflict and ignored it. When a staff member raised an issue that caused discomfort, the response was to blame the person for raising the issue rather than exclusionary look at the issue causing the problem. These places where I upheld elements of White dominant culture would eventually push staff of color out, or at the very least to an edge of extreme frustration and nonprofit fatigue.

There was clearly a great deal to unlearn. Over time, by embracing learning and taking accountability for these areas of ignorance, we founders became better at both preventing and addressing conflict, more committed, and accountable for the ways our sense of urgency made decision-making undemocratic. As a staff,[11] we worked to truly trust one another and take the necessary risks to share our fears, our weaknesses, and our challenges. It took years. We had to learn how to listen to one another with compassion. We created new ways to affirm each other and continuously shared credit for the success of the organization and the development of the curriculum.

Over time, the combination of practice, learning, and national research proved pivotal. Grants were secured, and by 2005, ten years after we'd begun, we'd grown to a racially diverse staff of ten, working with hundreds of girls across Seattle. Without a dedicated space, we would drag along our supplies, snacks, and pillows to reach the girls directly in schools, community centers, and detention facilities.

As a staff, we aimed to provide the opportunities we lacked in our own upbringing—healthy competition, conflict resolution, cultural critique, and confronting racism, along with health and educational opportunities. The curriculum evolved based on the girls' expressed needs and powers that mattered to them.[12] Interacting with girls, who ranged from twelve to eighteen, was what grounded every aspect of our shared endeavor.

The mixing of racially different groups of girls didn't appear to happen outside carefully orchestrated opportunities like ours. So at the beginning of each new school year, as the leaves began to fall and the girls switched out of jean jackets for heavier rain gear, we taught girls how to play Common Ground, a game designed to build trust among the group. We led the game by asking the girl, who had agreed to stand in the middle of the circle, to come up with a personal quality or detail about her life. If that quality was shared by other members of the group, they rush to find a new spot outside the circle, leaving one straggler in the middle, who then shared her own quality. We noticed that girls shared aspects of their lives they were proud of, and they were eager to discover who shared these experiences.

"I share common ground with anyone who has a grandmother who lives in another country," said Ruby, a sixth-grade participant from our very first middle school group in 1998. About half of the dozen players scattered, shuffled, and otherwise traded places, desperate to find a spot on the flimsy purple construction paper. "Okay, I share common ground with someone who speaks another language," Ruby offered, sounding a little less enthused this time. There was more movement. Girls ran and tripped over one another to get to an unoccupied spot on the side of the circle—to "win" a round of the game. Though on the surface they seemed frivolous, these games became bedrock to every week's group, a main vehicle for breaking down norms of mistrust. From playing games like these, we learned that the girls enjoyed friendly competition, and often didn't have outlets for it.

Space, we learned, was pivotal. Anywhere we led a group, we remade the surroundings to reflect a culture that resonated with girls. Wherever our group work happened, we created a teen girl's sanctuary, a place of refuge, equal parts cozy and edgy. We taped posters of Venus and Serena Williams, Mia Hamm, and other athletes on the walls. Christina Aguilera, Mariah Carey, and unrecognizable-to-me female musicians enshrined the room. Zebra-striped beanbag cushions circled around an offering of popcorn, carrots, and juice boxes. A handful of dented, candy-striped hula hoops and a skateboard encouraged movement. A large poster on the wall advertised, in curvy, bold typography, the agreements for being a community, such as "Step Up, Step Back" and "What Happens Here, Stays Here."

Introducing girls to alternative sources of media—and teaching girls to critique media—was essential and foundational from the very first groups we ever did in 1998. A media literacy class gave them critical thinking skills to turn away from cultural images and expectations that sexualized, diminished aspirations, or otherwise limited a girl's potential.

That same year we created a Relationships 101 class. The workshop's focus was on teaching girls about how to tell the difference between healthy and unhealthy relationships, and the rights and responsibilities they had within them. Girls left the workshop with an understanding of what they valued in relationships and what made them feel safe, healthy, and respected. We also began to meet individually every other week with a handful of girls to hold a space for them to share what was most pressing, challenging, or in need of a compassionate ear.

In the early 2000s we began working with a local artist to invent Lulu, a life-size, brown burlap fabric, anatomically correct doll for teaching sex education. Lulu had imperfectly shaped breasts that were attached with Velcro and poppy-red cording for a vulva. Her velvet uterus was a regal purple color. Lulu's mission was to help girls understand the body's functional aspects—how many holes females have and what their purposes are—as well as the role emotions play in the decisions a girl makes about her body.

In 2005, we worked with community organizers to develop an identity and community class, which helped girls explore membership in different communities and asked them to explore how belonging shapes or defines who they are. For most girls, the class was the first time they talked openly about stereotypes and their impact. Learning of the real-world impact of racial and economic disparities on those standing next to them was something that stayed with them.

Alongside individual differences, common threads emerged: Each girl needed to establish a robust self-definition to defy pervasive gender- and race-based stereotypes. They learned that collaborating with other girls became crucial to fostering a healthy culture both at home and at school. They set high expectations for themselves and others, made peace with their body images, and gained a real-world understanding of sex.

These qualities formed the foundation for the girls to forge a healthy girl culture and find belonging with each other, qualities that defied mainstream socialization. Recognizing these qualities as sources of power, I observed that girls who consistently used and developed these powers reaped numerous benefits. Some measures of success were immediate, such as girls questioning the media that sexualized them or refraining from participating in bullying on social media. Others manifested over a handful of years, like girls abandoning the tendency to blame their mothers for the economic failures they suffered. The skills they'd learned bolstered the girls' ability to confront obstacles, maintain healthy relationships, and believe in their choices, all of which helped guide them toward their desired futures. Conversations with the girls revealed a shared urgency to ensure that younger sisters, neighbors, and coworkers developed and asserted these same powers. Accidentally learning of their existence was not only unnecessary, it was what one girl called "sisterhood malpractice."

Still, I frequently wondered and worried. What, if any, would the lasting power really be? Despite our best efforts, would the girls we had grown so fond of be doomed to the confidence-stealing, toxic cultural expectations? What lessons would stay alive for them as they grew up?

"I have seen this girls group and the mentoring have a positive trickle-down effect on the other girls in the school," said a ten-year veteran school counselor. She pointed at a mannequin in the school's glass-covered display window covered with healthy messages about body image. "And it looks like *that*."

Introduction

These were good omens, but only time would tell if my hopes or my fears would prevail. My first hint came in 2014 when I literally ran into a girl I'd worked with at a state senate hearing in the marbled halls of our state capitol. "What are you doing here, Ann? Sooooo good to see you," she cooed in a collegial voice. Turns out we were both there to testify on a youth development bill being vetted that morning. We left having promised to get together for coffee to talk about Powerful Voices.

Seeing her made me curious about so many of the girls I'd worked with at Powerful Voices over the years. Where were they? What, if any, was the power they derived from having a lens-shifting experience as girls early in their adolescence? How were their lives shaped as they grew up?

As an evaluator of girls' programs, I was immediately drawn to the challenge of studying what worked. After all, we knew what *wasn't* working for girls. I was able to use social media to reconnect with fifteen girls, most of whom had been out of the program for more than a decade, and I began meeting with them, documenting what had stayed with them.

I talked with most girls at local coffee shops. A few I met on the campuses of universities and community colleges they were attending. Our conversations lasted for an hour or so, and though focused on the research questions I prepared, they were invariably like catching up with an old friend. They wanted to know about other girls ("So how's so-and-so doing?"), the other organizers ("Does so-and-so still work there?"), or me ("How old are your kids now?"). Our reunions were brief, but fulfilling. They always ended with a "words-can't-express" thank you for the culture, tools, and people they encountered at Powerful Voices. At times I felt sad about the hardships or challenges they'd faced since we'd first met. By the end, I was indebted to each girl for agreeing to work through ideas of power and to name how she had used what the program had tried to teach.

Introduction

Fostering a Strong Girl Culture at Home

On-the-job learnings such as these provided valuable skills for parenting my own expanding family. While navigating girls' work, I simultaneously raised four daughters. Throughout this book I wear two hats, that of a mother and that of a girls' advocate. My daughters, all now in their early and mid-twenties, each bring unique experiences and perspectives to our family dynamic. Two of my daughters, Bella and Lena, were born in Seattle and were the first to join our family. Two of my daughters, Betelhem and Adanech, were born in Ethiopia and faced the loss of their biological parents before joining our family at ages six and four.

Countless lessons gleaned from my work with Powerful Voices had a profound impact on our home life, and establishing a healthy girl culture was a daily commitment. By emphasizing the celebration of individual accomplishments instead of promoting competition, my daughters became adept at supporting and applauding each other's successes. Intentional media consumption was the habit long before smartphones became ubiquitous. Trust-building activities were a regular part of our nightly routine. Teaching conflict resolution and effective communication meant instilling in these girls, from a young age, the importance of distinguishing between intent and impact. Identity development in the context of a multicultural, transracial adoptee family included attending the Ethiopian Orthodox church for two of my daughters, arranging for them to regularly speak Amharic, and surrounding our family with supportive members of the Ethiopian community. Confronting racism at home involved believing our daughters when they shared experiences of racism at a playground, acknowledging the White privilege that half the family had, and working through racial and ethnic tensions between us that arose as a result of that privilege. As a family, we set a proverbial place at the dinner table to share difficult topics and experiences where honest feelings could surface.

Introduction

I have looked into the "parent mirror" many times only to see a reflection that challenged the best intentions I had as a mother. I am of a generation with a very different level of involvement and connection to my daughters than my mother and father had. I tried to balance—and possibly worried that I overstepped—the boundaries of being close to my daughters without stifling their sense of self and independence. I feared I may have filled my daughters with faulty expectations of how the world would treat them, or airbrushed the reality surrounding their roles and opportunities in the world. At times, I was at a loss for how to answer questions about sex or the media's portrayal of females. Other times, I tried (and failed) to give constructive criticism about friends, school, or their preferred activities without sounding judgmental or like I was shutting down or judging their choices.

I remember clearly the times I royally flubbed up or fumbled for the right advice. Like when Betelhem, at age eight, said, "Mom, there is a red stain on my underwear," and I had to fight *my* denial that she had gotten her period. Or when Bella was twelve and came to me wearing a pencil skirt instead of her usual soccer sweats, and my eyes widened. "Is something wrong?" she asked with a crinkled brow. I grasped for a response that didn't inadvertently shame her choice while still trying to express how the outside world might treat her because of her outfit. When Adanech was sixteen, I tried to provide constructive criticism about how I felt her friend group was becoming a negative influence. My well-intentioned input came out too harsh, leaving her defensive. "You're just judging my choices again!" she told me. Only recently, eighteen-year-old Lena reprimanded me, "Mom, it is the equivalent of dissing your weight," for the negative comments about aging I made. Still, when mothers and parent figures who know about my day job would ask, "How can I use the tools you've learned at work?" I attempted to respond to their heartfelt curiosity through this book.

INTRODUCTION

Imagine that parenting is also about you wearing the hat of a trusted coach, teacher, or counselor; a guiding instead of controlling force; an adult who puts aside an agenda of expectations and instead creates a space for an open exchange of ideas centered on what accessing power means for a girl in today's world—not what it would have meant for you when you were younger. Fostering a strong girl culture at home depends on it. I also pose a question back. Are *you* willing to do the work of peeling back your own layers?

How to Use the Book

My insights from both work and home inspired the creation of *Powerful Girls*. Crafted as a guided journey through fostering the powers that are so crucial to the girls I worked with and raised, this book is essentially the story of how I observed these eight powers play out for the girls you will meet within its chapters. This book's framing of power in terms of relationships, choice, identity, body, and leadership will help you learn about power with a lens for cultural critique and in a way that is centered in the world girls occupy today. It is also the story of how I developed these powers within myself, and it asks you to do the same. Throughout *Powerful Girls*, keep in mind that:

- I use "girls" as shorthand for "girls and young women," as the practices apply to girls and young women up to age twenty-six.
- to protect their privacy, I have changed the names of the girls who participated in the groups and one-on-one activities.
- to protect their privacy, I have changed the names of the instructors and mentors who led the groups.
- I use the terms "girls of color" and "Black, Indigenous, and people of color" (BIPOC) girls. Using BIPOC highlights the distinct experiences of Black and Indigenous communities, rather than grouping all people of color together. While

BIPOC is widely used by many, others prefer not to use it. I aim to respect how girls have referred to themselves, and so use both terms throughout the book.
- I use the terms lesbian, gay, bisexual, transgender, questioning, intersex, and asexual (LGBTQIA+) to respectfully acknowledge sexual orientation. I use "girls" to refer to anyone who identifies as one, including cis girls, trans girls, nonbinary youth, gender nonconforming youth, genderqueer youth, and any girl-identified youth to respectfully recognize their gender identities.
- I capitalize White throughout the book because choosing to not capitalize White while capitalizing other racial and ethnic identifiers sets Whiteness as the standard and norm. Capitalizing White recognizes the way Whiteness functions in institutions and communities.

You can start working with any one of the powers. Some of the best ways to explore these powers are close to home. At the kitchen table or while driving carpool, you can talk to girls about power and choice. You can adapt the activities throughout the book to start these conversations. Same goes if you are working in a school as a mentor and/or working in an out-of-school program. Adapt the workshops, classes, and activities to fit best with your workplace culture and environment.

The chapters start off by providing a clear definition of what each power is and why it matters. Next, we take field trips to a workshop or a one-on-one experience that brings the power to life. We visit workshops on healthy girl culture, relationships, and gender mending. We travel to places such as Microsoft's Digigirlz program, designed to get more girls into science, technology, and engineering fields, and the Girlvolution conference sponsored by Powerful Voices, which seeks to engage and represent girls in policymaking in places where they are not. Then I give you some specific tips to take into the fold of your relationship with the girl or girls in your life.

Every chapter includes a personal story about how I developed the capacity we're exploring. By sharing my vulnerabilities, I invite you to do the same. Revisiting past experiences isn't always pleasant, but understanding your own journey in developing a particular form of power deeply impacts how you support a girl in doing so. Each chapter provides reflective questions as an exercise to take you back in time. Whether you're using the entire book or not, I encourage you to answer these reflective questions in each of the power chapters.

Finally, using their own words, I share what girls tell me are some of the lasting impacts from connecting with adults in the ways described in the book. The present-day places where policy, programming, and research connect to these impacts are put into context as well. I have closed each chapter with an activity related to developing a particular power. You can use these with a small group of girls or with an individual girl. If you have a handful of girls in your neighborhood, you could start there.

CHAPTER 1

The Incomplete Revolution
Maintaining Momentum for Girls

In today's world, my experience with Claire and the girls' group is called mentoring, youth development, girls' empowerment, or what I call girls' work. These are common terms within the nonprofit sphere where I've worked for the past twenty-five years. However, some still wonder, "Is there a need for conversations about power with girls?" They ask rhetorically, "Aren't girls getting college degrees at a higher rate than boys and enjoying less restrictive gender roles?" I often hear, "My daughter has it way better than I did." Or they point to prominent female figures like Kamala Harris, Michelle Obama, Hillary Clinton, Simone Biles, and Greta Thunberg, suggesting girls already have role models and opportunities. Some even ask, "What about the boys? Why focus on girls when no one is doing well?"

While broader advancements for girls and women have occurred, these don't erase the individual struggles many girls face in finding their places. The trailblazers who paved the way often endured ridicule, harassment, and trauma. Nor should we negate the need to support boys' development, as outlined in books like *Boys Adrift* by Dr. Leonard Sax and *Raising Black Boys* by Jawanza Kunjufu. Continuing the conversation on persistent challenges and barriers for girls *can and must* happen alongside care and concern for boys.

Chapter 1

The girls I have worked with have a lot to say about why they need our continued support and focus on their well-being. As they navigate their formative years, "they are absorbing sexism and racism as unconsciously as they breathe." They tell me that everywhere they go, they are at risk of or are experiencing multiple forms of violence, including sexual assault, unwanted touching, abuse, incest, harassment, catcalling, and stalking—because of their gender, race, sexual orientation, and/or gender identity. Regardless of their race or economic background, they are acutely aware of "the diminished value American society places on their contributions." This awareness often erodes their self-confidence, leaving them doubting the worth of their ideas and opinions. Many grapple with feelings of isolation and a lack of belonging among their peers, unable to articulate the injustice they sense. Mental health challenges, especially anxiety and depression, are epidemic among the girls I work with. In the face of such adversity, there is hopelessness, despair, and an inability to assert themselves in relationships.

What girls tell me is backed up by research across many fields. Particularly alarming is the prevalence of racialized, heteronormative, and gender-based sexual violence.[1] From media portrayals to interpersonal interactions, girls encounter environments where such different forms of violence are disturbingly normalized. About one in four girls will be sexually abused before they turn eighteen.[2] Almost half of the women who have been raped were first raped before age eighteen.[3] About eight in ten women report experiencing street harassment for the first time prior to age seventeen.[4] As they grow into adulthood, BIPOC girls will experience gender-based intimate partner and sexual violence at disproportionate rates,[5] with Indigenous girls, in particular, enduring staggering rates of sexual violence.[6] Hate crimes have reached their highest level in a decade, with two out of three being motivated by a bias against race, ethnicity, or ancestry.[7] Almost one in four high-school-aged girls who identify as lesbian, bisexual, or questioning (LBQ) reported experiencing some form of sexual violence in the prior year.[8] Transgender youth are also especially vulnerable to sexual violence. In one recent study, almost one out of four had reported being raped in the prior year.[9] While legal protections have grown in the last quarter century[10]—such as consent laws, the establishment of the legal definition of *rape*, and the establishment of statutes of limitation for particular sex crimes—they have done little to dissuade or alter the dangerous, toxic, and pervasive cultural norms that feed a culture of "acceptability" and "expectability" of gender-based violence. The trauma inflicted by such violence often manifests in mental health issues, including PTSD and depression, disproportionately affecting girls. Despite legal protections, campus rape remains rampant and largely unpunished and unpublished, contributing to a culture of fear and vulnerability among female students. Even at the highest levels of achievement girls are unsafe, exemplified by Olympic gymnasts Aly Raisman and Simone Biles, who bravely spoke out against the sexual abuse they endured from their team doctor.

Meanwhile, there is a growing mental health crisis among girls. Even before the pandemic, girls were more likely than boys to experience emotional abuse, anxiety, and depression, with BIPOC girls bearing a disproportionate burden. Data from the U.S. Department of Health and Human Services showed that in 2019, 25 percent of Black girls and 24 percent of Hispanic girls had experienced a major depressive episode in the past year, compared to 20 percent of White girls.[11] A study in *JAMA Pediatrics* found that Hispanic girls had higher rates of suicide attempts compared to White girls between 2009 and 2018.[12] Native Hawaiian/Pacific Islander girls also had elevated suicide attempt rates.[13] After the COVID-19 outbreak, there was a drastic spike in emergency room visits for suicide attempts among all teenage girls. One report found that while emergency department visits for suspected suicide attempts were higher among adolescent girls compared to adolescent boys before the COVID-19 pandemic, suspected suicide attempt visits rose 51 percent among girls ages twelve to seventeen in early 2021 compared to the same period in 2019.[14]

There is ample evidence that social media is exacerbating the mental health crisis girls are facing. A 2019 study published in *The Lancet Child & Adolescent Health* found that higher social media use was associated with increased rates of psychological distress, suicidal thoughts, and suicide attempts among adolescent girls.[15] A national survey by the Associated Press-NORC Center for Public Affairs Research found that 48 percent of teenage girls say they struggle with anxiety related to their social media use.[16] A longitudinal study published in *JAMA Psychiatry* tracked adolescents over several years and found that each additional hour per day on social media was linked to increased odds of depressive symptoms, psychological distress, and suicidal ideation among girls.[17] Platforms like Instagram, with their emphasis on unrealistic beauty standards, have been implicated in exacerbating body image issues among young girls, particularly those from marginalized backgrounds. One recent study suggests Instagram's promotion of unrealistic beauty standards and "thinspiration" content can contribute to body image concerns, eating disorders like orthorexia, and psychological disorders related to appearance among vulnerable young female users from marginalized groups.[18]

For girls of Black, Indigenous, or other marginalized identities, the challenges are also more pronounced when it comes to educational barriers. While it is true that compared to generations before them, academic outcomes have improved for girls who identify as BIPOC,[19] it is also true that despite many, many years of calling out the problem, race and gender disparities in opportunity and academic achievement *continue* to disproportionately lead to higher high school dropout rates, limited job opportunities, and increased risk of poverty for BIPOC girls. BIPOC girls are much more likely to attend schools that are underresourced and to have inexperienced or underqualified teachers,[20] and eventually make up the majority of American adults in poverty.[21] In schools that are heavily attended by BIPOC students, girls have fewer opportunities to play sports—a potential road map to higher education scholarships and access—than boys have in the same school.[22] And despite BIPOC girls holding leadership aspirations at inspiringly high rates, they face a number of barriers to realizing those aspirations, including unfair treatment from teachers and administrators because of their race.[23] For Black girls, in particular, harsher treatment in schools is amply evident. Minor offenses, such as dress code violations, talking back to teachers, and defiance, lead to high rates of "pushout" from school.[24] In fact, Black girls in high school are six times more likely to be expelled, three times more likely to be suspended, and four times more likely to be arrested than White girls.[25] BIPOC girls who go to college holding high hopes of a better economic future are juggling classes along with assumptions they are less talented. At institutions of higher learning, overt acts of racism remind them that progress remains elusive, perpetuating cycles of inequality and disenfranchisement.

It is no wonder, given the myriad societal pressures and biases girls face, that their desire and willingness to take on leadership roles tends to decline as they get older. Research has revealed a concerning "leadership labyrinth" where from a young age, girls' leadership aspirations get derailed. A study published in *The Journal of Abnormal Psychology* found that as early as age six, girls rated themselves as less capable leaders than boys did. By age ten, this disparity widened significantly, with girls being much less likely than boys to associate positive leadership qualities like ambition and perseverance with themselves.[26] Longitudinal studies tracking the same girls from childhood through adolescence showed their initial associations of leadership with self-confidence, achievement, and other positive traits became increasingly negative over time.[27] A large-scale international study further reinforced these findings, documenting declines in girls' self-confidence and leadership aspirations across cultures during the adolescent years. The researchers identified gender biases, lack of role models, and societal pressures as key driving forces behind this concerning trend.[28] While girls are growing up to hold strong professional ambitions, the research suggests that societal forces and biased messages increasingly dampen their leadership self-perceptions and motivation during the crucial developmental stages of childhood and adolescence.

This decline in girls' will to lead is particularly vexing when contrasted with data showing young women's career aspirations are simultaneously at an all-time high. The Pew Research Center's 2012 report *Young, Underemployed and Optimistic* revealed that among eighteen- to thirty-four-year-old women, 66 percent rated having a high-paying career or being successful in a high-paying field as "one of the most important things" or "very important" in their lives—higher than the share of young men who felt the same way (59 percent).[29] Meanwhile, high-paying careers remain elusive. The tech industry is a case in point. While making some gains, women and especially women of color remain underrepresented in tech/STEM occupations. As of 2019, women comprised only 27 percent of workers in computer and mathematical occupations. For Black and Hispanic women, the shares were even lower at 15 percent and 7 percent respectively.[30] As of 2022, women working full time earned about 83 cents for every dollar men earned, an improvement from 62 cents in 1979, but a persistent gap. The gap is even wider for most women of color.[31]

Alarmingly, this generation of girls is witnessing a rollback of the rights and opportunities that their mothers and preceding generations of women fought to secure. The erosion of reproductive rights, epitomized by the overturning of *Roe v. Wade*, has set back decades of progress. Political maneuvering, from Title X restrictions to attacks on Title IX protections, further imperils the rights of girls and women. With each shift in political power, the struggle to safeguard and expand these protections intensifies, leaving girls vulnerable to the whims of partisan agendas. It is no wonder when women's political representation in Congress and in state government remains unequal. The 118th US Congress had record numbers of women serving, with 28 percent of voting members being women (149 out of 535 total), but this still lags far behind gender parity.[32] At the state level in 2023, women hold only 31.6 percent of state legislative seats.[33]

Given the challenges girls face all around them, it's crucial to confront the negative cultural narratives that pit girls against each other. So often in our society and communities, girls are taught they should compete with, fight with each other, or build alliances against each other. They participate in creating a negative culture that reinforces the stereotype that girls are catty, competitive, shallow, and gossipy. Without girls' work integrated into how we educate and support girls, when the bars are this low, it's no wonder we see girls behaving aggressively toward one another or using the silent treatment, exclusion, or indirect attacks with gossip.

If we want to shape a radically different, equitable, and better world with girls, these are among the forces we must confront. Until the day arrives when a girl has a greater chance of being mentored in the ways outlined in this book than of being victimized, until there are as many girls in living-wage jobs and on corporate boards as men, we will need to teach girls about how to negotiate and build power. In that spirit, the purpose of *Powerful Girls* is to spark intergenerational conversations about what power is for today's girls, create a fuller version of what power means, and recast girls as change makers in the world. We have our work cut out for us.

Chapter 2

The Eight Powers and How to Catalyze Them

Power need not be a dirty word, but most girls grow up without a way to talk about it. By creating experiences to address this gap, we build momentum for social progress, a chance at living in a world in which no girl is limited by her circumstances. Directed at all who provide care for and mentor girls, these are the powers that are the focus of each chapter:

1. Creating Healthy Girl Culture
2. Shifting Conflict Norms among Girls
3. Developing Race Consciousness and Confronting Racism
4. Using Choice, Not Chance
5. Trusting Her Instincts, Voicing Consent
6. Celebrating Identity, Not Image
7. Deciphering the Codes of Dominant Culture
8. Embracing Horizontal Leadership

Girls benefit significantly from exploring their powers, especially during their teenage years. They expect more from those around them, seeking dynamic relationships that nurture them creatively, spiritually, intellectually, and physically. Unmasking and interrupting shame related to gender, race, sexual orientation, gender identity, or class, they believe in the value of their choices without filtering them through culture-bound expectations or adopting a victim mentality. They seek genuine belonging, cultivate resilience against discrimination, and aspire to higher goals. By connecting emotions to decisions about their bodies, they are better equipped to handle body-image issues and practice effective self-care. They can navigate cultural norms traditionally associated with White middle-class males while pursuing their desire to make a difference as leaders. As they grow up, girls become comfortable with conflict and gain confidence in decoding culture. Many show vulnerability in the presence of other girls, becoming advocates for one another. Their lives open up through experiencing a healthy girl culture and recovering a sense of belonging there. Significantly, many girls begin to forgive their mothers by expressing hard emotions like betrayal and anger, shifting from anger and shame to pride and compassion. As one girl shared, "I started asking my mom more questions about herself . . . We began to fight less and listen more." Another said, "Here I built self-confidence and understood my mom, instead of just getting mad at her point of view." This shift often arose as girls developed a social critique of how women and people of color are devalued in mainstream culture, fostering compassion for the same forces—poverty, low expectations, lack of opportunity—their mothers experienced.

Prerequisites for Doing Girls' Work: Cultivating the Eight Powers within Yourself

"So, what exactly is girls' work?" a social work student asked me during an internship interview.

"Girls' work is mostly about getting out of a girl's way, but first we show up with big aspirational ideas about healthy girl culture, choice, race consciousness, identity, connection to your body and emotions, and striving for leadership in a way that fits with her values. We name and teach concrete skills that go beyond these ideas, so girls build upon feelings of competence in these areas. Then we get out of the way."

"What qualifies you or anyone to do girls' work?" she probed. I could see why her curiosity mixed with a very healthy skepticism. As I ran through a list of top-of-mind considerations, qualifications like the abilities to normalize conflict and disagreements, use elements of girl culture as a point of connection, blend what girls want to learn with what I think they need to know, and support a girl in seeing multiple forms of leadership in herself, I sensed the deeper question she was asking.

"Girls' work isn't a one-person job," I offered. "Girls need to see a community of folks from racially different backgrounds who practice antiracism and affirm sexual orientation and gender identity so they know what that looks like. The creation of the 'we,' the community of adults, mentors, teachers, mothers, fathers, and other mothers, who can help girls see themselves outside the boxes they tend to be in, is essential. Each of the girls you are engaging needs to see herself in relation to a broader set of potential role models. For girls of color, it is especially important to see women of color who can relate to the experiences of being 'othered' because of their race."

Equally important, I told her, is the work a person needs to do in order to do girls' work. This involves the peeling back of one's own layers of identity, privilege, powerlessness, trauma, and motivation for doing this work. That's true whether you are a mentor or a parent. The following are the bedrock considerations on which the work is built:

- How connected to your own identities are you? Have you engaged in addressing any shame that you are holding in relation to these? Do you feel pride in who you are?
- Are you willing to do the continuous learning of owning your racial privilege if you are White? In an ongoing way, have you considered what you have lost or gained as a result of your racial identity in a system of racial oppression? Have you considered how you will use what you've gained to recover what we've all lost?

- How do your experiences of power or powerlessness as a youth impact you now?
- What are your main motivations for doing girls' work? When you look inward, what motives do you see for wanting to help empower girls? Are you willing to step back if what drives you is more about your needs than their needs?
- What are your experiences with a healthy or unhealthy girl culture growing up? How do these experiences shape your beliefs about the potential girls have to support one another?

If you can't commit to developing self-awareness related to these aspects of working with girls, you may not be using your time well. Or worse, you can do harm to a girl. The bottom line? It is essential to engage these questions for yourself to successfully use the tools shared here. Doing so is a prerequisite for doing girls' work.

At Powerful Voices, we also integrated girl-centered practices with effective youth development practices using the Youth Program Quality Assessment (YPQA) framework to evaluate our girl-specific programming.[1] While sharing common features like safety, peer culture, social skills, and belonging, our girl-centric model added value by intentionally attending to the cultural context in which these girls lived their lives. For example, our framework, shaped by the Ms. Foundation study[2] and Powerful Voices' fieldwork, views safety specifically in terms of developing healthy girl-to-girl and mother-daughter relationships. The leadership skills developed in the girl-specific framework help girls shape empowered identities as girls of color. They become leaders who challenge society's oppression of people based on gender and race as well as other societal disadvantages such as class, sexual orientation, and ability. Similarly, the girl-specific model promotes social change and activism opportunities as critical to girls' struggle for identity and their ability to respond to injustice. Progress was not linear but dynamic; often one step forward was followed by two steps back. For example, as girls developed trust with instructors and as instructors held higher expectations, some girls disclosed issues of abuse or family chaos that prevented them from working in small groups, a desirable facet of interaction in the YPQA pyramid. For these girls, the safer they felt with instructors, the more they needed outside support before they could engage with the group as a whole, undertake projects, and meet higher expectations.

As one instructor noted, "The [YPQA] model tied really well with what we were already doing, while giving us a youth development language that was widely spoken." By blending the two models, Powerful Voices created a holistic approach speaking to girls' unique needs while adhering to quality standards. The YPQA has been widely adopted by youth-serving organizations across the United States and internationally, suggesting its practical usefulness and acceptance in the field. However, like any evaluation tool, the YPQA has limitations, such as the potential for observer bias and the need for ongoing training.[3]

Guiding Principles for Raising Powerful Girls

Throughout the years of running girls' groups, the curriculum and learnings have gelled into a framework of practices that translate into girls' empowerment. Through my own experience and practice, I have come to believe that there is a wide and well-grooved path toward socializing girls for power in a world that systematically strips them of it, so long as we walk alongside them.

Socializing girls for power is an ongoing experience, and these principles and practices are the foundations that steady that experience. If you become fluent in these and frequently review these as measures of change, you will begin to notice, even in small doses, a shift in a girl's attitude, behavior, and beliefs.

1. A girl's power is *personal*. It's about developing her sense of agency, and a belief that she has a right to use her agency in her life given her values, identity, and community.

2. A girl's power is not about *her* power only. Socializing a girl to access her power succeeds in direct proportion to *her* ability to stop blaming other girls for the toxic girl culture that surrounds her, and to acknowledge the privileges and oppressions that accompany her racial and sexual orientation, gender identity, and expression.
3. When a girl holds an equal understanding of both her free choice and where an illusion of choice exists, she is socialized to access her power.
4. Socializing a girl to access her power is dynamic and nonlinear.
5. Her power is not *your* power. Stay aware, and catch yourself when forcing your expectations or needs onto a girl.

CREATING PRACTICES TO BUILD THE EIGHT POWERS

There are pivotal tools in girls' work that you will need to become familiar with using. Some are about paying attention to what you need to learn or unlearn as an adult. Others are about paying attention to and providing what girls need. Some are centered around the process of creating a healthy girl culture together. These are primary benchmarks for holding yourself accountable to providing a solid experience, and a healthy girl culture, whether in a group or individually. Others are centered on diving more deeply and consistently into understanding your own identity, privilege, power, powerlessness, trauma, and motivation for doing this work.

A successful experience in which adults are fostering girls' inherent power requires the consistent use of all of the tools that are mapped here. This section broadly and conceptually covers what I call "power tools." In subsequent chapters, I drill down into how they can be put into direct practice when developing each of the powers. These girl-centered practices were forged not only in girl-specific programming, but also with practices known to work best in the broader youth development field.[4]

POWER TOOL #1: TEACHING THE HEALTHY GIRL CULTURE CODE

Many girls are taught to believe that dominant cultural expectations should define their worth and value. Many have not had very positive experiences with other girls and blame girls for the conditions created by dominant cultural expectations. Many accept negative stereotypes about themselves and their identity groups. By pointing out what healthy girl culture looks like and giving girls opportunities for authenticity, girls build an appreciation of their own cultural group and subgroups. Practical ways you can work with girls to create healthy girl culture in groups and one-on-one are:[5]

1. Teaching girls how to create and agree on community norms of respect for one another, such as give-and-take, stage sharing, using your own experiences, owning White privilege, and practicing antiracism. These are ways you can create a culture of respect together and not assume what safety means to a girl in a group.
2. Teaching girls the difference between intent versus impact when they commit microaggressions based on race, religion, disability, and/or sexual orientation and gender identity. Recognizing that even if one's intent was not harmful, the impact of one's words or actions on others is significant.
3. Holding girls accountable for adhering to these community norms of respect. By consistently doing so, the behaviors, attitudes, and language that fit with the values and goals of the community become solidified.
4. Witnessing and engaging in conflict among girls, not shutting down the conflict. Don't be afraid of tensions, conflicts, or disagreements. You may be tempted to move too quickly out of the conflict to deal with your own discomfort. Instead, normalize conflict so girls become adept at engaging in conflict themselves.

5. Possessing an awareness of the needs and concerns of girls' communities. Knowing the common values, identities, location (neighborhood, city, school), culture, religion, and historical background of a girl's community is essential to earning her trust, and supporting her to see potential sources of pride and resilience all around her.

Power Tool #2: Igniting Critical Consciousness, Fueling Girl Leadership Development

As a result of internalized stereotypes, many girls hold serious doubts about their own potential, including their abilities to lead. When we use strengths-based language as we challenge girls to grow their skills, we help them develop confidence in their belief that their actions make a difference. Practical ways you can work with girls to create and expand girls' critical consciousness in groups and one-on-one are:[6]

1. Introducing and defining language that develops a critical lens to see sexism, racism, and other forms of oppression they experience. When we support a girl to see and make personal meaning of these forces, she can begin to name and undo how power dynamics impact her present and future opportunities.
2. Fostering growth by facilitating opportunities to reflect on successes, set goals, and plan concrete steps to achieve them. Supporting a girl to reflect on and practice decisions, choices, and behavior with future goals in mind leads to a stronger sense of hope, perseverance, and self-control.
3. Calling out what skill development is, especially with authority figures. When we grow a girl's understanding of why skills like engaging effectively in conflict, making informed decisions about present and future goals, and tapping adults for the types of support they need, she sees how these are applicable to her real life.

4. Providing activities focused on pride in identity, achievement, and activism. By doing so, you are actively combatting negative beliefs, shame, and a lack of agency that can accompany a girl's self-perception.
5. Helping girls articulate multiple forms of leadership. When we actively help a girl develop a language for seeing her individual strengths as a leader, there is a greater chance she will hold onto her will to lead as she grows up.

POWER TOOL #3: CHECKING YOUR OWN ASSUMPTIONS AND BIASES

Girls are often mistreated and disrespected simply because they are young. As adults, many of our behaviors and attitudes are based on the (often unconscious) assumption that we know better and are entitled to act upon young people without their consent. When we check ourselves and model authenticity and accountability, girls express greater vulnerability and develop trust in us as facilitators. Practical ways you can work with girls to check your adult biases are:[7]

1. Refraining from projecting your experiences onto girls. Making the assumption that a girl experiences or feels things the same way you do can seriously thwart her ability to connect with you. This cuts you off from really understanding the reality of her life, and it cuts a girl off from defining her own experience.
2. Being aware of racial biases. Work to understand how your background and experiences are shaped by race and racism. Educate yourself about the impact of racism and its history, and be open to feedback and hold yourself accountable when acting in ways that perpetuate racist beliefs and actions.
3. Articulating your role and limitations as a facilitator. Be prepared to say what you can and cannot do to support a girl.

Be aware of the tendency many adults have to try to "rescue" rather than truly support a girl in tapping her own power.
4. Admitting when you do not know something and being committed to your own learning. Be aware of the behaviors and attitudes you hold that are based on the assumptions that adults are better than and know more than young people.
5. Acknowledging the privileges and oppressions that accompany your identities. When you can name the power you hold or do not hold in relation to your identities, you are better able to upend power dynamics with youth and can better support girls in authentically developing their own power in relation to their identities.

POWER TOOL #4: MAKING SPACE FOR GIRLS' FEELINGS

Emotions are an important factor in girls' decision-making, yet girls may mask their feelings because they have learned that others don't react well when they express them. *Validation* is the recognition and acceptance of a girl's thoughts, feelings, sensations, and behaviors as understandable, given her history and biology. It's important to normalize the range and depth of emotions that any girl might have in a growing process. Practical ways you can work with girls to make space for girls' feelings in groups and one-on-one are:[8]

1. Validating girls as they give voice to their own feelings and opinions. Girls often prioritize their relationships when making decisions and can place their own needs secondary. By reflecting back what they say they feel and believe, you can support a girl in prioritizing her own needs and aligning her choices with her values.
2. Helping girls make the connection between their emotions and the choices they make. This is especially helpful for helping a girl see how decisions she makes about her body—for instance, what she eats or wears—are influenced by others

and instead become more aware of how she can take control of decisions she makes about her body.
3. Supporting girls as they hold ambivalence and frustration with the dominant culture and the oppression it perpetuates, and as they develop skills to actively challenge it.
4. Encouraging girls as they hold an appreciation of their own cultural group. Support a girl in developing a deeper understanding of what truly makes her who she is: her history, beliefs, and identities.
5. Validating girls as they navigate dominant culture and combat stereotypes. By developing an understanding of stereotypes she has experienced as discriminatory and harmful, she can begin to reject these and identify experiences and people that help her gain pride in her true identities instead.

These guides are simply a way of making sure you are growing and tweaking how you show up so that girls' needs remain at the center of the experience. Generally speaking, projecting your experiences onto girls is something to diligently watch out for. Although these boundary violations can show up in a handful of ways, they typically take one of the following forms identified by girl program researchers:[9]

- romanticizing girls
- sheltering or underestimating girls
- overidentifying with something they've experienced

By consistently using these tools, I learned more about what girls *say* they need, and what powers mattered to *them* individually.

All these practices have a hand in shaping the power we are socializing girls for. All of them hold adults accountable in ways that are essential to the process. In working with this book, I hope you will experience rewarding, guided engagement with how you developed your own power: your healthy and unhealthy experiences with other girls, the sources of pride in your identities, your hopes and fears that blossomed or were dashed because of the power you were socialized with, and the style of leadership you came to value. Instead of saying, "God, I wish I had a program like that growing up," I hope you will feel a sense of community with others who are dedicated to *being* that program for girls in their communities.

So, are you ready to practice girls' work? Feelings of humility and discomfort are excellent signs. Are you slightly afraid? Are you saying things like, "What do I know?" or "Who am I to step into a girl's life in this way?" These are signs that you are self-scrutinizing the way you use power in your relationships with girls. This is the work you will *always* be doing in girls' work. It's a good sign.

CHAPTER 3

Creating Healthy Girl Culture

POWER #1

A girl who understands the power of creating a healthy girl culture knows how to build trust, embrace healthy relational dynamics, and reject societal norms of female competition and power struggles. By elevating expectations for how girls treat one another—reframing give-and-take, fair conflict resolution, meeting emotional needs, and sharing passions—she takes a new yardstick of belonging out into the world. Setting a higher bar for the girls around her has profound influences beyond just the girl culture she inhabits. This also has a ripple effect on the intimate partners and relationships she cultivates as she matures and elevates the society she helps create.

In recent years, historians, social scientists, and psychologists have helped to paint a fuller portrait of how social mistrust among girls gets passed down.[1] "Girlfighting is not a biological necessity, a developmental stage, or rite of passage. It is a protective strategy and an avenue to power learned and nurtured in early childhood and perfected over time," states scholar Lyn Mikel Brown in her 2003 book *Girlfighting: Betrayal and Rejection among Girls.* Brown's study examines the phenomenon of relational aggression and conflicts among racially and economically diverse groups of girls ages eight to eighteen. "Girlfighting behaviors" like gossiping, exclusion, bullying, and physical aggression to jockey for power and status in and outside their friend groups are grist for a toxic girl culture.

Brown contrasts "girlfighting" with more positive forms of female community based on empathy, loyalty, and directness, and criticizes how adults often dismiss or trivialize girls' relational conflicts as "just drama" rather than taking them seriously. But girls rarely (if ever) have had the opportunity to build an inclusive culture rooted in the values, behaviors, and agreements that align with a vision of healthy female friendships that this power seeks to instill. Instead, as they move through puberty, many internalize destabilizing competitions, limiting gender roles, and expectations that make authenticity in relationships all but impossible.

Subsequent researchers have built upon Brown's findings, amplifying the understanding of relational aggression and its implications. Tracy Vaillancourt and Dorothy Espelage are preeminent scholars investigating what underlies relational aggression behaviors like gossip, exclusion, and rumor spreading, ranging from individual traits to environmental influences. Vaillancourt has focused on the long-term impact of relational aggression, as well as bystander roles, on mental health, academics, and social adjustment. Espelage has explored intersections between relational aggression and other bullying forms like physical and cyberbullying, particularly for marginalized groups like LGBTQIA+ and disabled students. Both have developed and assessed interventions promoting healthier relationships and social-emotional skills through classroom curricula, school policies, and community initiatives. Collectively, their work illuminates the complex dynamics of relational aggression while providing evidence-based strategies for fostering more positive, inclusive environments for youth.[2]

Years of viewing media, and now especially social media, is a huge culprit in perpetuating unhealthy girl culture. Girls are exposed to hundreds or even thousands of images and photos every day, as young girls are asked to "compete" with airbrushed models and celebrities who spend hours a day in the gym. Endless and unconscious scrolling leads to an internalization of beauty ideals that are unattainable for almost everyone, resulting in greater dissatisfaction with body weight and shape. A 2022 survey by the Pew Research Center found that 29 percent of teenage girls say they are online "almost constantly," compared to 20 percent of teenage boys. This same report revealed that 35 percent of teens say they have been bullied, harassed, or threatened online, which can compound issues like poor body image. Moreover, 46 percent of girls ages thirteen to seventeen report often or sometimes being called offensive names or having rumors spread about them online.[3] The prevalence of girls' near-constant engagement with social media documented in this report aligns with concerns about its potential to amplify toxic pressures and behaviors surrounding body image and self-worth.

The divisions inherent in an unhealthy girl culture are amply evident among girls of different racial backgrounds. Although the cultural climate has increasingly accepted and promoted racial solidarity, particularly following the 2020 murder of George Floyd, racial solidarity remains the exception rather than the norm. Rather than becoming easier, interacting across racial differences is increasingly challenging as racial segregation in schools—crucial environments for fostering integration—continues to rise.

In the 2020–2021 school year, over six million students attended public schools that were racially or ethnically segregated, with at least 75 percent of students belonging to the same race or ethnicity.[4] And while diverse schools offer the potential for cross-racial interactions, research has consistently shown that even in these settings, students tend to self-segregate along racial lines.

This phenomenon, known as "second-generation segregation," is characterized by voluntary clustering of students within racially homogeneous friendship groups, extracurricular activities, and social spaces. Factors contributing to this include peer influence, shared cultural experiences, and social identity formation. These divisions can perpetuate racial stereotypes, limit meaningful interracial contact, and undermine the intended benefits of diverse educational environments, despite physical proximity.[5]

There is a negative cumulative impact on girl culture when girls are denied the opportunity to engage with one another and explore power in healthy ways. So often in our society and community, girls—no matter their background—are taught they should compete, fight with each other, or build alliances against each other. They are taught to make enemies of one another. Then they are blamed for participating in creating a negative culture that reinforces the stereotype that girls are catty, competitive, shallow, and gossipy. When the bars are this low, it's no wonder we see girls behaving aggressively toward one another or using the silent treatment, exclusion, or indirect attacks with gossip.

What do we lose when what's communicated as culture is debasing and degrading? What gets lost, consciously or unconsciously, is the hope that girls and women will have your back, that there is an antidote to confront the shallow, socially conditioned impulses that stack us against each other. It's time to restore the hope that healthy girl culture is entirely possible.

DEFINING POWER #1: THE HEALTHY GIRL CULTURE ANTIDOTE

When she first started middle school, Ruby was a shy newcomer grappling with her undocumented status and cultural identity as a Mexican immigrant. She looked for a seat in the back of each class to avoid being called on, but she also wanted to break out of the isolation she experienced as someone hiding her immigration status. Being undocumented overshadowed many aspects of her school experience, with fear pushing her into the background. An encounter with a classmate led her to visit our girls' group in the fall.

Ruby deeply connected with the program's values of mutuality and equity. These values were fostered in community with other girls who had earned her trust. A healthy girl culture provided her with a space to appreciate her Latina identity while challenging the limits imposed by her culture. Simultaneously, it helped her navigate the exclusionary norms at school. The group served as a focal point for exploring the health of all her relationships. You will meet Ruby in this chapter, and her journey will be shared as we learn about this power.

Ruby's example isn't unique. Girls who form communities in this manner are encouraged to earn each other's trust and expect respectful treatment from others in their wider circles. We often miss the obvious, that healthy relationships like the ones Ruby developed in the group are the antidotes to social toxins. Extensive research over the last three decades consistently illuminates that relationships are uniquely influential on a girl's development and behavior.[6] If her social world offers few healthy relationships, she experiences pervasive negative impacts and more emotional strain, because she has been socialized to focus on relationships.[7] This is particularly true in adolescence, when relationship conflict can make her feel rejected and depressed,[8] and she is at higher risk of more severe forms of intimate partner violence (IPV) and will suffer more severe consequences as a result of IPV, such as mental health decline, economic insecurity, and/or academic underachievement.[9]

Teaching about harmful societal expectations in girl relationships helps girls stop blaming each other and allows for them to shift their focus to building alliances. Developing awareness, coupled with a belief in a girl's agency to transition from toxic to generative cultures, is crucial. Hands-on methods to nurture healthy girl culture enable girls to build positive alliances and elevate the quality of all their relationships over time.

I've observed numerous positive changes as a girl develops the power to create a healthy culture with her peers, such as a girl growing in her capacity to:

- express anger constructively when feeling disrespected.
- embrace her authentic self, shedding the pressure to feign niceness.
- disengage from media that undermines her or another girl's self-worth.
- reject body shaming, embracing body satisfaction.
- decline unwanted sexual advances, identifying her own needs in romantic and sexual relationships.
- display kindness through body language, such as offering smiles to unfamiliar girls in the hallway, signaling allyship.
- make an effort to pronounce each girl's name correctly.
- avoid stereotyping girls with identities or experiences different from theirs.
- advocate for choice and equity, eschewing values based on appearance.
- foster language and expectations that respect all girls.
- create media and art that challenge stereotypes.
- define her personal style freely.
- hold romantic partners to higher standards of thought and communication.

Reflecting on environments where girls encounter either healthy or unhealthy girl cultures—whether in sports teams, dance teams, school musicals, church groups, homes, carpools, or online communities—provides insight into the positive impact we can have. It's in these spaces where we can envision what is possible for girls, creating a culture that truly honors them.

DEVELOPING THE POWER: HEALTHY GIRL CULTURE 101

On a crisp autumn day, amidst the vibrant fall foliage, a one-story church turned community center becomes a haven for a girls' group. Encouraged by school counselors, teachers, and parents, a dozen teenage girls from various urban schools in Seattle come together to explore empowerment within a community of their peers. At their schools, some are in student government, some are excelling in academics. Others feel like they are on the margins, invisible. Some have been truant.

The space, despite its faded charm, radiates a sense of calm and refuge, somehow blending cozy and edgy vibes. A large poster of group agreements centers the tone of sanctuary and respect. It leads with "What Happens Here, Stays Here."

Vivian and Nat, the group leaders, welcome me. Vivian, a second-generation Filipina, has an independent spirit that is reflected in her eclectic, thrift-store clothing ensemble. Nat, a petite White woman with an array of tattoos, speaks in soothing tones. "Managing this group has been challenging," Nat admits. "Some members interrupt frequently, while others remain quiet or disengaged. We are actively working on more supportive dynamics."

We pause the conversation as the girls arrive and start to settle in. "Today's class is on building a healthy girl culture," Nat announces to the group. She outlines the objective: to understand what this culture entails, what it doesn't, and how to cultivate it.

To kick off, Vivian introduces the game Common Ground, designed to help the girls find shared interests and experiences. "I share a love for pizza," one girl states, prompting a flurry of movement as participants find commonalities, from family dynamics to music preferences. The game, punctuated by ten rounds, lightens the mood before we pause for snacks.

The activities here are designed to grow awareness and build self-confidence as girls become mindful of the dynamics of female competition, racial differences, divisions, and where they experience their own power. At lunch, in the hallways, and during most other "free" social times, the mixing of racially different groups of girls rarely happens outside carefully orchestrated opportunities like the ones provided here. Trust *building* in describing this activity is a misnomer. Trust *earning* is more accurate. Games can be a fun, engaging way to build a culture of respect, but there is also depth to what games can provide. For instance, games are a way of exploring the many differences in the ways respect is shown at a girl's home, which deeply influences how she gives and receives respect elsewhere.

As I watch the girls run, trip over one another, and play, I notice, too, that while girls across different backgrounds and identities are very eager to discover who shares their experiences and interests—having a sibling, celebrating religious holidays, following certain social media influencers—there is a temporary gloss over the holes in their understanding of where they hold privilege and power, and indifference toward the impact of these.

For instance, having pets, taking extended summer vacations, and babysitting younger siblings instead of playing sports or participating in after-school activities are markers of differing levels of socioeconomic privilege—who has it and who doesn't. Surfacing these markers as we work to name common experiences in the girl community can feel like a balancing act. Is this fair to ask, I wonder? Is it too much of a burden? But where else, if not here, will they have any opportunity to break open the assumptions they have about the other girls in the group? Healthy girl culture thrives in the light of open dialogue.

The game winds down, and Vivian tees up a new conversation.

"Where do we get these messages on how a girl should act or look?" she asks in a more serious tone. "What does it feel like to be a girl in your world?"

The girls consider the communities they inhabit, from family, neighborhood, and friends to school, religious, and extracurricular activities. Nat writes on the slab of paper, "What do you think 'girl culture' means?" The girls get more animated and involved as they tackle this question. They pass around pieces of paper with names of locations on top—bus stop, mall, home, school—drawing and writing how they act and interact with girls in these different places.

One draws a big thought bubble and writes "Rumors" in bright orange. Underneath it are notes like, "It [starting rumors] happens for all kinds of reasons like jealousy, to stir it up, insecurity," and "Some girls are willing to make other girls' lives worse by starting lies." Another thought bubble reads "Using."

Under this, girls write, "When a girl hangs out with someone so she can get something from her, getting higher on the social ladder, help on homework, get a guy."

Nat probes, "What are girl interactions like here? What do you see and hear? And, finally, why do girls treat each other like this?"

At this final question, the room falls silent. Girls clearly find this difficult, and after pausing a bit, Vivian steps in to break the ice. "Is this the best we've got? You all know it doesn't have to be this way."

And they do. In the group and others like it, some girls will learn to curb their need for center stage, while others will become more comfortable in the spotlight. Girls agree to keep their conversations confidential and not make assumptions about other girls based on looks. As the school year unfolds, the girls explore the question of why there is often a debilitating default to negativity among girls. They brainstorm ways this can be countered to create a positive girl culture.

"Early on we support girls in thinking critically about how they relate to and think about other girls. That's not enough, though," Nat relates. "This is a place where they discover a previously unnamed set of values, such as critical and appreciative thinking, activism, and access to their personal experiences."

CHAPTER 3

Six months later, I see a department-store-type mannequin in the display case at a school attended by some of the girls' group members. Instead of displaying trendy clothing, the lifelike figure wears artwork. She greets each guest with written messages that express positive images of girls and more relatable messages about their bodies. At the girl group closing event that spring, girls in unison chant, "Do you hear us? We are HERE." One school counselor leans over to me and says, "I have seen this girls' group multiply a positive effect on all the other girls in our school. They hold off on judging, block out the noise. They know they have to expect better from each other."

Moving forward, this group of girls commits to practicing the positive girl culture they experienced in different places—at the dinner table, on the job, in the locker room. A little bit of healthy girl culture goes a long way as they begin to recast female competition into a more generative model. They understand the need to shed a scarcity mindset of not having enough and shift to a collaborative model rooted in abundance.

KEEPING IT GOING: RELATIONSHIPS CLASS

In the bustling atmosphere of the Healthy Relationships class, Ruby found her place among her peers, settling into the informal circle with an air of quiet anticipation. The group, alive with the chatter and laughter of her classmates, would dive into discussions that promised to stretch beyond the conventional curriculum.

Hana and Cole, two biracial AmeriCorps volunteers leading the group, have a unique approach to guiding the girls through the group's content. They share personal stories, drawing from their diverse backgrounds to connect and teach. Hana, with her sharp wit honed in Philadelphia, engages immediately. "She's all truth, no fiction," one girl says, appreciating Hana's directness. Cole, a Pacific Northwest native, complements with her calm and balanced perspective. Together, they're a powerful duo, demonstrating through their interactions the essence of healthy relationships.

As the session begins, more girls trickle in. Hana sets the tone: "Today, we'll explore what makes a relationship healthy or unhealthy. We'll be thinking about what you value in relationships and how to express your boundaries." She emphasizes the importance of creating a safe and supportive community, inviting the girls to redefine safety on their terms.

Hana offers a check-in question, making eye contact, clockwise, with each girl. "What's a relationship that either makes you feel free or cages you in?" This question isn't just about relationships; it's about understanding and asserting one's definition of safety, often for the first time.

"My mom cages me when she tells me what to wear or how to act as a girl," ventures Ruby, who is especially engaged in the conversation today. Many girls echo her sentiments, defining safety as being able to trust the adults around them to not shame or punish them when they try to freely express themselves or share their thoughts and opinions. The other responses vary, touching on personal freedom, racism, and family expectations. The discussions highlight the importance of trust, respect, and the freedom to express oneself without fear of judgment or reprisal.

In her slanted handwriting, Cole writes the next topic on the whiteboard: "Write or draw symbols for ten things you want in a relationship. When you are done, cross off five from your list, then another and another and another, until only one thing is left."

What she was introducing was the idea of how many of us give up what we want in relationships without really thinking about it. This is often rooted in a lack of understanding of our own needs and wants in a relationship.

After five minutes of writing and relative quiet, Cole prompts the girls, "Whatcha got?"

A girl wearing a Seahawks jersey calls out, "Loyalty, kindness, protection, fun."

Hana writes these on a poster-size paper under "Healthy Relationships." A number of comments follow: "respect" "has your back" "laughs." Another girl adds, "MR. RIGHT."

"How do you decide on Mr. Right?" Hana probes. "What does that mean to you? And what if you don't want a Mr. Right?" She steers the introductory conversation back to the topic of emotional safety. There is a pause as they consider. "Has anyone heard the expression 'girls who live to give'?" she asks. "It describes someone who puts the needs of everyone else over their own. As women, we are often taught we should be selfless and nurturing, and this is often at our own expense." Hana has the girls' attention.

"One of the most valuable skills a girl can learn is to set boundaries," she continues, "to be vulnerable with someone but not defined by that person. And today we want to talk about what this looks like."

These conversations give girls the rare permission to question the quality of their relationships and to define safety for themselves. Girls get in touch with their boundaries—around preferences for physical space, touching, emotional neediness, and criticism—and discover that they can reject being defined solely by the needs of another. They learn to ask themselves when it is safe to be vulnerable. They develop a growing awareness that mutuality is a right, give-and-take is a communication skill, and self-advocacy is a language they can practice and improve.

One-on-One Power Building:
Values Exploration Visit

As the Relationships 101 class progressed, it became clearer to girls that a healthy relationship should reflect their deepest values. Hana had asked the girls to think carefully about the values that make them feel safe, healthy, and respected in a relationship. These values were so important that they warranted a deeper conversation in one-on-one mentoring time.

On the day that I come to do that follow-up exploration of relationship values with Ruby, we meet at a quiet table in the corner. To be clear, this is not counseling. In girls' work, we adapt a values-based model of coaching to help Ruby identify and explore the personal values she is uncovering.[10] Simply put, the goal is to focus on the present, the values that Ruby holds dear, and the choices she can make to fully live those values as she works to achieve her goals.

Ruby knows the nature of the mentoring program is to talk about what she values and what she is learning on a one-to-one basis. She is aware that confidentiality will be honored with the important exception of if her or another's safety is at risk. In the event Ruby needs to work through past trauma, we have established an additional level of support from the school counselors.

We start with a check-in. Ruby feels more at ease, much more than she did on her tentative first day with the group. We then move to the conversation cards. I display images of noted activists, a half-blooming field of red poppies, and more. We call these symbol cards, and you can use these to explore experiences of personal power and activism. Ruby's eyes show interest as she adjusts herself to reach for one. "You can choose a few that grab you, and then tell me about a time that you found yourself connecting to something on the card."

There are so many spread out, covering most of the space between me and her, that I start to wonder if this was overwhelming. I resist any impulse to hurry her. Ruby selects the symbol cards of a girl jumping off a diving board into the deep end, lonely dunes, and a doll. She says to me in a whisper, "I want to tell you about where I was born."

Over time, we talk about Ruby's life experience, values, and interests. Just as in the group we establish a culture of trust between women and girls. Our hope is simple. We want Ruby to hear herself say what she needs as a starting point for forming healthy relationships. We want her to understand the power of give-and-take, of not automatically giving in to someone to avoid conflict, and of viewing herself as an equal in relationships.

POWER TOOL: PARENT/MENTOR TIPS FOR CREATING HEALTHY GIRL CULTURE

- Reframe Female Rivalry, Reject Scarcity Mindsets

  Being well versed in power dynamics means you are not feeding the idea that "she's just jealous" of you because you meet a societal expectation like being pretty or popular. It is important to shut down the "girls are just mean" refrain. Rather, it's essential to scrutinize societal norms and the cultivation of competition among girls. Clinging to the "mean or jealous girl" stereotype reinforces the status quo. Let's inspire girls to champion unity and dismiss the scarcity mindset that these narratives reinforce.

- Create Safe Spaces for Girls Facing Multiple Oppressions and Shared Identities

  Beyond nurturing gender affinity, it's vital to create environments where girls contending with various forms of oppression can connect with peers who have similar life experiences. You can further grow their sense of safety in the world by connecting them with supportive individuals who share their race, ethnicity, sexual orientation, gender identity, religion, and/or disability, among other identities.

- Connect the Dots by Emphasizing New Behaviors

  You can support a girl in forging healthier relationships by praising when you see the new behaviors she's learning. Although she may understand the importance of healthy boundaries—like respecting different perspectives, empathizing with others' emotions, seeking permission, and fostering independence—she might still revert to unhealthy patterns during interactions with peers, intimate partners, and adults. Encouraging her to consistently practice these new behaviors elevates the quality of all her relationships.

- Explore Healthy Boundaries and Expand Notions of Safety

  The concept of safety for girls often focuses solely on the absence of violence, neglecting their unique needs for feeling secure. It's vital to encourage girls to broaden their perspective on safety and consider what they individually need to feel protected. When addressing safety and healthy boundaries, it's important to do so without casting judgment on their current behaviors. Understanding the context of their lives, including challenges such as poverty, violence, racism, or familial rejection, is crucial. Acknowledging these factors leads to a deeper understanding of their experiences and allows for safety rooted in the reality of their experiences.

- Maximize Girl Talk, Minimize Adult Talk

  One effective approach is listening and limiting your role to giving simple directions, asking clarifying questions, and making observations. This allows a girl to take the lead in the conversation, speak in her own voice, and name valuable information about her needs.

My Girl Culture Story

Claire, my mentor and girls' group leader when I was twelve, had arranged an overnight retreat during which fifteen middle school girls of all types—popular, sidelined, athletes, bookworms—could come together for a winter weekend in the Wisconsin woods. This would be my first time away from my parents since my sister's murder.

I took a seat a few rows behind Claire as she chirped, "Pack 'em in tightly, girls. Sleeping bags left, backpacks right." I had Laura Ingalls Wilder's *The Long Winter* with me and I immediately cracked open the book. Wilder's series, and this book in particular, had become a comfort to me, a metaphor for that difficult period of my life. I opened to the chapter "Alone," where Laura aches as she realizes that her sister Mary will leave one day, for she desperately wants to go to college. My post-tragedy

Chapter 3

social status at school had left me something of a "celebrity of tragedy" in the popular girl camp. For that reason, I gravitated to introverts who liked to talk about books instead of feeding on my family's story. It surprised me when the two girls who took van seats around me were from other groups entirely—athletic girls labeled as tomboys and some quiet girls who mirrored my nervous state.

On our way to the highway, I focused on the scenery, the train station, Butler Lake, and Ascension Cemetery. From the road, through the snowdrifts, I could imagine a burst of color beside Kim's gravesite. Kim's many friends and their families made sure she did not go forgotten. Often, a collection of artificial flower arrangements decorated her grave, giving a surreal imitation of life in the frozen terrain. My parents, lost in grief and self-blame, visited frequently. I hated going with them. Hated the lifeless flowers and the sight of my parents' future plots adjacent to Kim's. I closed my eyes and feigned sleep.

"Ann, you seem like you aren't enjoying this," Claire offered. "Is there anything I can do?"

"I'm fine," I said, my voice quivering as I held back tears. "No, I'm fine, really."

An hour or so later, light snow had begun to fall, and we arrived at the lodge. Cabin assignments were promptly doled out. "Ann, Joanne, and Sue are together in Madison Cottage," I heard Claire say.

No. This was not good—I didn't want to be with them, because I had never really talked to either one of them. Plus Sue had accidentally launched a soccer ball in my face at recess earlier in the year. I felt intimidated. In reality, though, Claire could have said any names and it wouldn't have been good.

Silently, I made my way toward the cabin and set up in the bunks. That night, the others fell asleep quickly. My bunkmates' breathing was comforting, and eventually, I fell into a deep sleep, dreaming about pine trees, snow, and a frozen river, the bucolic scenery I'd seen from the van. Then my sister . . .

I awoke to a concerned voice: Joanne, saying loudly, "Are you all right, Ann?" I opened my eyes on the unfamiliar room, the darkness of that cabin. "You were screaming in your sleep," she said.

Something in me thawed. I was grateful for her kindness, such a simple, disarming thing, like the snow flurrying outside the window. Joanne and Sue did their best to comfort me, wiping my tears. I leaned into their care.

The next morning, they left me to sleep late. They brought breakfast to me with a hot chocolate, making excuses for my absence at the mess hall. "We're going horseback riding today—can you believe it?" said Sue, pulling up her jeans, trying to cheer me up. "In the snow?" As I dressed that morning, we had officially bonded.

"You girls ready?" asked Claire as we saddled up. Nothing had prepared me for the thrill that came next: cantering across a snowfield on a horse. "I feel like I'm in a movie," I shouted, bouncing as my bottom hit the saddle and then rose again. Though the thrill was momentary, it was something I hadn't tasted possibly ever; the feeling was such a contrast to what had become a normal state of withdrawal from the rest of the world.

When we got back from the barn, Claire pulled me aside. "How are you doing, Ann?" I will always remember the way she looked at me when she asked. Her eyes signaled she would accept whatever I had to say and, importantly, *however* I said it.

"Everyone stares at us at church, everyone feels sorry for us," I blurted, unaware until that moment just how much pity added to my suffering. What surprised me most—and her, too, I bet—was how readily the raw anger came, how loud and violent it was for such a seemingly sweet, compliant girl like myself. Claire, without judgment, and for the rest of that long winter, connected me to horseback rides in the snow, brought me navy blue tights when I needed them for a choral concert at school, and helped me taste again, even for a moment, the feeling of joy, of hope, that had been long absent from my life.

Chapter 3

As an adult looking back, I can see my relationship with these girls and with Claire deeply informed how I now show up for girls' work. Claire validated my feelings as they snuck out of the crack she helped create with me. She accepted how I grieved and didn't tell me how to feel. She listened carefully to my anger, my pain, and my personal values of freedom and joy. The presence of girls around me who deeply cared about my emotional well-being was met by feelings of inclusion and camaraderie. All of this reflected a template, a standard, for healthy girl culture. In my work now, I refrain from saying things like, "I know exactly how you feel" or "That happened to me." Even if something similar has happened, I believe that having an adult who holds space to simply witness versus comment on a girl's experience is a gift for her to unwrap and hold.

At the same time, as I work with girls, there are places where I fail to see where the ground has shifted since I was a girl, or where I operate out of unconscious assumptions about what all girls do or do not have access to without considering the damage—the internalized oppression—caused by racial stereotypes. Early in my professional work, for instance, I began to reckon with the racially biased lens I had developed growing up and how it had limited my exposure to the world around me. My unexamined "isms" meant I was deeply unaware of the struggles of violence and racism that faced communities of color. What does healthy girl culture mean in the context of being followed around in a store and being suspected of shoplifting? Of you or your loved ones being harassed by the police? When have I been unable to buy makeup or Band-Aids in my skin tone, or greeting cards and picture books in which my race and culture were represented? What does girl culture mean if you can't physically access the spaces where meetings are held? What if you don't feel safe using the bathroom because of your gender identity?

My own standards for healthy girl culture—and what needed to change to make it healthy—needed to be examined with a lens for viewing the unconscious assumptions I held.

Parent/Mentor Self-Reflection Power Tool

Recalling and reflecting on your own experiences of girl culture can provide valuable insights to better support girls in developing this skill for themselves. Unpacking memories and understanding how your day-to-day life has been influenced by these experiences can enhance your ability to guide and support them. Do a little sleuth work so you are better equipped to support the girls in your life. Ask yourself:

1. What information about your experiences of girl culture is helpful to recall? Are there memories that you can unpack so that you are better prepared to support a girl in developing her power to create healthy girl culture?
2. What do you need to do with what you've learned to develop your ability to support a girl in building this power?
3. What is your attitude toward changing your behavior related to this power? Why do you think that is?
4. What existing habits might you need to unlearn?
5. What about your current environment at home or work prevents you from being successful in learning this new habit?

Seeding Hope

It's a January day in 2013 and I'm meeting with Ruby. Many years after we first met, as a hazy sunset advances, Ruby strolls into the coffee shop where we agreed to meet. She wears square-shaped sunglasses and a white scarf, her hair freshly bobbed. She reaches out and offers me a warm hug. We settle into small talk about work and family, and she describes her career as a home health care worker. We eventually move to questions I had sought to ask her: What had she gotten from her time in the girls' group? Are the lessons about power in relationships lasting? Are her experiences and choices in relationships as she gets older shaped by a community where healthy girl culture was the norm? What could we as mentors have done more of to support her?

Chapter 3

"Even now, when I see magazines or commercials, I tell my sister it's not real," Ruby begins. "As women, the media portrays these perfect people, stereotyping us in certain roles. The stereotypes are walls. I wanted to break out of these and speak my voice," she continues. "Who better to help you than other women who have gone through what you have? I don't want my younger sister to go through what I did."

With a shifting tone, she tells me the story of a boyfriend she had mentioned all those years ago in the girls' group. His rage first showed up at the end of middle school. By then, Ruby and Jessie had been dating for over a year. When he found her talking to a fellow male classmate, he grabbed her arm. In time, Jessie became more controlling, accusing her of cheating and threatening to tell authorities she was undocumented.

Ruby continues, "At seventeen he had his first breakdown, and in his early twenties he was diagnosed with bipolar disorder. I watched his symptoms of paranoia and got him admitted. I loved his mother, but she let me find out about his issues on my own. He never hurt me physically, so I kept trying to catch him before he hit rock bottom." Jessie continued to pursue the relationship in ways that made Ruby feel uncomfortable and afraid, with late night calls and some unexpected visits. She had developed an understanding of her own needs, safety, and boundaries and went through the complicated task of obtaining a restraining order and shutting down her social media accounts so she could not be tracked. Ruby moved on once she realized she was sacrificing her own happiness and security.

The benefit of the teachings had come in a time-released way in Ruby's case. "I still have the poster I made of what a healthy relationship is hanging on my wall, and one night when I couldn't sleep, it just all clicked."

As the sunlight disappears from the café wall, Ruby offers, "The feeling of power that I got when I was younger helped me realize that it's going to be okay. I could have gone a different path, gotten depressed, and tried to keep working things out. But I know I'm powerful and I didn't let it bring me down. I see often now, my patients, women, depend on their husbands. Even if they are in a domestic violence situation, they don't have money or kids, they are dependent on men. They don't have the power or strength to leave. I knew that wasn't going to be me. I don't want to be in that situation. I was not going to live that way."

As Ruby can attest, moving from a mildly unhealthy relationship to an exploitive one is a short distance, even when you have the benefit of a girls' group or supportive adults. But her story gives us a window into what lies beneath a girl's ability to negotiate power in her relationships, even under extreme circumstances. Ruby successfully challenged the stereotypes of subverting her own needs, rejecting society's view of men as sometimes violent and dominant individuals and women as passive and subordinate objects. She went into an intimate relationship with a definition of what she wanted in a healthy relationship, even if it took time to surface in a way that manifested a healthy change.

In her younger adolescence, she had learned to value equality and open communication. She became media literate, recognizing the false and often violent images of women and people of color that show up. Ruby eventually recognized and confronted her unique challenges to leaving Jessie: fear of letting down someone whom she cared about who was mentally ill mixed with feeling bound to cultural values she had been taught about the role of a woman and wanting to honor her mother. With her coworkers, Ruby had also replicated having a community based on values of empowerment, values she had first named and experienced in her girlhood group.

Her story is about the power to recognize an unhealthy relationship in time to establish a different standard, about choosing differently because she knew she deserved better. She held a higher standard. As the last sliver of sunlight disappeared from the café wall, Ruby offers, "I learned to be independent, to take care of myself." She pauses as she reflects. "I define empowerment as knowing my own worth."

These are the kernels of hope that are seeded by caring adults in our lives. Earlier I shared why arming a girl with hope about the power she has to shape the girl culture around her is transformative and vitally important to healing. What if every girl experienced the power of creating healthy girl culture? The power whose essence springs from the hope that girls can have agency in their lives and communities, and therefore freedom? An entire field is dedicated to the study of hope and how it heals us.

Shane Lopez, author of the book *Making Hope Happen*, explains it this way: "Hope is half optimism. The other half is the belief in the power that you can make it so. There is a profound difference between hoping and wishing," he suggests. Wishing encourages passivity, whereas hope represents an active stance. In 2004, a California theology professor, Duane Bidwell, and a pediatric nephrologist, Donald Batisky from Emory University in Atlanta, Georgia, found that children suffering from chronic or end-stage illnesses accessed hope through a variety of pathways that included maintaining identity, believing that they were not alone, claiming the power to self-advocate, using contemplative practices, and finding ways to give back.[11] These pathways to hope do not only map to terminal illness or medical systems. They can support the disruption of the dynamics of powerlessness and oppression.

POWER TOOL: A HEALTHY GIRL CULTURE ACTIVITY YOU CAN DO WITH GIRLS
Introduction

It is important for a girl to recognize the power she gains or loses from her relationships, and the weight she gives to relationships when she makes a life decision. This activity provides a way to have a thoughtful conversation about which relationships in her circle elevate her, which bring her down, and which do both.

It also helps her reflect on skills she needs to develop mutual, healthy relationships.

Conversation Tip
Don't step in too early or too much as a girl explores the healthy and unhealthy qualities of her relationships. You may want to overprotect, interpret, or "rescue" her from how she truly feels. Try to share using a three-to-one rule (for every three things she says, you say one).

Goals
- Develop a deeper understanding of characteristics of unhealthy and healthy relationships and people in her life who fall onto these lists.
- Develop a fresh understanding of skills needed to end unhealthy relationships and build healthy ones.

Do This Together
1. Draw a line down the middle of a piece of paper. On one side write characteristics found in valuable and healthy relationships (i.e., fun, common interests, respect, you can say what you really think, you can disagree and still be friends). On the other side write characteristics found in nonvaluable and unhealthy relationships (i.e., "I never feel good when I hang out with them," "they are mean to me," etc.).
2. Explore the differences in the lists. Have her write down three people in her life that fall onto one list, the other, or both. Ask her: How does she feel when she spends time with various people she's listed? Why does she spend time with people that are on the "unhealthy" list? What is at risk if she cuts off an unhealthy relationship? This can be complex—for example it could be a relationship with someone that she doesn't feel she has a choice about (i.e., on her team at school or in her family).

3. Explore the idea of expecting more from relationships. Ask her: What are the skills she brings to relationships? How could she use these skills to strengthen the relationships she likes or better negotiate the ones that she struggles in?
4. Now reread the definition of the power of creating healthy girl culture and the skills that it takes to build it. Ask her this closing question: What is a skill she needs to develop related to this power? Who can help her?

CHAPTER 4

Shifting Conflict Norms among Girls

POWER #2

Renorming an understanding of healthy conflict among girls expands the power a girl has to engage in conflict in ways that defy gender and race-normed expectations and allows her to stay connected to what her emotions—especially anger—are telling her about what she needs. By developing this power, a girl learns to identify and build on common values as a foundation for resolving conflicts, acknowledge her role in disputes, and communicate feelings of anger without fear of jeopardizing relationships.

Creating a foundation for a healthy girl culture paves the way for transforming the complex dynamics of conflicts among girls. Healthy conflict involves openly and respectfully expressing differing viewpoints, needs, and boundaries while valuing all parties. It permits open discussion of disagreements without personal attacks, shaming, or underhanded relational aggression tactics. Learning to navigate conflicts respectfully allows girls to realize that disagreements need not sever relationships.

Conflicts among girls are often rooted in societal pressures to conform to unrealistic feminine ideals that prioritize appearance and popularity over authenticity. Girls face rigid gender norms that teach them to avoid conflict, yet punish them for defying these expectations when they exhibit confrontational behavior. These conflicting pressures surrounding femininity are further complicated by intersecting factors like race, ethnicity, and socioeconomic status.

A common challenge is that social expectations frequently lead girls to suppress anger, which can manifest unhealthily during interpersonal conflicts, especially with other girls. The difficulty arises when cultural norms imply girls should feel ashamed of their anger, despite anger being "an important compass" that helps them "navigate challenges and boundaries," as Lyn Mikel Brown writes.[1] While anger can be an empowering response to systemic oppression, girls are unfairly stigmatized for expressing it. Even young girls are evaluated more negatively than boys for expressing anger,[2] highlighting the gendered socialization around anger. When adolescent girls violate feminine norms by expressing anger, they face social consequences and higher depression.[3]

When girls are unable to express or examine their anger in a healthy way, an unfortunate consequence is that they may direct it toward one another. Unexamined anger can lead to relational aggression, a form of bullying where girls, as a marginalized group, turn their frustrations against each other. Examples include gossiping or spreading rumors about other girls; excluding them from friend groups; bullying them on social media; making cruel comments about their appearance, clothing, or bodies; and in some cases, physical aggression like pushing or hitting.[4] Often, suppressed anger can look like silenced opinions, critical remarks about their bodies, and the relentless expectations that shadow them through girlhood. Girls may lash out at each other through put-downs, fat-shaming, slut-shaming, or policing how "properly feminine" another girl is acting or dressing as a way to vent their frustrations about restrictive gender norms.[5]

Learning to express anger and resolve conflicts constructively is especially powerful for girls who have experienced trauma. Facing higher rates of traumatic experiences compared to boys,[6] girls are frequently met with blame rather than support from adults when they respond to trauma with anger or a sense of powerlessness. Rather than attributing fault, adults can help these girls develop power through healthy conflict negotiation and effective communication of needs. Research has shown that teaching adolescent girls skills in constructive conflict resolution leads to "improved family relationships, better peer relationships, and less involvement in dating violence."[7] One longitudinal study found that adolescent girls who learned healthy conflict management strategies had "decreased rates of suspension, school discipline, and fighting" at school over time.[8]

The transformation is particularly notable in mother-daughter disputes. By focusing conflicts on mutual understanding and respecting both parties' values and needs, studies indicate mother-daughter relationships can significantly improve through this "mutual perspective-taking, compromise, and emotional self-regulation."[9] Learning these skills helps reframe mother-daughter conflicts from power struggles into opportunities for deeper understanding.

Moreover, equipping a girl early on with conflict resolution tools does more than just help resolve her personal conflicts and clarify her values. It also challenges the institutional and societal norms that fuel toxic conflict behaviors among girls more broadly. This shift moves the discussion away from simply questioning why a girl might perpetuate aggression or endure violence in conflicts. Instead, it examines our collective role in reinforcing feelings of powerlessness and lack of agency that contribute to girls' conflicts.

As a girl grows into adulthood, holding this foundational power of understanding conflict-resolution behavior can shape her approach in public and professional arenas. Women who develop skills in managing conflict constructively tend to report greater satisfaction and effectiveness when dealing with workplace conflicts.[10] Enabling girls to transform interpersonal conflicts in their youth has a ripple effect across many facets of their lives.

DEFINING POWER #2: SHIFTING CONFLICT NORMS AMONG GIRLS AND GOING TO THE VOLATILE

When Alicia, a second-generation Iranian seventh grader, first joined the girls' group, she was socially outgoing yet struggling with financial and family instability. Around the same time her father had abruptly left and she lost contact with him, Alicia began lashing out at girls at her new school, repeatedly landing her in trouble. Noticing an after-school girls' leadership club flyer, Alicia's mother signed her up, partially to deal with the gap in after-school care during their increasingly challenging circumstances. During this turbulent period in Alicia's life, Ty, the group leader, reached out to begin one-on-one mentoring with Alicia in addition to the group sessions.

In her dedicated one-on-one mentoring time, Alicia explored, without fear of judgment, the way conflict and anger showed up in her life. Though initially resistant, she began exploring the underlying needs and perspectives fueling her conflicts with her sister and other girls. Through thoughtful questioning, her mentor Ty guided Alicia to reframe these clashes as opportunities to find mutual understanding rather than zero-sum power struggles. As Alicia built skills in perspective-taking and compromise, she gained newfound confidence in voicing her needs while considering others'. This approach allowed her to have more productive disagreements and take on leadership roles in the girls' group.

At home, Alicia brought these activities into family time, shifting dynamics with her mother and sister. In a supportive environment challenging rigid norms around feminine conflict avoidance, Alicia learned to express herself honestly and empathetically. You will reconnect with Alicia later in this chapter, and her story will be shared as we learn about this power.

For girls like Alicia, demystifying the how-to of conflict proved profound. Many are unaccustomed to articulating their needs, much less advocating for those needs when disagreements arise. Yet by role-playing conflictual situations, Alicia built muscle memory for using the language required for healthy conflict. Diving deeper into how it felt to reframe conflict helped solidify what she was practicing. And while encouraging her to use her voice didn't guarantee it would always be heard, the very act of expressing herself was an empowering first step.

Renorming girl conflict expands the power a girl has to engage in conflict in ways that defy gender-normed expectations, allowing her to stay connected to what her emotions are telling her about what she needs and to express her need in a way that honors her values. It is the power of being able to use anger and frustration in constructive ways in her intimate relationships and beyond. Growth in the power of shifting conflict norms means a girl is exploring these topics:

- How can she foster an understanding of her conflict style and its impact on her relationships?
- Which values contribute to conflicts in her relationships, particularly with other girls and women?
- What level of contribution should she aim for in a relationship to ensure mutuality? What is her expectation from her counterpart? Is it equitable?

Exploring these subjects shines a light on the subtle ways a girl is conditioned to relinquish power by avoiding or failing to navigate conflict effectively. This awareness enhances a girl's judgment in selecting her circle and managing conflict constructively. It develops her capacity to build relationships grounded in shared needs, values, and interests, moving beyond the reflexive expectation to please others. By cultivating the ability to navigate conflict, a girl learns to:

- express anger openly rather than repressing it.
- address perceived injustices with strength and confidence.
- remain authentic without succumbing to the pressure of contrived niceness.
- leverage social media to bolster, rather than undermine, the self-esteem of others.

Engagement in conflict equips a girl to:

- encourage others to acknowledge their role in disputes.
- identify and build on common values as a foundation for resolving conflicts.
- communicate their feelings of anger without jeopardizing relationships.
- hold boys and romantic partners to higher standards in expressing consent or rejection.

You can support a girl in developing this power by not passing down fear of conflict. Developing the power of engaging in conflict goes hand in hand with growing a girl's belief that mutuality is something she deserves. The power connects her to a new language. The vocabulary of give-and-take is also an important communication skill and a significant form of self-advocacy. Inviting girls to think, feel, and speak about their values and about conflict in the context of their own lives fosters a freedom to communicate in fresh ways that are revolutionary in a girl's life.

DEVELOPING THE POWER: CONFLICT SKILLS WORKSHOP
In an activities room at a large middle school, Amina and Ty, two group leaders, are busy setting up for a lesson. Amina, an Eritrean immigrant, accentuates her outfit with a vibrant scarf, a present from her sister in northern Ethiopia, as she arranges plush pillows

and hums to SZA. Ty, who grew up in the Pacific Northwest, is White and has recently started their gender transition journey. They set up a colorful flip chart listing the session's goals.

"This group is always full of life," Amina remarks to Ty. "Today's discussion on conflict is super relevant. We've seen some passive-aggressive behavior among the girls—eye rolls, subtle acts of exclusion, and snide comments about attire." As the girls gradually enter, music fills the room, setting a peaceful tone. One girl eagerly discusses her upcoming birthday month, while two others talk about their favorite influencer's latest Instagram story. Several snack on fruit roll-ups, and most are absorbed in their devices, sending last-minute texts before being asked to put them away. With the group now familiar with the routine, Ty dives into the day's agenda. "Today's workshop focuses on acquiring skills for healthy conflict resolution in your relationships," they announce as they launch a warm-up to help get the girls engaged. As the activity concludes, Amina transitions to the next topic. "Let's talk about values. These tell us what matters most to us, and this can have a big impact on conflict."

Amina then reminds the group of the definition of values. She says, "Values are a person's principles or standards of behavior, one's judgment of what is essential in life, and how they are shaped by our identities and who we are." She next asks each girl to write one value on a small paper for use in a trust-earning game that explores how her values steady her and can also be at the center of conflicts that emerge.

"Now, it's time for a values snowball fight," she announces once they are done writing. "Ready, set, go!" she whoops in a playful tone. The girls crumple up their written notes into balls and toss them up in the air. The physical movement is fun and unexpected, the mood contagious. Then Ty yells, "Values!" and each girl picks up a "values snowball" off the ground and finds a partner to pair with for discussion.

Ty then instructs the girls to read the value out loud to their partners and define what they think it means and when they've used or could use this value in their life. The girls take the cues and begin to share out when Ty calls upon them.

"Beauty is the one I got. It means looking good," reveals one of the girls. "I used it today when I got out of bed, picked out my outfit, and put on my earrings." Her partner replies, "Caring. That's my snowball. It pretty much means when you understand how someone else feels, right? I think I could use caring more toward my little brother, I guess."

Another pair of girls shares. "Dang, I got 'love,'" quips one of them. "Love means you show up for someone. That's what 'love' means. I always use it." "Wisdom. That's really mine. I wrote that one!" says her partner. "It means using your experience to think differently."

The girls do a couple more rounds of picking snowballs and new partners. Afterward, Amina does a temperature check to see how the activity felt to the girls in the group. Once she is assured that the intention for the game and its impact are in sync, she moves the conversation on. "What is a time when your core values may have caused a conflict, say with your parents, guardians, siblings, friends, classmates, or teachers? Maybe a conflict you've been afraid of getting into," she asks, as she records the sources of conflict girls are naming on the whiteboard. Girls share disputes such as:

- My sister took my clothes without asking.
- My friend was not inviting me to a party when she invited everybody else in the friend group.
- My mother is policing what I wear.
- My boyfriend pressured me to have sex.
- A classmate sending a group text with sexist and homophobic slurs about another student.
- A teacher showing clear classroom favoritism toward some students and slighting others.

Amina then provides more context. She tells the group that one reason girls avoid conflict is that they are often conditioned to please others and will stay silent about their true needs to hold onto a relationship. For some girls, "When their values feel violated, they don't have coping skills to address what's happening, and they have fights or conflicts that get them in trouble with others," Ty comments. "Let's find a way to address both of these behaviors by redefining conflict, okay?"

The game Ty introduces is an activity to explore how to renorm conflict. Nicknamed PLOW, participants take an example from the earlier conflict brainstorm and "plow through" it in pairs. In a four-step process, they (1) pick a shared value to acknowledge the other person and (2) let their feelings show, expressing how an incident of conflict or a statement about conflict made them feel. Then they are encouraged to (3) own a part in the conflict up front, with the overall goal to get to a (4) win-win or a "let go" mindset, in which girls state what they would like or need next time from the other person involved in the conflict.

Alicia and Brea, two girls in the program who are partnered up, choose to address a real-life conflict that happened between them from a previous group experience. Brea, with a tentative look on her face, begins the conversation. "I appreciate how committed we are to a good relationship," she tells Alicia. "I also want to let you know that I felt really embarrassed and judged by you when you dissed my outfit. I am sorry I rolled my eyes and walked away. Next time, I would like it if you asked me why I chose this outfit and why I feel good about wearing it. I'll be less rude and consider your feelings about the outfit instead of rolling my eyes."

Alicia stays uncharacteristically silent for a few moments, and then she responds, "Makes sense to me. I hear you."

The workshop closes on an understated but revelatory note as the girls are asked to verify what matters to them about the experience of renorming conflict. One girl reports, "I didn't really think that could be so easy. Why didn't anyone ever tell me I could say what was bugging me?" Another girl says, "Now I can try this when my mom and I are fighting about after-school stuff she wants me to do." Still another says, "Next time my boyfriend pushes me to do something I don't want to do, I can use some of these responses and I won't be so afraid."

KEEPING IT GOING: ONE-ON-ONE CONFLICT POWER BUILDING

At the conflict skills workshop, Amina and Ty emphasize understanding that girls' values—and values differences—can play a central role in how conflicts surface in their lives. This connection warrants a deeper conversation with Alicia, which Ty carefully notes so that they can discuss during an upcoming one-on-one mentoring time.

When Alicia first joined the group, her mother, an interior designer, was on hiatus from her job and had homeschooled Alicia and her only sibling. Her parents had divorced, and when Alicia's dad refused to pay child support, her mom had to go back to work, which meant she wasn't able to homeschool her daughters anymore. Most nights around the dinner table, thirteen-year-old Alicia, her high-school-aged sister, and their mother shared worry and anger over the father's abrupt departure. When homeschooled, Alicia would spend hours painting and creating other types of visual art. Her new school, however, did not offer that luxury. In fact, she was told by a neighbor girl that unless she did a sport outside of school, she would likely be stuck taking a dreaded physical education class.

As Alicia watched her mother buckle under the pressure of suddenly losing her financial stability and her community stature, along with the man she still loved, Alicia was having struggles of her own. She had recently landed in the school resource officer's[11] office on the day she was to start the girls' group.

"Alicia, what were you thinking, throwing that at Nora?" the officer had asked, in a high-pitched voice. "How in the world is it *her* fault that Mack cheated on you?" she continued, not waiting for an answer. She sounded exasperated and disappointed. "If this keeps happening, we will need to start helping you look for a different school. We don't tolerate any kind of violence here."

Under these increasingly challenging circumstances in Alicia's life, Ty reached out to begin a one-on-one mentoring relationship with Alicia in addition to the girls' group. Characteristically, Ty began working to break down social and cultural barriers between them. In working with Alicia, Ty observed the ways that Alicia, a second-generation Iranian girl, connected or did not connect to her heritage. How do expectations that gird her culture influence her life and her family's life now? In what ways is her culture a source of joy? In what ways is her culture a source of conflict with her mother?

Ty also noted what Alicia needs individually, what Alicia says she wants to be different in her life, and what she wants to do to make that so. Recognizing that Alicia is having unhealthy conflicts with other girls and has a hard time having healthy conflicts in general, Ty came up with an individualized activity to help. They supplied paints and craft materials and asked Alicia to invent a new superhero—a supergirl. "You can create whatever you like. She's your 'shero,'" Ty tells her. "What superpowers would you give her if you were her?"

"I would give her the power to make coin, that's for sure," Alicia responds matter-of-factly. "The power to freeze time would be good, so she can redo things when she messes up. And the power to shoot darts at girls in a fight. And electric underwear to stop a rapist."

Ty hones in on the dart's power. "Let's go a little deeper into that power, Alicia. I've noticed you have a lot of anger toward girls at school and your mom. Can you tell me about a conflict you've had at school or home?"

Alicia resists at first, but eventually, she talks about an issue with her sister. "My older sister, Ava, had a big test coming up and had just sat down to study. I came home and turned on the television. Ava got up and ordered me to turn off the TV. Then I mocked her and turned the television back on."

Ty pauses there and says, "Okay. I have some questions for you to think about. What do you think Ava needs? And what do you need? If Ava won, what would she get? How would she feel? If you won, what would you get? How would you feel?"

Ty continues to work with Alicia on analyzing the conflict by asking for ideas about how it might end, with more probing questions: Does Ava get what she wants? Do you? Then what kind of an ending is that?

Alicia finally arrives at a solution where both sisters would benefit. "Ava can study for thirty minutes, and I can go in my room for thirty minutes," she says. "I thought either I would win or she could win. Not both of us." A lightbulb had gone off in Alicia's head.

As time goes on, Alicia becomes more invested in her relationship with Ty. She starts trying to get along with the girls in the group, and her willingness to trust and show vulnerability makes it possible for her to have more productive conflict with other girls in general. Her instructors give her more responsibility in the group as well.

"It's your day to assist, Alicia," Ty tells her at one group meeting. "I need you to cut up those magazines and start spreading the pictures, so the girls get the full effect when they walk in." Ty instructs her to take out all pages featuring pictures of sexualized women and girls, leaving only photos that, in Alicia's opinion, aren't overtly demeaning or disrespectful.

Not wasting a minute, Alicia snatches up the *Vogue*, *Cosmo*, and *Teen* magazines and starts tearing out pages. When the other girls arrive, the room is littered with glossy images, a layer of magazine photos strewn about. Meanwhile, Alicia holds a stack of magazines, virtually emptied of their contents.

Alicia brings these same activities home with her, and they are a source of bonding for Alicia, her mother, and her sister.

Dinnertime conversations begin to shift, more often centered on subjects learned or an argument in the girls' group that day.

Power Tool: Parent/Mentor Conflict Renorming Tips

- Go to the Volatile Moments

   Conflicts between girls can arise during any of the activities or within any of these conversations about power. Don't be afraid of tensions, conflicts, or disagreements. You may be tempted to move too quickly out of the conflict to deal with your own discomfort. Don't do that. Call out the conflict you see. Your role is to channel the disagreement toward a deeper understanding of what's being communicated between the girls. Go to the volatile, or girls will get the message that conflict avoidance is valued.

- Bullying vs. Conflict: Knowing the Difference

   Differentiating between conflict and bullying among girls is important to ensure appropriate intervention and support. Bullying involves a power imbalance, where one person repeatedly targets another with the intention to hurt, intimidate, or control. It goes beyond a simple disagreement, often causing the victim to feel unsafe and powerless. When you become aware that a girl is being bullied, approach the girl privately and create a safe space for her to share her experiences. Listen without judgment and validate her feelings. Let her know that you are there to support her. Ask about her safety and whether she has a plan or any existing support in dealing with the bullying.

- Reframing Anger

   Rather than judging anger as a negative emotion, we can view it as an invitation for personal growth. Validating a girl's anger and supporting her in developing healthier ways to express and manage this emotion are crucial. Societal messages that discourage girls from expressing anger or associate it with conflict can hinder their ability to navigate healthy conflicts. Inviting a girl to understand the underlying emotions behind her anger can be transformative. Is it a response to feeling violated or unfairly "policed" for expressing herself? Is it an empowering reaction to the oppression of girls and women? By providing context about reframing anger as an opportunity for self-reflection and growth, we can support a girl in rejecting cultural norms that imply she should feel ashamed of her anger. Rather than directing anger inward or toward other girls, we can encourage a girl to embrace anger as a valid emotion deserving of healthy expression.

- Eyes on the Horizon: Encouraging Future Focus

Supporting a girl in reflecting on and practicing decisions, choices, and behavior with future goals in mind leads to a stronger sense of hope, perseverance, and self-control. You can support skill development in this area by helping her develop meaningful and realistic goals through identifying strengths and support systems while planning action steps, considering obstacles, and monitoring progress.

IDENTIFYING MY CONFLICT NORMS

My mother is from a South Side Chicago Italian and German immigrant family. She grew up in a neighborhood surrounded mainly by people who spoke Italian like her grandparents and parents before her. By outward appearance—hazel-brown eyes, high cheeks, olive skin color—she favors the southern Italians. Her personality, however, leans toward her punctual, precise, and stoic German roots. My grandpa gave her, the youngest of three daughters, a nickname that followed her throughout her life: Baber, which means baby. She is anything but a baby, though. My mom is tough as nails.

"Can you hand me a hair tie, Annie? Let's get your ponytail done," she said to me when I was six years old, as I played with the ties I had selected from the bathroom drawer. That day, she was coming off the night shift at the hospital and running on no sleep. She'd already finished packing six school lunches by then and tied four ponytails.

"But I want a braid," I chirped, unaware that what I was asking would push her over an edge.

The comb abruptly stopped midway down my back.

"Give the brat a braid," my mom instructed my older sister in an exasperated, clenched voice I did not recognize as she went to her bedroom to grab four hours of sleep before she picked me up from half-day kindergarten.

Over time, my asking for what I needed earned me a dreaded nickname at home: Demanding Ann. Indeed, I always seemed to "push it" or ask more than any of my sisters. "How do I look?" my sixteen-year-old self inquired of my mom as I descended the short flight of stairs. "You are not leaving the house looking like that, Ann Carol," she replied. Without giving me a second glance, she added, "Go upstairs, and take half of that makeup off your face, too." I followed the do-as-you-are-told rule publicly with my parents. Privately, not so much. The rule breaking—lying to my parents about my whereabouts and staying out way past what they would allow when on a sleepover, for instance—ramped up significantly when one of my best high school friends gained access to a car. I developed the power of being sneaky to avoid conflict with my parents altogether.

At eighteen, I saw the ways unspoken rules of conflict played out with my sisters. By then, we had squandered countless opportunities to learn how to engage in healthy conflict. My younger sister, for instance, diligently took care of her clothes. We are talking marathon ironing sessions. I would help myself to her closet without permission whenever I wanted, and there was no consequence to me for doing so. This may seem innocuous or silly, but my sister never told me how much this deeply angered her until much later in life. Brushing conflict under the rug was simple. In no particular order, here is a snapshot of the codes of

CHAPTER 4

conflict conduct I'd learned growing up at various developmental moments.

1. When I asked for what I wanted and felt I needed (like a braid), I got labeled something pejorative for a girl: demanding.
2. My childhood adversity impacted my conflict style and the values I honored when choosing to engage in or avoid conflict. For instance, I valued avoiding conflict to protect my mother's well-being.
3. Slut shaming wasn't a known "thing" back then, but my mother routinely implied it by commenting on my clothing and makeup. Most of our potential points of conflict were at the intersection of me trying to express my fashion or sexuality and my mother's rules for what was "appropriate" in her eyes.
4. Anger was not expressed *among* women and girls.
5. My mother had reasons for avoiding conflict with us. These ranged from her own racial socialization and gender-based norms, which meant trying to "protect us" from being unmarriageable or slutty, to having limited experience with the new culture we girls faced in a post–feminist movement era. The intergenerational conflict codes among girls and women were only beginning to be rewritten.

In my years of swapping stories about conflict norms with mentors and mothers, I have noticed similar patterns. In fact, it is the rare person who has a relationship with the feeling of anger such that, when it arises, they know how to engage it in a way that could be characterized as healthy conflict.

Many years later, living and working in Seattle, I realize I have brought these norms of conflict out into my workplace. I think to myself, "Why is everyone ten minutes late to our staff meetings?" I don't say this out loud. In my family, being on time was expected, a way to feel like you had control over something.

Different expectations around time were only one of the sources of conflict. Music levels in common spaces were a source of conflict. Completing reports on time was a source of conflict. Our workplace struggles with one another appeared everywhere, and some of these related to cultural factors that had a bearing on the way we negotiated workplace relationships and got stuff done.

Expecting girls to have healthy confrontations with one another when I struggled to do it myself was ample motivation for change. But where to begin?

By examining the template from my own childhood codes of conflict conduct and arranging for a staff training called "What's Culture Got to Do with It?", I had an important opportunity to grow.

"Look in each of the four corners," said our workshop facilitator. "You will see signs for 'I completely agree,' 'I am unsure,' 'Sometimes,' and 'I completely disagree.'" She further prompted us with, "In my family, it is important to be on time," and asked us to silently walk to a corner.

Those of us from the dominant White culture were usually clustered over in the "I completely agree" or "Sometimes" corners. At the same time, our coworkers of color stood in the "I completely disagree" corner. They joked about "people of color" time and how difficult it was to adapt to cultural norms in which everything feels urgent and people value quantity over quality in their work.

The trainer asked us to repeat the exercise, only this time she asked, "In my home, there is a lot of noise." Our office space was at a premium, and staff—except for the other directors and me—work elbow-to-elbow. Between voice levels and music, the noise was an issue.

The workshop allowed us to view our workplace expectations and judgments and see how they played into real-world tension. Once we surfaced these, we could create norms for our workplace culture that could shape a greater sense of belonging for more of us.

Chapter 4

Sometimes our opinions about the best way to work with girls surfaced as conflicts. Although this dynamic did not occur often, we saw it when adults in different roles (e.g., researchers and agency staff) or adults in different positions of power (e.g., staff and administrators at our agency) experienced serious disagreements about how an aspect of a girl's case or a group should be handled. Invoking language reminiscent of a custody battle, we sometimes said things like, "You obviously don't understand the needs of *our* girls," or "I've been working with young people for [number] years—I think I know what I'm doing." We could also get possessive, as in saying "She's my girl" instead of "They are our girls." This was especially true when administrators and instructors were at odds.

Like players on opposing teams, we shut down what we could have learned from others with different perspectives. Worst of all, we missed the opportunity to model collaboration and constructive conflict resolution for girls. At times, girls were put in the unfair position of choosing a side: this mentor or that one.

A breakthrough came when we practiced what we preached. We learned to name a shared value—a deep commitment to a girl's well-being—in order to acknowledge the other person. We let our feelings show, being vulnerable by expressing how the incident made us feel—frustrated or hurt. We owned a part in the conflict up front and aspired to a win-win, communicating what we would like or need next time from the other person.

Importantly, this experience helped me understand how conflict was based in my cultural understanding, with White American society dictating the way I communicated. How do I consider tone of voice, word choice, or elevated expression during conflict? Where does my cultural experience—either believing these aren't the "correct" ways to engage with conflict, or people being told they are "wrong" for exhibiting non-White characteristics in conflict—impact how I lead conflict transformation?

This type of personal reflection is crucial for supporting girls in developing the power of engaging in healthy conflict. Initially, supporting girls as they develop the power of renorming conflict may bring up a heightened level of anxiety. You may sense simmering tensions between girls or between you and a girl. You may be tempted to ignore things like eye rolls directed at you, a girl who is overly invested in approval, negative comments about clothing or hair directed at a girl, or jockeying to sit next to the girl with the most social capital. All can be signs of developing conflict. It is essential to discern entry points and "go there" when possible. Remember the end game. The power to *engage in* conflict equips a girl with a valuable tool to meet the limits of the cultural messages about conflict that girls are soft-wired to pick up. Giving girls opportunities to think, feel, and speak about their values and conflict in their own lives is transformative.

Parent/Mentor Self-Reflection Power Tool

Your experiences of conflict can provide valuable insights so you can better support girls in developing this power. Unpacking memories and understanding how your day-to-day life has been influenced by these experiences can enhance your ability to guide and support them. Your homework? Ask yourself:

1. What information about your own experiences of conflict is helpful to recall? Are there memories that you can unpack so that you are better prepared to support a girl in developing this power?
2. What do you need to do with what you've learned to develop your proficiency in supporting a girl in building this power?
3. What is your attitude toward changing your practice related to this power?
4. What existing habits might you need to unlearn?
5. What about your current environment prevents you from being successful in learning this practice with a girl?

CHAPTER 4

Not Your Mama's Conflict Norms

A few years have passed, and Alicia, tall, dark-haired, and professionally dressed, arrives for our meeting about twenty minutes early. Alicia now lives in Seattle and is a college student. She's just completed a grueling series of exams, but her exuberance and warmth outweigh any residual grogginess. Alicia's long history with our girls' program involved joining the after-school group as a seventh grader, participating in two summer programs through eighth grade, returning as a marketing intern near the end of her high school sophomore year, and being a teen instructor the final summer before she left for college.

Today, I meet up with her to see if developing the power to engage in conflict as a younger person has impacted her experiences and choices in relationships as she has gotten older. Alicia opens our conversation by talking about her lasting impressions of the project on media literacy. "We looked at magazines, listened to music, and talked about oppression. We were not using that word, but now I know it. A girl in the group really got it, and she wondered, why does this happen? Our instructor had said, 'This is political and hard to break down, but it's inherent in our system,'" she reflects. "I didn't engage in that and didn't feel the need to ask, and I knew it was bad, but I wasn't ready for that—the why."

What she was ready for was developing confidence in her ideas and getting more comfortable communicating these in a group. "In class, I lacked confidence in my ideas, my appearance, all of it," she tells me. "I felt ugly. I learned the skill of speaking up and having my own opinion. At school, for some reason, it seemed like there were way more boys, and I didn't want to speak. Later, after the group, I learned to speak up and open up to my own space."

What also strengthened was Alicia's desire to encourage people around her to use healthy communication skills to get to a deeper level of relationship. "Even in my group of friends, since we were fourteen, every time we get together, we're asking each other the deeper reason why we do things," Alicia explains. "I also learned how to be part of a counterculture," she says, "which was very important to learn at a young age. I understood politics and system stuff, which shaped me because everything I do now is about pushing for something better and expecting more out of something when there should be."

"It was liberating and life-changing to understand that and feel that desire to give back," she adds.

Beyond her intimate friends, this was true of her family relationships and relationships with girls. Her dad, whom she had lost contact with right when she turned thirteen, had left her family without any means. It left her angry at her mother for being "so weak." Alicia describes how devastating this was and how she would lash out at other girls and get into fights to cope with her anger before being involved in the group. "There's a huge element of nonviolence as part of the culture in the girls' group. We discussed how if a girl finds out her boyfriend is cheating, she tends to attack the woman instead of confronting the man. What commonly happens is we go after women and have campaigns of hate. Besides that, I realized I needed to learn how to communicate my anger to fix things," she explains.

Alicia suggested that dinnertime conversations with her mother and sister be centered on subjects learned or an argument had in our girls' group that day. "I was coming home teaching her more than she was teaching me," she says. "Every night, we had long conversations, and she respected that. My mom felt like she had an obsolete career and sold out because she's an interior designer. Now she's engaged in domestic violence projects in Santa Barbara and feels the need to engage."

Alicia is adamant that it should be essential to not just have your mother as a mentor. Having others in that role can strengthen your relationship with your mother. "My mother saw the group as such a positive thing. I think if my mom acted out of authority or jealousy, this would have changed my reaction," she offers. "Ty was the first person outside of my mother who was a mentor."

Alicia shares the familiar theme that women leading the girls' groups broke down social and cultural barriers and supported her in exploring what she wanted to change in her life, and how she wanted to do that. The cycle of empowerment happens in this way. When Alicia herself became a teen intern, leading a group, one of the girls gave a speech about how she had begun the program as a sixth grader, when she didn't have any friends. "Alicia, you were my sidekick, encouraging me to reach out," the girl told the entire group.

"I was honestly shocked she felt this way," Alicia says. "That girl was testing my patience the entire time." Alicia mentions with a knowing smile, "I saw so much of myself in her."

We talk some more. I realize this giving back, this higher expectation, applies to friend and family relationships and the school community. "Of course, our girls' group was a positive environment," Alicia says, "but in the end, it was a positive culture and spread out into the school. Any chance we had to bring up the political and historical conversation in class, we would. We'd go in with our armor on."

Alicia's story is not atypical of girls who transform complicated relationships with girls and their mothers. It is the story of a girl digging into the societal roots of why unhealthy conflict between girls is commonplace. It is the discovery that blaming the girls around you is a reaction to the social context. It is the story of being raised by a single mother and, at times, playing an adult role in that relationship. Of channeling feelings of betrayal, anger, and neglect that start at a young age into a life path that is more defined by connection to what she needs, by commitment to nonviolence in her relationships, and by building solidarity with the girls and women in her life.

The Big Picture: Growing Empathy

In 1995, researcher and *Ms.* Foundation president Marie Wilson addressed numerous inquiries about her pioneering work on mother-daughter relationships at the UN Women's Conference. Her research dissected the cultural forces that engender feelings of betrayal and powerlessness in mother-daughter relationships. Wilson and her colleagues uncovered that the dynamics between mothers and daughters serve as a primary setting for learning unhealthy conflict norms, such as shouting, silent treatment, shaming, or complete avoidance. These behaviors, in turn, become the template for the individual's interactions with peers and romantic partners. This revelation expands and opens the pursuit of anything that offers practical advice for unraveling the complexities of improving the mother-daughter conflict dynamic. This dynamic, rife with tensions that evolve with each generation, holds the key to significant benefits for girls.

Decades after the initial research in which feminist scholars like Wilson first shed light on the subject, brain science has deepened our understanding of the mother-daughter bond and the critical importance of transforming conflict norms. A pivotal 2016 *Journal of Neuroscience* study revealed that the part of the brain responsible for regulating emotions, including empathy, has more similarities between mothers and daughters than in any other intergenerational pairing.[12] These studies say that, if you are a girl, your mom is more likely to understand where you're coming from when faced with a struggle because her brain is more like yours. Mothers are uniquely positioned to empathize with their daughters, enabling a profound understanding during conflicts. Moreover, science underscores another crucial aspect: a strong connection to their mothers significantly boosts girls' self-esteem. Feeling connected to each other is a natural by-product of putting in the work to have healthy conflict. This connection, strengthened by healthy conflict resolution, surpasses other intergenerational family bonds in its impact through all life's stages.[13]

Developing healthy conflict resolution skills is one potential tool for preventing mother-daughter conflicts that can land girls in the juvenile justice system. In-home assaults, often stemming from conflicts with their mothers, is an issue that disproportionately impacts girls of color, who are overrepresented in detention and secure facilities for domestic assault charges arising from such familial disputes.[14] Without the ability to navigate disagreements with their mothers in a constructive manner, girls risk escalating tensions that can spiral into violence, arrests, and entry into the justice system's pipeline.[15] Equipping girls with skills to de-escalate and manage conflict is vital to disrupting this troubling cycle.

Embarking on the journey toward healthy conflict resolution with mothers in particular offers girls a crucial starting point for shifting away from lingering feelings of anger and shame and toward a deeper connection with empathy. This process not only empowers girls in their relationships but also reshapes their understanding of conflict dynamics and the intrinsic bond between mothers and daughters. The shared capacity for empathy, particularly during conflicts or in the face of complex emotions like betrayal, becomes an invaluable tool for all.

Consider the transformative ways you can empower girls in their relationships, armed with our current understanding of reshaping conflict norms and the innate connection between mothers and daughters. Accessing the profound empathy they share proves immensely beneficial for both mothers and daughters. Imagine you now have the opportunity to paint a picture of how different a girl's world would be if she knew how to shift the conflict norms she reflexively learned.[16] What supports and outcomes would reflect this reimagined dynamic? Here are a few to consider:

- A girl would cultivate a broader network of support, as unresolved conflicts wouldn't end a friendship.
- She would worry less about being liked and more about being heard. She would prioritize being heard over the need for approval.

- She would learn to dismantle horizontal aggression toward peers and, later, colleagues, fostering healthier relationships.
- She would demonstrate ease with conflict, showing that disagreements are normal. This confidence would translate into the workplace, creating an environment where diverse ideas are welcomed and safety is paramount,[17] making it feel more inclusive and safer for people to raise their ideas.
- She would gain confidence in public speaking, unfazed by responses or criticism.
- She would engage confidently in discussions with anyone, regardless of gender.
- She may be better equipped to defend herself against assault or violence in intimate relationships, understanding that unresolved conflict can escalate to violence, but effective conflict resolution skills can significantly reduce instances of harm.[18]

POWER TOOL: A CONFLICT RENORMING ACTIVITY YOU CAN DO WITH GIRLS

Introduction

A huge reason girls avoid conflict is because they are often conditioned to please others and will stay silent about their true needs in order to hold onto a relationship. This activity provides a way to have a thoughtful conversation about conflict and to practice skills a girl needs to engage in healthy conflict.

Conversation Tip

Tell the girl about a time when you felt great about having a conflict. Tell her about a time when you felt lousy about having a conflict. Explain what helps you overcome your fear or hesitancy in having conflict. Then listen actively. Stay focused on what she is saying. Don't answer the question for her. By jumping into answering the question for her, you are taking away her power.

Goals
- Develop a deeper understanding of characteristics of unhealthy and healthy conflict and people in her life who fall into these lists.
- Develop a fresh understanding of skills needed in order to have healthy conflict.

Do This Together
1. Explore the idea of conflict in general. Ask the girl to think of some examples of conflict (with parents, siblings, friends, classmates, or teachers). Has she ever been afraid of conflict? Why?
2. Explain the concept of PLOW (have the points below written on a poster board). Ask the girl to think of an example of a conflict she has had in her life and how she could have used PLOW to move through the conflict.
   - **P**ick a shared value to acknowledge the person: "I really appreciate how committed we both are to having a good relationship."
   - **L**et your feelings show: "I felt judged, angry, and ashamed when you made fun of my outfit."
   - **O**wn your part: "I'm sorry I was rude to you and walked away."
   - **W**in-win/let go mindset: "Next time, I would like it if you ask me about why I chose this outfit and if I feel good about myself wearing it. I'll be less rude and talk to you about your comments instead of rolling my eyes."
3. Role-play how the girl could use this in a specific scenario she is having in her life.
4. Now read the definition of the power of shifting conflict norms among girls and the skills that it takes to build it. Ask her this closing question: What is a skill she needs to develop related to this power? Who can help her?

CHAPTER 5

Developing Race Consciousness and Confronting Racism

POWER #3

A girl who develops race consciousness and embraces an antiracist perspective actively recognizes and confronts racial bias. She acknowledges the detrimental impacts of internalizing racism, understanding the emotional and psychological harm it inflicts. Proactively, she challenges biases within herself and strives to dismantle systemic racial injustice. Developing this power means engaging in open and honest dialogues about the consequences of internalized racial bias, fostering an awareness of privilege, and acting to challenge and disrupt racist structures.

There is no number of steps you can take to arrive at a "final place" of being race conscious and skilled at confronting racism. Anyone doing girls' work or racial justice work for any length of time can tell you that. Still, before successfully supporting girls in navigating the power of race consciousness and confronting racism, *you* will need to successfully navigate how to build this power in yourself. Depending on how you racially identify, you will be exploring a whole host of ways in which you can begin to undo the psychological harm of racism.[1] If you're White, internalized superiority, fragility, and guilt have behavioral implications you must confront. If you identify as BIPOC, internalized racial oppression, horizontal racial aggression, and racial stereotypes all have an impact you will need to examine.

The extent to which we equip girls with the power to become aware of racial history and comprehend how their actions can disrupt historical patterns or reinforce them, is the extent to which the dreams of girls of color will no longer need to be at odds with the structural context in which they find themselves.

While educational barriers have improved for girls who identify as BIPOC compared to previous generations, race and gender disparities in opportunity and academic achievement continue to disproportionately lead to higher dropout rates, limited job opportunities, and increased poverty risk for Black, Hispanic, and Indigenous girls, who are much more likely to attend underresourced schools and have inexperienced or underqualified teachers.[2]

More than two in five Black high school students (43 percent) and more than half of American Indian/Alaska Native students (53 percent) do not have access to the full range of math and science offerings, compared to 29 percent of White students.[3] Furthermore, in high-poverty schools, little more than half (52.1 percent) of science teachers have advanced degrees, compared to 71.1 percent in low-poverty schools.[4]

In schools heavily attended by BIPOC students, girls have fewer opportunities to participate in sports, which can potentially lead to higher education scholarships and access, than boys in the same schools.[5] Despite BIPOC girls holding leadership aspirations at inspiringly high rates, they face numerous barriers to realizing those aspirations, including unfair treatment from teachers and administrators due to their race.[6]

For Black girls, in particular, harsher treatment in schools is well documented. Minor offenses, such as dress code violations, talking back to teachers, and defiance, lead to high rates of "pushout" from school.[7] In fact, Black girls in high school are six times more likely to be expelled, three times more likely to be suspended, and four times more likely to be arrested than White girls.[8] Ultimately, BIPOC girls drop out of high school at higher rates and eventually make up the majority of American adults living in poverty.[9]

Racism's insidious impact is felt when, if a girl of color perceives an unfair system as fair, *she is left to see herself as the problem.* This harms her self-esteem, classroom behavior regulation, and perceived discrimination. Racism's influence is felt by girls of color who inherit a family history of institutionalized disadvantage and the effects of historical trauma, even as the structural mechanisms that created the disadvantage and trauma are still intact. Adding to all of these impacts of racism is the burden of explaining racism and the racist acts of White people, which is frequently placed on girls of color. "Emotional labor," or the time and energy a marginalized person uses to educate someone who exists in a more privileged position in society, takes an enormous toll on girls of color.

Developing the power of being race conscious and confronting racism is equally as crucial for White girls. With contemporary forms of racism, racial discrimination, xenophobia, and related intolerance all on the rise and continuing to deeply impact the lives of girls of color,[10] White girls must shoulder the onus of responsibility for confronting White superiority and White supremacy. White girls can know what unearned White privilege is and how, in today's world, they benefit from it. White girls can learn to pick up the emotional labor from their peers of color and refrain from asking a girl of color to explain how a particular behavior was racist. White girls can learn to honor the resilience and leadership of Black and Brown girls, know the history of oppression and strength of their peers of color, and celebrate their immense contributions in all facets of society. If White girls are to work against systems that perpetuate inequities, possessing this form of power is essential.

Chapter 5

Defining Power #3: Developing Race Consciousness and Combatting Racism's Psychological Toll

Lara, a Black participant in a girls' group, faced periodic homelessness during her teenage years while financially supporting her mother, who struggled with addiction. Through the group's activities, she connected her lack of housing to the structural racism prevalent in Seattle due to redlining practices. This knowledge helped her understand that the housing instability she and her mother chronically experienced was not solely her mother's fault but was a result of an unfair system. This realization opened her to other insights and informed her career path as an educator committed to social change.

Rhea, another participant, learned about "stereotype threat"—the fear that one's actions might fuel negative ideas about one's racial group—and how it had impacted her ability to take tests. With the sense of belonging she found in the girls' group, she was more likely to participate in discussions, build essential relationships, be open to feedback, and persevere in the face of difficulty, increasing her odds of academic success.

Sara, a biracial Asian youth who joined the group at fourteen, realized she was uncertain and cautious around her White friends due to the anxiety and stress of decoding racism for them. She eventually learned to invest her emotional energy into relationships that built her sense of self-worth, reflecting this understanding in her community choices.

The experiences of Lara, Rhea, and Sara in developing the power of being race conscious and confronting racism are not unique; they reflect the common journeys of many girls I have worked with. This power gives girls agency to challenge racial bias, understand the presence of systemic racism in their everyday encounters, and consistently challenge unconscious racial bias, oppression, and privilege. It involves having honest dialogue about the impact of internalized racial oppression and White privilege and standing up for other girls experiencing racism. It opens girls up to having uncomfortable conversations about bias within themselves and in the systems around them. Over time, girls who hold this power can move the dial in their communities toward antiracism. A girl who is building her capacity to be antiracist can:

- establish a shared language about antiracism within a girl community.
- develop a lens that can see and understand the harm of microaggressions, the subtle, often unintentional, acts or comments that can convey bias or discrimination toward marginalized groups.
- disengage from media that objectifies girls of color.
- refrain from adopting the fashion, iconography, trends, or styles from a culture that's not her own.
- challenge peers and adults who tell a joke that mocks or degrades a racial/ethnic group.
- pronounce a girl's name correctly even if is not from her cultural/ethnic background.
- talk to friends and family about the effects of racism. Call out racism when she sees it.
- shift the emotional labor of educating others about racism from people of color.
- challenge school policies around hair, dress codes, and student conduct so these practices do not continue to push girls of color out of opportunity.
- seek racially diverse perspectives in her life through media, relationships, and experiences to deepen understanding of other viewpoints.

Developing the Power: The Community Agreements Antiracism Workshop

Creating antiracist community agreements, or behavioral norms for how the girls are expected to treat one another, is an activity that we use to build this power of race consciousness and confronting racism. The activity goal is to name what being race conscious means to a girl and what practicing antiracism looks like in our girl group community.

Sandra, a mid-twenties Black Seattle native and aspiring public health master's student, and Chris, a White Seattle suburb native and recent graduate from a West Coast liberal arts college, are the leaders of a newly formed school-based group who will take us through this activity. Earlier in the week, the two met to check in about group dynamics. Both agreed that the group was ready to dive into the conversations about race. The first two meetings focusing on civil rights and covert racism in Seattle had a high level of engagement.

"Before we dive in," Chris tells the group of six, "let's warm up with a game called Pin the Superpower on the Girl." The girls look to her curiously for further direction. After a fast-paced first round, and frantic pinning of superpowers, the once-barren silhouette of a girl is covered in neon sticky notes with powers like "a squirt gun that shoots down catcalls and sexual harassment," "a tool belt to break down racism," and "tinted sunglasses that see your future."

Chris turns the group to conversation. "Today we are going to focus on building one of those superpowers in ourselves. Let's get started on that tool belt. Our main activity is to create a community agreement that reflects how we demonstrate antiracism with one another." Chris opens the conversation by asking, "What does antiracism mean to you?" The girls look away from one another. One looks straight ahead as she peels an orange. Initially, no one offers to share. Chris allows the silence, unfazed. The girls are clearly taking time to consider the question.

As they hold space for girls to think, Sandra writes definitions on the whiteboard: "Racism is . . . " "Antiracism is . . . " "Microaggression is . . . " These become the backdrop for the conversation.

Developing Race Consciousness and Confronting Racism

"Antiracism means people stop asking me where I am from *when I am from here*."

"Antiracism is White people, even nice ones, not expecting less from me because I am Black."

"I think it means breaking down ways out there that you never knew you were giving privilege to one person over another."

"It means you are mentoring people who sit in bad spots because of our systems."

"It's saying that racism lives in me."

"It is about creating justice and equity for people."

Chris listens to what the girls are saying while noticing which girls were silent. It is not uncommon for girls to be quiet in this conversation. For some, this may be one of the first times race as a topic has been discussed in this way. This is especially important to note because this is an activity where girls of color could be set up to do the emotional labor of educating their White peers.

Sandra also offers, "Defining racism should be more like several pages, not a few sentences like the one we wrote. Racism doesn't look the same for every person. You got folks coming from privilege versus folks coming from having to survive. We don't live single-issue lives." Based on the conversation, Chris and Sandra put together guiding themes for the community agreements on what antiracism means for the girls' group and ask for a thumbs-up or thumbs-down. They are:

- Antiracism is a range of thought and actions opposing/countering racism.
- We make a commitment to fight racism wherever we find it (even when you find it in yourself).
- We are part of a larger, collective effort to dismantle—take apart—racism and build equity in its place.
- We dismantle White supremacy by addressing individual, interpersonal, and systemic issues.

- We center our understanding of antiracism on present-day impact, not just as a historical thing in the past.
- We acknowledge we participate in antiracism from different identities, perspectives, and experiences.
- No one is entirely antiracist. We acknowledge that we also participate in White supremacy culture and strive to actively confront it within ourselves.
- Accountability and openness to feedback are essential for our growth.

The girls get more involved as they move on to answering the next question. "What are ways we can practice antiracism in our girl group community?" A big thought bubble is sketched. Girls write what comes to mind.

"Step up/step back. Everyone should contribute to holding the group to the norms of antiracism."

"Hold back from being defensive when someone calls an 'oops/ouch.' That is an opportunity to work through an unintentional offense."

"Be aware of the difference between intent and impact. Recognize that impact is real and important, regardless of your intent. Don't try to defend yourself by saying you didn't intend any harm."

"Do a literacy check. Explain concepts or jargon so that everyone has an understanding."

The list keeps growing. Sandra sums up the conversation, and says, "Folks have talked about how certain systems and organizations can hurt communities of color. You also have to understand your own biases and beliefs of inferiority. We need to be aware of these issues so we don't hurt people. Because even if we give more opportunities, create more space for folks of color, if these places still have racist attitudes, it's going to end up causing more harm."

Chris offers her perspective as a White woman working in spaces where girls of color are more impacted by structural and historical racism. "How do I openly discuss racism and antiracism, so people of color aren't trying to protect me from feeling uncomfortable? I have a responsibility to see and call out racism. I am a constant learner and invite others to be as well."

The instructors notice that the group's time is coming to a close. They let the space fill with the discomfort of nonclosure. They avoid trying to sweep the discomfort of discussing racism under the rug.

Sandra closes the group by underscoring that today was not a one-and-done discussion. She encourages the girls to keep thinking about additions to what antiracism looks like for this group's dynamic, how to successfully move the group forward when it's impossible to be entirely antiracist, and how to practice bringing these actions out into the world. "And please, if you need to, reach out with any thoughts or questions that surface."

With Sandra's help, Chris untapes the silhouetted supergirl and the antiracist agreements poster. Both are filled with new representations and actions, a new narrative of the culture the girls aspire to create together, tucked safely away until the group next meets. They will be added to the growing decorations that are reposted each time the group assembles.

KEEPING IT GOING: A SYSTEMIC RACISM POWER ANALYSIS ACTIVITY

After girls develop a shared understanding of what antiracism means in their daily lives and can envision practicing antiracism within their girl community, we can then confront racism in the larger structures and systems they encounter outside the group.

To do this, we teach girls how to analyze the dynamics of racial power within those systems. The school system provides an excellent starting point for this analysis, as it is a context deeply relevant to their lives. Through a power analysis activity, girls create a visual representation that breaks down how racial prejudice and power intersect and manifest in their community. This tool helps them conceptualize racism and oppression, while also connecting their experiences to broader efforts for change.

Dylan and Maya are two girls who stand out for having developed the power to confront structural racism and use that power to benefit the lives of others in their school community. Maya, a biracial girl, and Dylan, a Black girl, attend a large, racially diverse urban high school where an accelerated placement programming policy from the 1970s that had intended to integrate the school and create educational equity for students of all races has had a counterproductive impact on racial justice. There are two schools within the school now. The accelerated academic classes are overwhelmingly affluent, White, and Asian. Even though the high school is located in a historically Black neighborhood, the Black students are stuck on the lower rungs of academic coursework. This racial segregation and its ongoing harm is a huge source of acknowledged but unspoken tension in the community.

Dylan and Maya met when they were selected to become Congress on Racial Equity retreat facilitators. The high school's Congress of Racial Equity (CORE) engages students of all racial backgrounds and is a rare place where racial understanding and tensions can surface and be addressed. The club's quarterly retreats allow students an opportunity to openly discuss issues of race, gender, sexuality, family dynamics, and more that are all but avoided in the classroom.

The high school program has a particularly noteworthy history that the girls are proud to tell me the story of. "The Congress of Racial Equality (CORE) started way back in 1942," Maya emphasizes. "It is an interracial American organization established by a civil rights activist named James Farmer who wanted to improve race relations and end discriminatory policies by helping people take direct action in community. Like Martin Luther King Jr., he was inspired by Gandhi's nonviolent approach to combating racial prejudice," she explains.

As trained CORE facilitators, Dylan and Maya explore ways to improve interpersonal relationships across races. They appreciate that the conversations are novel for the students at their high school, who were largely divided along racial lines in sports and classes. However, the openness that is fostered at CORE retreats rarely impacts the segregated scenery once students return to school. "It is so frustrating that we go on these weekend getaways, we break the ice, we break bread, and then come back to these classes where students of color are second-class citizens," Dylan tells me in an exasperated tone. "We need to shift focus and connect to the community in new ways. We need conversations that get at the root of why all these divisions exist in the first place," she adds.

That opportunity for dialogue soon presents itself when the two are asked to lead a virtual town hall for girls to discuss how to address school policies that negatively impact girls of color. At the event, Dylan and Maya use a tool called a power analysis. They ask girls to share stories and experiences that relate to how racial prejudice and power play out in school, in the court systems, and in the mental health services available to girls in their community. Gathering these insights helps create a visual, conceptual breakdown of racism and oppression and connects with broader change efforts.

Although adults are attending, the goal is to center the experiences of girls of color. They look to elevate opportunities for girls of color to speak up. "What is power?" poses Dylan to the fifty-plus faces on the computer screen. "And why do you think it is important to talk about racial power when improving schools and developing better services for girls?" Participants quickly pop comments in the chat. Some take a poll to respond.

> *"Power is your choices and influence, but BIPOC girls don't have a choice regarding discipline policies. They get expelled way more often for the same behaviors as White girls."*

CHAPTER 5

> *"Power is the agency to act on things that matter to me, but I want to do after school activities. I can't because I'm an Asian girl scared to ride the city bus because of the rise in hate crimes against Asians. The school has no safe transportation for me."*
>
> *"Power is being able to use my energy to be creative. But I'm sapped and often feel down. As a Black girl living through hardship and trauma because of historical racism, I think we need to talk about mental health counselors and counselors of color and the lack of that in schools."*

"Seems like you all have a good grasp on power," Maya comments as she takes the mic from Dylan. "You've mentioned them here, but I want to share some firmer definitions of systems, power, and institutions that will help us to understand how power plays out with girls at school. The first one is the 'system.' System means the connected pieces, people, and places that work together for a collective purpose. A school is a system, for instance. The second is 'power.' Power means the ability to do and influence people or events. The third is 'institution.' Institutions are the people, power, and policies supporting the system. How do you think power operates at the different intersections? Who's impacted, who benefits, who has access, and who doesn't?" she poses before turning her sights to the screen to see what girls have to say. The girls rapidly raise their hands to be unmuted or start popping comments into the chat.

> *"Police presence and law enforcement seem totally wrong to be at our school. Some of these resource officers have inappropriate behaviors around us girls of color . . . really crossing the line and boundaries and getting away with it."*
>
> *"Addressing the impacts of colorism and other harmful beauty standards on BIPOC girls' mental health. And did you know that females participate in self-injury at higher*

rates than males? In some schools, girls are actually penalized or punished for self-harm. These policies are harmful. Unbelievable."

"Most of the time, people just say that we are making drama and are all show to get attention. In reality we are saying what we feel. If we get to that point, it's because we have been hurt, and it takes a lot of encouragement to talk about it."

"I feel like some teachers treat us differently than boys."

"Things like dress code really annoy me, the policing of what I wear. It's everywhere. When walking outside in the parking lot or street, students start criticizing what you wear, how you look."

"I feel like the school principal and security do not take my friends or me seriously. They do not believe girls when we report something."

Emojis like hearts and thumbs pepper the screen, a widespread recognition that the systems, the power, and the institution were working against many girls at school.

Building on what the girls are saying, the adults comment on how educators and people with authority impact a girl's power.

"Girls are supposed to seem nice. To fit into that mold, they hold back from having something to say. When they do, they are troublemakers."

"There is a lack of commitment from schools and districts to make schools antiracist and gender-affirming."

"People upholding rules don't know what the policy's original intent even was. For instance, dress codes are designed to NOT sexually provoke boys. It always comes down to girls being the provoker. Policies around dress codes are geared toward boys, not girls. Girls are sent home for how they are dressed."

Chapter 5

> *"The people making decisions haven't ventured outside their area, they don't leave, and haven't experienced hardships outside their little world. They make decisions for girls of color and don't understand their needs."*
>
> *"Curriculum is taught in the White perspective."*
>
> *"Policies punish youth for self-harming behavior. They are expelled for doing things that harm themselves. Districts are supposed to have a care team and a detailed plan, and none of the language says you can suspend students for self-harm. But they are expelled for self-harm."*

Dylan and Maya shift the conversation to the power girls of color do have. "We need more sessions to promote girl voices and stand up for action. We cannot continue to look the other way. Groups like this need to be at school boards," says Maya. They close by calling folks to action by inviting them to join another town hall, an opportunity to dive deeper and consider, "What do youth need to be fully supported and heard? What kind of individual or systemic change do youth need to witness to experience caring service from the adults? And, as adults, what can you do as an organization and community partner to continue elevating and centering the youth voice?" Dylan and Maya skillfully model the importance of nonclosure, the message that conversations about race consciousness and antiracism are never done.

POWER TOOL: PARENT/MENTOR TIPS FOR DEVELOPING RACE CONSCIOUSNESS AND CONFRONTING RACISM

- Call Out Racial Microaggressions

    It is crucial for a girl to be able to recognize and address subtle, unintentional expressions of racism. While a girl may have good intentions, it is important to acknowledge and address the offensive impact of her words or actions on others. Equipping a girl with a shared understanding of antiracism fosters awareness and encourages her to speak up against racism when encountered.

- Rewrite the Racial Narrative

  Facilitate a shift in the conversation, moving away from focusing on "what is wrong with girls of color" toward examining "what happened to girls of color." You can support this shift by analyzing racism within systems and institutions and creating spaces for girls to critically evaluate and question structures of power. By understanding power dynamics and intersections, girls can better grasp who is affected, who benefits, and who faces barriers within these systems.

- Prevent Girls of Color from Doing the Emotional Labor

  Pay careful attention to who speaks up and who remains silent when discussing and participating in group activities. When addressing the impact of racism and microaggressions, it is important to avoid placing the responsibility of educating others on girls of color in the group. If needed, direct questions about racial privilege and power to White girls in particular to encourage self-reflection.

- Keep Systemic Change at the Forefront

  Engaging in a single, isolated conversation about systemic change can be overwhelming for girls. To ensure the continuity of this crucial dialogue, it is essential to assist girls in crafting actionable next steps. This involves guiding them to set goals that prioritize equity and providing clear definitions of inclusion and equity. By doing so, girls can actively contribute to the ongoing pursuit of systemic change, fostering a lasting impact. You can use the SMARTIE goal-setting process, which is a great resource for creating goals that are smart, measurable, actionable, realistic, time inclusive, and equitable.[11]

My Racial Bias Story

Examining race and racism—even in the post–civil rights movement era of the 1970s and 1980s—was not something I consciously grew up doing in White suburbia where I was raised.

Chapter 5

Rather, I was left to *unconsciously* absorb racist behaviors from the people closest to me and eventually construct an unexamined attitude of White superiority, a behavior that traveled with me well into my twenties. When, at sixteen, I hoped to invite a group of Black teens I had become close to at a Teens Encounter Christ (TECH) retreat to my house, I vividly recall my aunt from the south side of Chicago telephoning me personally to try to convince me that this would be unsafe because my house would be robbed. Despite my aunt's attempt to dissuade me, my new friends did come visit, but her attitudes cast a long shadow over the day.

Something I also remember from my childhood was my dad sitting in front of the television yelling racist comments at the Black players on the Chicago Bears or Cubs teams. Though I did not know this or name this as racism at the time, I knew what he was saying was wrong. I knew that because on those stifling hot afternoons I would see my mother closing the windows, maybe even turning on music to hide the foul language emanating from a normally quiet corner of the house. After the game, my dad would emerge and return to his normal, loving form, a personality that made understanding his racism deeply conflicting for me.

Like my aunt's behavior, I came to understand my dad's as a byproduct of notoriously segregated Chicago in the years just before the "White flight" to the northern suburbs. My dad was from the north side of Chicago, Rogers Park, an enclave of Irish, Germans, and Luxembourgers (my dad was the latter). Over the years, Rogers Park's population grew increasingly racially diverse and older, and his narrative became one of "my neighborhood got taken over" by "other" people. He would say these things, but these contradicted another piece of his history. Rogers Park is also home to a venerable Jesuit institution, Loyola of Chicago. My dad, a graduate, adhered to the core spiritual characteristics of St. Ignatius of Loyola, a belief that all men and women are created in God's image and destined for eternal life. To him, a life of faith required reflecting on one's experiences and a belief that we are all invited to follow Christ by reaching out to those on the margins of society. It was uncommon for White people of my father's generation to interrogate their racism and the conflicts it presented with their moral beliefs. It was even more uncommon for them to be competent in undoing the psychological harm of racism.

At one point in my mid-twenties, on a return visit for the holidays from my new home in Seattle, I accompanied him to the storage closet to take down boxes for his Christmas village. For him, the Christmas season brought rites of the highest order, and the village became one of them. I was there to help him set it up, this diorama of what he valued and loved. But I couldn't hold back, not after witnessing his racist reaction to a Bears game that afternoon.

I wondered aloud, "Dad, you've always taught me that hate is wrong. I think you saying those racist comments is a form of hate. I don't understand how you taught me one thing but do another," I voiced, fearful that speaking up would turn into a shouting match. What followed surprised me in a profound way.

He paused as he stared at the village. I could see a pensive emotion in him. "You are right, Annie," is all he said, with tears in his eyes.

How does one reconcile the memory of hearing racial slurs hurled at sports figures with the memory of a man who deeply loved his family and community? Extricating racist behavior from myself when it is passed down from someone I loved so deeply is my lifelong work. The legacy of racist behavior is a generational curse. Before I could ever imagine supporting girls as a mentor or a mother, I had to actively deconstruct layers upon layers of how I came to learn what race and racism were and how to break past the rhetoric of these terms, past the White guilt, and move into practicing antiracism in my day-to-day life. I am still learning, still making mistakes. But practicing antiracism has changed the internal dialogue from guilt to one of self-reflection and accountability.

Chapter 5

After thinking back on these memories, I came to these conclusions about the racism I internalized as a young person and later as a young adult:

1. I knew overtly calling someone a racist name was shameful and wrong. I understood this when I heard people around me say it and when I later made racist comments. Still, I had no language for why it was wrong. It would take leaving where I was from to develop the skills to do that.
2. My childhood adversity made me avoid conflict around challenging my dad's racism. Calling out my dad's overt racism wasn't something I could do until I was much older. When I was young, I was more afraid of hurting him than I was of undoing the psychological harm of racism in the larger world.
3. "White superiority" wasn't a common term back then, but the segregated suburbs around Chicago spelled it out loudly and clearly, so I internalized it. School buildings, downtown buildings, housing. Traveling a handful of miles in one direction or another made visible the redlining practices codified after Chicago's White flight. As seemingly idyllic as my hometown, Libertyville, was, its "idyll" came at the peril of North Chicago and Waukegan, the Black and Latinx towns to the north and west.
4. Racial prejudice was more covertly expressed toward women and girls of color. "White pity" was somehow "granted" to the women of color who were cleaners or hospital workers who came to our all-White town to support the functioning of people's lives. When I wanted to invite girls of color to my house after the TECH retreat, there were no questions asked by my aunt. Something about Black boys and White girls was taboo in her mind.
5. When adults "otherized" kids, they somehow thought they were protecting me. My aunt honestly thought she was "keeping me safe" by pumping me with racist beliefs *about*

Black boys I had met on a religious retreat. And there was never regard for the safety of the people she otherized.

Our work to become more race conscious and able to confront racism, however uncomfortable, couldn't be more essential, nor could the stakes be higher. And it is almost always easier for us to identify the racism we see in others, as opposed to doing a deeper reflection on what it means to us. What is so insidious about White superiority/supremacy in the US is the way we all participate in it, regardless of race. What does it mean to participate in discrimination against any racial group other than our own? Additionally, the most important aspect allowing racism and discrimination to continue is for us to not name it when we see it, in order to "keep the peace" or to avoid conflict. What do we sacrifice when we do so? How do we continue to harm girls by *not* saying something?

PARENT/MENTOR SELF-REFLECTION POWER TOOL

When considering race and confronting racism, unpacking memories is essential preparation. Unlearning existing habits that hinder your effectiveness in supporting girls is crucial. Whether you are parent figure or a trusted teacher, mentor, or counselor, be an adult who puts aside an agenda of expectations and instead creates a space for an open exchange of ideas centered on what accessing this form of power means for a girl in today's world. Consider:

1. How have your background and experiences shaped your views on race and confronting racism? Are there memories that you can unpack so that you are better prepared to support a girl in developing this power?
2. How have you educated yourself about the impact of racism and its history and impact? How have you listened (or not listened) to the voices of marginalized communities?
3. What are the ways you transfer this knowledge and understanding to develop skills and proficiency to support a girl

in building this power? How do you support your growth alongside a girl's development?
4. How do you remain open to feedback and hold yourself accountable when you make mistakes or act in ways that perpetuate racist beliefs and actions? How do you ensure you don't repeat these mistakes?
5. What can you do to create and support spaces that are both inclusive and supportive? What actions do you take to foster equity and contribute to an inclusive environment?

EXPANDING RACIAL JUSTICE

Lara, now a driven college sophomore, is swarmed by others as she waits for her coffee. I feel pure joy seeing her across the coffee shop. Recalling our long history—she started in our girls' group back in seventh grade, then became a high school teen leader in the very same program from her freshman year through her junior year—fills me with questions about what was meaningful to her and what could have made even more of a difference.

"What impressions stay with you?" I ask, though the bustle and noise make it difficult to hear.

Lara explains, "The group was an opportunity to learn so much more than what I was learning at my school about social problems and what it means to be a girl. It went way beyond finger painting. Being a plus-size girl, I had trouble with being bullied. The airbrushing stayed with me forever. I was okay with my body, because how can I be something that was not even real? These women in magazines aren't even what you see. This whole media segment hit me hard and helped me be comfortable in my Black skin and raised my self-confidence and self-esteem. My favorite activity is when we created a shero and gave her all different superpowers like electric underwear to stop rapists, crazy glue to seal the lips of someone who is saying something that feels mean, and laser vision to see what people were really thinking. We were her."

I ask her to say more and tell me how this plays into skills she still uses.

"I learned leadership skills. I like the spotlight. I got to speak up and notice that people listened to me. I learned creativity, and the instructors didn't dumb the ideas down for us. They were adults with passion. Now I use this all the time in my sister-to-sister group at college, where I mentor a little girl named Deja every Saturday in a very rough area in Hampton, Virginia. The kids come from a hard-knock existence, and not all the mentors do. They teach us so much. That's how I know I'm heading in the right field of education."

Lara's activism and desire to give back are evident. She had spent the afternoon participating on a panel at her middle school on college life for sixth through eighth graders. "All I want to do is make a difference in one person's life. On the panel, I was the only one way across the country at an HBCU (historically Black colleges and universities). There is a lot of talk about whether or not HBCUs are still relevant. It hurts to the core. My experience at an HBCU propels me. If I would have gone to a PWI (predominantly White institution) it would have negatively affected me. I would have felt more isolated than I already feel. Now it's about economics, but at least it's not about color. Even at a HBCU, it's hard for people to understand where I come from. But the president of my school and my professors are proof that I can make it. There were only two African American teachers at my high school; this gave me the impression I can't make it. I mean look at my odds. It took me a while to get over the hump of sharing my story. I was the first in my family to graduate from high school and then went to college. Now my history is something I've embraced."

We talk some more about skills. I ask, If she could teach one thing to a girl growing up now, what would it be?

"Patience and perseverance are most important. Patience because growing up in this era with so many social issues. If it doesn't come fast, girls don't want to do it anymore. Things are worth more if you wait. Don't stop believing. What's it worth if you don't work hard for it? I stayed up a long night working on a paper and got an A. It was worth it. Understanding, too, that you don't have to be a product of your environment is important and that having a passionate dedication to addressing issues together really matters." Throughout the conversation I am sensing a high level of fatigue. Lara tells me about how stressful it is for her to come home and "couch surf" because her mother is still using drugs and it is too painful for her to be around it. She yawns and explains that she will be sleeping on her best friend's couch tonight.

I ask her about coping with pain and hardship on an ongoing basis.

"For so long, I was thinking the life I lived was normal: the evictions, and lights turned off, I thought this was normal. But it wasn't. Letting the mentors in my girls' group know I had a rough night or I don't like my mom doing this or that was how I learned to accept it. I definitely taught my mom some stuff. My mom would always come home and ask, 'What did you learn today?' Talking to the women leaders meant I could tell them and *not* come home and lash out at my mother. They helped me see that her circumstances were part of a bigger cycle."

Lara brings up how differently things turned out for her because of the mentors she had. She tells me about her cousin. The two grew up together. "Our moms raised us the same way, and we did the same things. My cousin didn't get her GED or go to high school. If she had participated in programs like I had, where you develop expectations for yourself, she'd be in a different place."

Lara acknowledges that she had it in her to be an academic, but that what she learned in the program "started the engine for me, the gas was finding people in the profession who were like me." Her vice principals had a similar background and showed her she could do it. But she explains, "Enough is enough, we have to have passion for these kids. I've had teachers who don't want to be there, so I don't want to be there. Attitude and anger, doesn't work to bring that into the classroom. In high school, my math teacher was an English teacher. There's a difference between getting a subject and teaching it."

Lara and I wind down our conversation as she tells me, "Coming from a dark place, my girls' group was the light. My only wish for how the program could be different is if we could bring others out the darkness with us. These programs shows you there is another route, but that path needs to be open more widely and intentionally. I think, wow, my life doesn't have to be dark. When you take that positive energy back to your dark home, it creates a crystal ball of positive energy. I knew I was going to be out of there. I'm growing every day. With that, you carry it, to middle and high school. Now I'm in college. I have a duty and responsibility as a citizen to change things. Now that I have this knowledge of how to create light, I want to pass it on."

The conversation with Lara and the connections make me think back to when I began my professional career doing girls' work. At that time, I knew about as much about race consciousness and antiracism, practically speaking, as the next White social worker, which is to say, hardly anything. Though modern social work schools had strived to shape antiracism practices, approaches were often outdated or insufficient for those working with girls. Even now if you read the professional literature on the websites of social work schools, you get the impression that the degree is all about "living your passion" to "make change." Passion built on an inadequate foundation doesn't bring about change in yourself or systems.

In reality, my job has always involved looking at all the ambiguity, the things that made me uncomfortable—my White guilt, privilege, and my upbringing around "colorblindness"—to assess the impact on the girls around me, on the adults around me, and on the field more generally. So the point of investigating my own

CHAPTER 5

history was to continually unlock *my vulnerabilities and weaknesses in* doing girls' work and where I could work on these so that developing this power *in girls* was truly centered.

I recall as a new White social worker, I attended a girl's court sentencing hearings. On that occasion, and frequently, we matter-of-factly heard a variety of very personal, sensitive information from primarily Black and Brown girls. This included the disclosure of physical or sexual abuse, a girl's mental health status, family and peer relations, and the type of offense she'd committed (e.g., prostitution, assault). Testimony included sharing and discussing this information in order to make recommendations about the girl before the court.

Despite hearing, day in and day out, about this high level of violence and sexual violence, I sat and watched as the court would take a paradoxical stance. Paternal, holding a desire to protect, but at the same time punitive for behaviors deemed defiant or deviant, "unladylike." Seldom was the connection made between behaviors and underlying causes. I watched, time and again, this being especially problematic for Black girls, who were viewed as less innocent and more adultlike than their White peers. As a result, Black girls were more severely punished for the same things and didn't get nearly as many second chances. This was not only my direct experience with racism; researchers began to notice the same thing.[12]

As a White adult who had never experienced these realities growing up, what did I know or understand about what BIPOC girls were expected to endure, on top of the sexism we all faced? And importantly, what could I do to confront this racism and advocate for BIPOC girls moving forward? Focusing on what I could change meant forging a Justice for Girls Coalition training called Beyond Pink for court workers, law enforcement, and advocates to ensure that trauma and adversity were understood through the lens of historical and structural racism. It focused on the need to understand the constraints of our thinking around girls and to challenge and confront these and other forms of implicit racial bias in how we treated girls.

At other times in doing girls' work, I learned to develop my racial consciousness and understanding of racism's impact. Early on, in groups, I frequently noticed that the girls were afraid to talk about the racism they had encountered. After one middle school group, one girl expressed that she was worried that if she said anything like "White people have done this, or rich people get to have that," I, as her girls' group instructor, would be hurt or upset. "Will you stop coming back if we tell you those things?" she probed. "I am afraid you won't let me stay in the program." Many girls in the program, outside of the home, perhaps, did not have a space where they could freely express their feelings of injustice and frustration and be heard and validated by White adults, whom they perceived as a huge part of the problem.

Yet, a considerable part of girls developing broader choices came from girls having the freedom to develop a language for the injustice they had experienced without fearing they would hurt my feelings or that I would pull away from them. I had made the assumption: *of course* the girls would trust me and could express these painful truths with me. My blinders had conveniently overlooked the myriad reasons why, across the racial and age privilege I had, the girls had every reason to *not* trust me. Checking those assumptions about trust without defensiveness and recognizing that trust must be earned repeatedly was vitally important. Owning where I am responsible for harm or injustice that stems from racism is a minimum standard.

This brings me back to the girls and what is at stake in helping them develop the power of being race conscious and able to confront racism at an early age. When I turn to build this power with girls, it is crucial for me to underscore that antiracism teaching is not new for girls of color. What is new is the expectation that White youth and White girls, that White people, will be the ones confronting their implicit bias and the institutional layers of racism in the world around them. It is an expectation now that White folks, those who in general benefit most from the present-day structural inequity that resulted from historical racism, pick up the emotional labor of confronting racism that folks of color have been doing for centuries.

Keith Edwards's work on ally identity development provides a helpful framework for understanding one's role as an ally. He identifies a continuum, where an individual's motivation reflects self-interest, altruism, or social justice. Self-interest involves doing the work for someone you know and care about without necessarily extending it to others. An ally motivated by altruism does the work for others but may not recognize how they are personally impacted by the issue or the need for systemic change. In contrast, an ally driven by social justice recognizes that they are also affected by unjust systems and works toward structural transformation.[13]

The point here is for me to be accountable for living up to my antiracism values and practice—*in all of my community work*—the personal, institutional, and structural. The National Association of Community and Restorative Justice (NACRJ) has coined the term relational justice, a reference that unites the racial justice and restorative justice movements. It expands the meaning of justice to apply in community work, not only juvenile justice work.

NACRJ reframes the concept of "justice" to reflect "how people live together peacefully, harmoniously despite their differences and root it in several fundamental principles—fairness, balance, decency, respect, and dignity between people within their communities and the larger society." Ultimately, justice "requires that harms and injustices be repaired or ameliorated, as much as possible, by those responsible."

If all girls are to become a part of moving the world in a more just direction when it comes to the impact of racism, we must equip them *all* to have the agency to confront the history of racism and work to undo its effects. We must equip them *all* to be able to stand up for other girls who are experiencing racism. We must equip them *all* with tools to have uncomfortable conversations about challenging unconscious bias. Only if we do is there a glimmer of hope that they will one day see a world where skin color has no bearing on what any girl is perceived as capable of.

Power Tool: An Antiracist Community Agreement Activity You Can Do with Girls

Introduction

In the collective journey toward racial equity and justice, each of us holds the power to shape and nurture a community that mirrors our most profound values. Within this space, a girl has the agency to define how she expects to be treated and how she will treat others. An antiracism community agreement serves as a guiding compass, establishing clear expectations for accountability.

Goals

- Develop an understanding of behaviors a girl defines as antiracist.
- Set ongoing expectations for how we interpersonally show up as antiracist in community.

Do This Together

1. Explore what antiracism looks like in the community. Take a piece of paper and draw a large circle in the middle. Ask her or them to write responses to the question "What does racial respect look like in our community?" inside the circle. (For example: seeing and calling out racism, being a constant learner about other people's cultures, being conscious of the burdens of policies on girls of color, etc.)
2. After she or they have offered a few suggestions, here are one to three key elements that could be included in the antiracism community agreement:

Intent vs. Impact: Recognize that even if one's intent was not harmful, the impact of one's words or actions on others is significant. Acknowledge that the impact is real and valid, regardless of intent, and refrain from becoming defensive or dismissing concerns by stating lack of harmful intent.

Sit with Discomfort: Emphasize the importance of engaging with uncomfortable and challenging topics surrounding race. Encourage individuals to reflect on why they feel discomfort before reacting defensively. However, prioritize ensuring that no one feels unsafe or violated during these discussions.

Speak from Your Own Experience: Use "I" statements and speak from your own lived experiences. It is okay to share how others' experiences have affected you, but don't share other people's stories or experiences.

3. After the middle part of the circle has filled up, ask her or them to write what she or they don't want on the outside of the circle. (For example: girls of color protecting White group members from feeling uncomfortable, etc.)
4. Finally, seal the expectations by confirming: Can we all agree to use our power and relationships to hold each other accountable to this agreement? Now have each person sign the paper to visually seal the commitment to the agreement.

Chapter 6

Using Choice, Not Chance

POWER #4

The Power of Choice, Not Chance awakens in a girl when she realizes she has the ability to make her own decisions. This power grows stronger when she understands which decisions she can control and recognizes how friends, family, and society affect her choices. Through honest reflection about control and powerlessness in her life, she develops the awareness and confidence to use her voice to transform chance into deliberate choice.

When a girl makes choices based on her values and believes that her actions make a difference, she takes the reins of her life and does not leave her life to chance.

Believing she has a choice is at the core of owning decisions about her life. By embracing her agency, she transforms her present circumstances and sets the stage for a future filled with fulfillment and meaning. An understanding of this power is transformational.

A notable caveat here is that the word "choice" has become narrowly defined. "That's a feminist word," is what many girls say when they hear the word choice. How in the world did the word

CHAPTER 6

choice become so taboo? I wonder. And how did choice become a cudgel for judging the choices of other girls? Activist Roxane Gay has a crucial point when she says, "I believe feminism is grounded in supporting the choices of women even if we wouldn't make certain choices for ourselves."

Psychologists[1] and youth development researchers[2] agree on the vitally important power that comes from replacing a "things just happen to me" mindset with one of "I make things happen for myself." They refer to the latter mindset as self-efficacy or self-authority. Girls that possess this power do so because they can harness two separate but related forces: self-efficacy and personal values.

Why does using the combined forces of self-efficacy and values make such an essential difference for girls? It matters because a big part of the coming-of-age experience for girls is second guessing or betraying their values in an effort to fit in with the mainstream. Girls need to know when their choices and the freedom they possess to be themselves are being squeezed out. Outwardly a girl may even look like she is succeeding in school or elsewhere—getting good grades, participating in class, and other external markers of "success." The reality may be a facade built on an ability to follow stereotypical expectations fueled by the world around her.

The power of using choice not chance matters for a girl because success maps just as closely with confidence as it does with competence. Girls are often self-doubters. This halts and holds them back as they grow up. Yet, the actions a girl is willing to take rest on her believing in herself, believing that her goals and aspirations matter. Katty Kay and Claire Shipman, authors of *The Confidence Code: The Science and Art of Self-Assurance—What Women Should Know*,[3] put it this way: "The natural result of low confidence is inaction. When women hesitate because we aren't sure, we hold ourselves back." In their groundbreaking work to understand and close the confidence gap, they had a critical finding: What most doomed the women in the research on confidence was not their actual ability to do well on the tests. *What held them back was the choice they made not to try.* Even when women had the ability to do well on tests, a cloud of self-doubt often undercut their confidence. This routinely caused them to pass on answers they knew or to not try. Shipman and Kay suggest, "to become more confident, women need to stop thinking so much and just act."

Population and public health researchers[4] add important texture to considering choice as a power. Social determinants of health, for instance, underscore how a girl's individual choices move against the strong current of the societal limitations she faces and the multitude of forces that are outside of her control, yet impact her well-being.

A clear example of a force beyond a girl's control is the pervasive threat of violence: in the media, on a date, walking alone down the street, at school, under medical care, and even in her own home. Everywhere they go, girls are at risk of experiencing multiple forms of violence, such as sexual assault, unwanted touching, abuse, incest, harassment, catcalling, and stalking due to their gender, race, religion, sexual orientation, and gender identity. While legal protections have grown in the last quarter century,[5] they have done little to dissuade or alter the dangerous, toxic, and pervasive cultural norms that feed a culture of "acceptability" and "expectability" of gender-based violence.

In developing this power, you must be mindful of, but not daunted by, the ways a girl's choices are limited by the conditions around her. This supports her ability to see the places in her life where she holds the power of using choice to make things happen for herself.

DEFINING POWER #4: USING CHOICE NOT CHANCE TO RECOVER A SENSE OF AGENCY

For Dominique, a girl you will meet in this chapter, developing an understanding of choice in relation to her personal values altered her life. Understanding choice meant she could discern where to put her energy, like participating in sports, engaging with her friends, and nurturing her relationship with her mother. Naming where she did not have agency was equally important. She did not have control over the dominant culture outside of her school, but didn't blame herself for it either. Dominique's example is emblematic of many girls I've met over the years.

Girls who develop an understanding of choice are motivated by a deep connection to their values. By developing an ability to use choice and not leave decisions to chance, a number of positive changes start to happen. A girl can:

- name situations where she feels she has a choice.
- name situations where she feels she doesn't have a choice.
- better understand how her choices are influenced by others.
- imagine the agency she has to change the things she wishes she could.
- determine what things she wishes she could change in moments when she feels victimized.

Seeing how this understanding plays out can be observed on a visit to Values Class, the first on-ramp we used with groups to build a girl's understanding of what choice means in the context of her life.

Developing the Power: Values Class

"Before making a big decision, what is one thing you usually think about that helps you decide what to do?" asks Cole, the girls' group leader, a biracial law school applicant. "Let's check in with that question today," Cole instructs at three schools as part of the middle school girls' group program, an effort to provide girl-centered youth development and support services.

Dominique, a recent enrollee in the girls' group, sits in the circle. A trusted school counselor had recommended the group to Dominique's mother. Fastidious by nature, Dominique is known to her middle school teachers for being a peacemaker, blessed with an ability to critique ideas in helpful ways. Dominique's mother, a Black woman, the brightest light in her world, and her White father, a significant, encouraging influence, had split up as she began middle school. Dominique is sought out as a role model for the other girls, but her expectations for herself were slowly eroding.

A budding track athlete, she had recently traveled along with her teammates and coaches to the mostly White, rural part of Washington state. On day 1 of the meets, they frequented a Denny's restaurant for breakfast and were shunted to a lone table in the back of the restaurant. "Everyone stared at us as if it was the first time they'd ever seen a Black person," she recalls to the school counselor. "Our coach explained the situation to us in a hushed tone." Turns out there was a White supremacist rally that same day. This left Dominique and her teammates terrified, with the sick feeling that they couldn't leave the dorm room, much less run the races. Though she and her team did end up participating, what stays with her, the indelible memory, is of fear instead of the accomplishment of participation.

"I think about how it will impact my friends. Like when I had a crush on a boy, and so did my friend. If I tell her, will we still be friends?" Dominique offers. "When it is something like a school decision, I talk to my mom," she adds.

Cole sets the stage further for Dominique and the group's next step: "Today, we're going to talk about the personal values that help shape who we are and the choices and decisions we make." A white poster board, like a huge flash card, clearly lists definitions.

"Values are . . . "

- Things (not physical) that are important to us, like love, honesty, or trust
- What we use to guide us in making our decisions, especially in critical moments

- Tools we carry in an imaginary backpack to use in difficult moments in life
- Chosen by us in relation to who we are, what we want, and what we do

Slow to share at first, Dominique and the other group members focus first on the material things they value, like food, money, and clothing.

Cole pushes by asking, "What do you like about money?"

"I can buy what I need and don't need to ask anyone," says one girl.

Cole responds, "So when you can buy what you need and don't need to ask anyone for help, how do you feel?"

"Free" and "independent" are the responses. Taped around the room are pieces of paper with examples of values written on them. Terms like activism, personal power, critical thinking, faith, and loyalty are posted. Cole then asks the girls to go around and write something—a word or a short memory that tells why the value is important to them. A little time passes, and she asks the girls to stand by one value they thought was essential and share why.

Without hesitation, Dominique writes, "Freedom to travel without experiencing racism." Dominique then shares three values she's written down: solidarity, racial equality, and faith in others. She tucks these away, along with her curiosity about the group and whether she will want to stay a part of it over time.

After a week or so passed, and having planted the "values" seeds, Cole next brings a Magic 8 Ball to the group, an old-school Mattel toy used for fortune-telling or seeking advice. The toy is a prop to be used in a game that conveys how arbitrary it is to not consider your own ability to say yes or say no.

On that day, Dominique and the girls root around the questions piled next to the Magic 8 Ball. The slips of paper ask girls personal things like, "Will I try out for basketball or volleyball?"

and "Will I sign up for drama camp or not?" But there is also a thread that pertains to choices girls often made unconsciously, choices like building up or breaking down other girls, choices that may have pleased others but didn't reflect what a girl really wanted for herself.

Questions like, "When a girl is being bullied on social media, do you stop reading it, or do you laugh and 'like' the comments?" and "If you were asked to smoke weed to keep a friendship, would you do it?" Others seemed far-fetched, presenting a life-or-death ethical dilemma like "If people were trying to escape a burning building, and the only option was to leave an elderly person behind so others could get out, what would you do?" The girls banter as they read the questions aloud. The room begins to feel like a late-night game at a slumber party.

"Oh, no, I'm not answering that," one utters.

"Actually, you don't have to," Cole quips. "You have a choice. Just don't answer it if you don't want to. Or make a question of your own," she tells the girls matter-of-factly, further emphasizing the point of the activity.

With uncertainty on her face, one girl shakes the ball and chooses the question: "Will I be able to go to college?"

"Definitely not," the magic ball foretells, which prompts a "what-does-this-ball-really-know" eye roll and affirms the whole idea of self-efficacy and choice.

For the rest of her first year of middle school, Cole, Dominique, and her girls' group (peers she now calls friends) will more deeply consider where they believe they have a choice and where they do not. Ultimately, in these seemingly playful activities, girls' work here is intended to help Dominique and the others see what they value and have control over and where their true values come from. Dominique begins to build a ladder to see where the larger cultural forces are impacting her world. This view allows her to interrupt the cycle of limiting and blaming herself for how racism, stereotypes, and structural barriers hold girls back.

Chapter 6

Keeping It Going: Media Literacy Class

When a girl uses personal values to guide decisions, she is on a solid track to developing the power of using choice. Alternatively, when popular culture drives a girl's choice, she loses agency and power. The values that populate mainstream culture among girls closely mirror what they've been taught by the media—objectifying other girls, looks matter more than substance, and violence is sexy, to name a few. Girls who become literate about media develop the power of knowing their true values and believing in their ability to make things happen for themselves. In my years of doing girls' work, what stayed with girls the most—no matter the program they've participated in—was learning media literacy skills. Girls who experienced our media literacy class frequently referenced the power they gained as they came to understand the mainstream currents pushing against an identity rooted in personal values. They came to embrace values that seemed counter to everything the mainstream media tells girls about themselves. Naming these forces gave them a chart to navigate and hold their agency despite the power of the currents.

Witnessing this understanding unfolding in girls' minds is a critical component of girls' work. This is one of the reasons I feel anticipation as I pack up for a group at a large urban middle school.

When I arrive in the classroom, I can sense the energy. Judging from the large bag of glue sticks and scissors on the floor and dozens of glossy magazines piled on the table, this room is ground zero for some media literacy training. "The goal today is for you to understand what media is and how to critically look at how media images are manipulated. I want you to understand the influence media has in your lives and the messages it portrays," explains Maria. Maria is a woman deeply connected to her Catholic Filipina heritage and has learned the skill of naming her personal values amid powerful mainstream forces that pressure her to assimilate.

"But first," Maria continues, "Let's check in. Write an open-ended question on the note card I am handing you. When you are done, find a girl to ask the question you wrote down. Be sure to not ask questions you are not comfortable answering," she notes.

After the girls have some time to be social, Shanda, a Black public health student in her late twenties cofacilitating the group, frames the conversation. "What is media?" she asks the girls. "Write down sources of media, as a means of communication like social media, television, newspapers, and magazines. Any source that reaches or influences people widely and everywhere," she says. Girls write many of the same things, though not surprisingly, there is a preponderance of social media channels like Instagram, TikTok, Twitter, Snapchat, and Facebook.

Next, Shanda directs the girls to review the definitions she's written on the whiteboard:

- Literacy is the ability to read and write coherently and think critically about the written word. Literacy can also include the ability to understand all forms of communication, be it body language, pictures, video, or sound (reading, speaking, listening, and viewing).

Media literacy is the ability to access, analyze, and create media in a variety of forms.

"Now let's check out this video made by Dove. It shows how advertising companies retouch photos," she instructs. As the girls watch, they initially seem disinterested. After a minute or so, however, their eyes focus and the sidebar chatter slowly ceases. The girls are mesmerized and, later, incensed. When the short video ends, Maria hands each girl a before-and-after picture. One is of Angelina Jolie, and the other is of Beyoncé. As they break into pairs, she asks them to talk to each other about what adjustments had been made to the photos and to consider why. The girls report back to the group.

Chapter 6

The second activity that day—How to Look and Act Like a Girl—is a work-by-yourself one, and girls appear ready for it. Maria passes out a collage of images of women in the media, a range of brands being advertised. Each girl is handed one as Shanda unveils two posters with these questions: What messages do the media tell us about how to act like a girl? What message does the media tell us about how to look like a girl? Inside a box on the page, she asks the girls to write down all the words and examples they had and instructs, "Just because you say a message doesn't mean you agree with it. Be respectful when calling out the judgments you hear, the assumptions people make." She guides the girls further and asks them to think about who they really are, how they look and act, and what parts of themselves are not represented in the images. Girls start writing these outside of the box.

When the girls look up at Maria, a signal they are done, she asks them, "Who created the box? What effect does the box have on your sense of identity and your self-esteem? Do you fit in the box? How do you get outside of it?"

"I created it," says one, in a self-blaming way.

"The media and other girls," says another.

"My mom tells me to act like a girl," announces a third.

I could tell Maria wishes there was more closure, a way to make girls feel better about what they've just been made aware of.

"What went well today? What did you like? What would you do differently next time?" Maria poses, closing the group out for the day.

"I feel relieved that those women aren't even real," announces another. "Gives me permission to be myself."

The media literacy class is an eye-opener and a confidence shifter for girls. It surprises me again and again how girls connect what they learn about photoshopping and developing an eye for what is false in the media's portrayal of girls and women to a greater sense of choice, of connection to their values, and of their self-efficacy. On hearing how the girls felt after the class, Maria, Shanda, and I are reminded of their appreciation for the truth, and willingness to have the veil of societally created expectations pulled back.

POWER TOOL: PARENT/MENTOR TIPS FOR USING CHOICE NOT CHANCE

- Build Her Values Literacy

  Naming a personal lexicon of values, such as justice, integrity, kindness, and courage, is crucial to a girl's sense of power. It is essential to prioritize values that align with personal beliefs rather than relying solely on popular culture influences. Values literacy should be coupled with an understanding of the significance of a girl's actions in effecting change.

- Respect Her Values Boundaries

  When faced with a girl expressing different values, be aware of your reactions. What signals do your body language, facial expressions, or words convey? Recognize your triggers and learn to stop yourself from influencing her to adopt your values. Keep digging for her values.

- Use Media Smarts to Explore Choice

  A media-literate girl can critically analyze and challenge sexist and racist media messages. Media significantly shape how a girl perceives herself and forms beliefs about her choices. Media consumption without critique can limit a girl's beliefs about her power. Support a girl in understanding how the mainstream media promotes a limited range of choices for girls.

- Highlight Media Literacy's Connection to Healthy Girl Culture

  Teaching girls the media's influence in perpetuating a negative girl culture is crucial. Media literacy is a vitally important opportunity to focus on the societal circumstances reflected there. The media mirrors, magnifies, and reflects the ways girls are taught to demonize one another and compete. By promoting media literacy, and the opportunity to critique what she is

CHAPTER 6

consuming, you are providing a girl with a way to envision an alternative. A girl can create media in new ways and use it to change the girl culture at home, at school, or anywhere.
- Reframe, Don't Demonize, Media
   Critiquing media without alienating a girl is key. Encourage a critical perspective on consciously and subconsciously absorbed imagery. Ask a girl to share empowering examples of media representation she appreciates. Engage in constructive analysis rather than direct criticism.

MY POWERFUL CHOICE

I was one of forty thousand women activists who had converged on Beijing, China, for the Fourth United Nations Conference on Women for a weeklong gathering to ratify a human rights agenda for women and girls from all corners of the globe. For a newcomer to international organizing, human rights were no longer abstract. Before, reading a UN report, I felt distant from the data, from the individual stories they reflected. We don't see ourselves as statistics, and this was especially true in Beijing. Here I met women in a daily struggle to overcome the forces of poverty, sexual violence, and/or limited access to education. Relying on limited NGO budgets and the strength of their relationships with one another, these women courageously faced bureaucracy, repressive governments, and the obstacles of patriarchal systems. I had come to meet these luminaries, but had never expected how profoundly I would meet myself. Attending the conference would transform my understanding of my work and choices I made as a girl and shape my understanding of the broader context of choice for all girls and women.

On one of the sunny September days in Beijing, ten conference attendees and I, from various continents and cultures, boarded the local bus for a dusty, potholed, diesel-scented ride through the valley to visit the Badaling section of the Great Wall. The view was unexpected and transcendent. A chorus of singing and prayers I will never forget spontaneously erupted from my fellow attendees upon sight of the Great Wall.

Being the very last person to exit the bus, I was buoyant. I wept. For much of my life I made choices within a box designed to protect my parents from any further harm. Coming to Beijing was one of the most inspired, independent choices I had ever made. This was the moment I felt like part of a movement. What my parents saw as my recklessness, I saw as freedom. What my parents—my dad in particular—saw as selfish and rebellious, I saw as the whispering of a sense of agency, of my ability to make my own choices. His fears and protective instincts were at the forefront of every conversation where risks were involved. "Why? What are you in search of?" he'd asked. The weight I'd carried to that point had, at last, yielded to the recognition of my own free will to decide what I wanted, my power to act. I was freed to fully experience my *own* hope and my *own* choices. My choices *and* the gender-based fears for my safety as a young woman were for once held in the right balance.

The decision to go to Beijing held profound significance, not only for the experience itself but also for the personal insights it brought about. While in China, I embarked on a journey of self-discovery, delving into the depths of my childhood adversity and its impact on my sense of agency. It was a pivotal moment during which I began to articulate and understand the ways in which my past experiences had shaped my identity and perceptions.

One of the most significant realizations during this time was the recognition that my childhood adversity was not solely a collective family experience but had uniquely affected me as an individual. This acknowledgment was a turning point, allowing me to view the past trauma of my sister's murder through my own lens rather than solely through the perspectives of my family members.

Years later, the formalization of my understanding came with the emergence of the term "adverse childhood experiences" (ACEs) by the Centers for Disease Control and Prevention. On some level, understanding the complex interplay of trauma and its effects on behavior allowed me to empathize and support girls in their own healing journeys. This framework was particularly helpful for understanding those girls who had faced multiple adversities, including various forms of abuse, neglect, exposure to violence, parental separation, or living in environments affected by substance abuse or mental health issues.

Overall, my experiences in Beijing and the subsequent understanding of ACEs not only facilitated my personal growth and healing but also equipped me with the knowledge and empathy to support others who have faced similar challenges. It underscored the importance of acknowledging and addressing childhood adversity to promote resilience and well-being in individuals and communities.

Scoring high on the ACEs chart is not a desirable label, but it is crucial to assess the potentially traumatic events a girl has faced. As for myself, I discovered that my childhood adversity had somehow enabled me to turn a blind eye to violence. Denying the possibility of violence was a psychological defense mechanism deeply ingrained within me. It acted as a protective shield, but it also hindered my ability to confront and address realities.

Being socialized as a girl taught me to tolerate casual violence. There is a continuum of gender-related violence that ranges from catcalls on the street to more blatant acts like being groped at a party or being subjected to slut shaming based on my attire. I often reasoned that as long as I hadn't experienced rape or something worse, the situations I encountered were somehow manageable. If I could overlook this much everyday violence in my own life, what about the violence in the lives of the girls I would meet? How does denial by adults of the violence a girl experiences impact her choices, especially when they are charged and entrusted with her healing and well-being? Understanding what is beneath the surface forces any care provider to witness instead of looking the other way when we see a girl's suffering.[6]

Cultivating an ability to consciously observe, acknowledge, and articulate my initial encounters with choice has enhanced my effectiveness as an advocate and a mother. This skill has enabled me to become more attuned to moments when a girl's experiences of tragedy or violence elicit personal turmoil by resurfacing my own past experiences. Engaging with girls frequently evoked memories of feeling a lack of control and authority over decisions in my own life. Consequently, it became imperative for me to grasp the importance of delineating between personal emotions and my professional role when working with girls.

Recognizing the importance of separating the personal from professional realms represented a significant advancement in my work. It involved actively working to interrupt my pattern of being emotionally consumed by these experiences as swiftly as possible. This conscious effort to navigate the intersection of personal history and professional practice has not only deepened my understanding of girls' needs but also enhanced my ability to effectively support them on their unique journeys.

What also exists in this experience for me is my Whiteness. What considerations are there for women of color, who must navigate casual sexual violence in a society designed to provide maximum punishment to the men in their communities? Or for those who have experienced sexual violence from those within the systems of power purported to be "protecting" the community? From boarding schools for Indigenous children in the Americas, to forced sterilization for incarcerated women of color, to the focus of police brutality often being on Black men and not the Black women also victimized, it is important to put "choice" into the context of existing in a social system that targets women of color.

PARENT/MENTOR SELF-REFLECTION POWER TOOL

Recalling personal experiences is valuable in understanding the impact of choice. To build your muscle for supporting a girl in developing this power, explore your comfort level with how choice affects your day-to-day life. Ask yourself:

1. What information about your own experiences of exercising choice is helpful to recall? Are there memories that you can unpack so that you are better prepared to support a girl in developing this power?
2. What do you need to do with what you've learned to develop your proficiency in supporting a girl in building this power?
3. What is your attitude toward changing your practice related to this power?
4. What existing habits might you need to unlearn?
5. What about your current environment prevents you from being successful in learning this practice?

Recovering a Sense of Choice

"My mom says 'hi,'" Dominique announces as I sit across from her at the café. We order red velvet cupcakes and soak in this reunion moment. Fifteen years later, we are here to discuss her involvement in the girls' group as an adolescent. In her late twenties, Dominique still possesses her calm, contemplative demeanor. With a red shirt, silver earrings, and short curly hair, she is both impeccable and understated.

"I remember always being excited to go, loving what we would talk about, leaving feeling happy, and telling my mom about it. I remember Cole. She was soft-spoken. She even gave me her old bridesmaid dresses for eighth-grade graduation, a gorgeous lavender dress that my mom made a shawl to match. And though confidence isn't a skill, I know this is what I gained," she tells me matter-of-factly.

"When you're that young, you're so impressionable. We saw all these things going on that were uncomfortable, and we had a safe space to talk about it. When we got into that room, we were united, on the same team, helping each other, helping ourselves, a feeling of solidarity where there is usually division among girls." This feeling Dominique describes is healthy girl culture, and I learn that day that she continued to seek out and create healthy girl culture at every subsequent phase of her life: Sister Circle in high school; the Beta Jean club, a "Divine Nine" sorority, at the University of Washington.

"Validation of my choices was critical, too. I wanted to feel heard and to try on my choices without judgment. I wanted to know that others understood why I felt the way I did and why I might want what I wanted. Then I could move forward honoring my values," she tells me.

The longer-term impact of joining a girls' group set off a cascade of choices that reflected Dominique's growing sense of power. In high school, she stopped watching music videos after a Sister Circle in which they discussed the impact of these videos. When she wrote her letter of intent to her sorority, she wrote about girls' empowerment as foundational to her life. In her senior year of high school, Dominique founded the Beta Jean Petal Club, a younger version of the Black sorority she hoped to join in college. Now all younger women who join learn who Dominique is as part of the club's history "Everything I do I think of my sisters. We are all positive, Black women always pursuing success, uplifting each other. No matter what I did, it was the sisterhood that got me through."

More broadly, Dominique's experience reflects a big shift in what happens for girls when they successfully make decisions from a place of belief about their abilities versus following socialized expectations. Hers is also an excellent example of viewing choice more broadly, seeing what tools she needed to begin to confront societal forces, the racism threaded throughout the systems and institutions in the United States. It was about seeing why the choices available to her in the world around her were limited and that she could join forces with other girls, at every stage of her life, to challenge these.

Chapter 6

A handful of years after our coffee shop reunion, Dominique and I meet again in the conference room of her nonprofit workplace. She has joined the board of directors where I work, and we recently hired additional staff so we could take on a more significant role in state-level legislative policy advocacy. We bury our minds and hearts in local data and talk of the places we want to grow girls programming. On a whiteboard on one side of the room are community norms that provide texture for how we hope to meaningfully engage others who join in our organizational culture, where communication is expected to be free and open and inevitably a bit messy. Toward the back of the room, written on another whiteboard, are the first key concepts of a federal grant, where the funds are expansive and plentiful but require a hefty amount of time to acquire. Beyond the glass window directly in front of us is the food and clothing bank that draws girls and families to the center and a dutiful sign that reminds us to consider big ideas for change in the context of a girl's choices, as they exist, at that moment.

With Dominique's leadership, we start a girls' advocacy program, which provides girls in Washington state an opportunity to provide legislative testimony on issues related to juvenile justice, mental health, child welfare, housing and homelessness, education, and more. With chapters across the state, girls leverage the collective influence of policymakers based on the prioritized needs identified by the chapter members. This includes speaking at events, testifying in a public hearing, appearing at fundraising engagements, writing, traveling, and training alongside our staff. One of the chapters is at the state's youth rehabilitation facility.

What this entails for girls' work moving forward is that we will make sure the policy tables—juvenile justice, child welfare, housing, school, mental health, and youth development, for instance—have more chairs for girls directly impacted by the policies that aren't working. Another useful role is to bring new resources, get funds redirected using a race and social justice lens, and teach girls how to do all of this through internships. Pushing to continue to divide all the data we collect from these systems by race and gender so we can highlight disparities and respond with more targeted support; continuing to acknowledge the history of racism, past and present, against communities of color across Washington state; ensuring our organizational budgets are formed using antiracism and social justice tools; and continually expanding racial representation and youth voices in staffing, board, and membership. All are within our control.

It is not insignificant that Dominique and I, as relatively young women, had started our girls' work journey with a personal understanding of choice. Choice is a word that no longer trips us up. It puzzled us because we thought that the people who tended to use the word negatively, including those inside and outside our political circles, were the ones who blocked the discussion from moving forward. "I think we should expand the word *choice*," Dominique tells me.

I asked her what she would say it meant, and she paused for a long moment. "That a girl's life choices are generally improved," she says finally, "but in such a way that it encourages an overall rise of girls themselves in making policy, in getting elected to office and holding the purse strings to fund change."

This is the ultimate hope of girls' work at this stage. The more girls have choices, the more they want to ensure these choices are more widely available to others. It is the power of wanting all girls to have greater choices.

The Big Picture: Change the Rules Not the Girl

En route to an inaugural girls' rights summit in Washington state, I observe a truck's mud flaps. Initially, I assume they are the typical sexist mud flaps, the ones depicting a female silhouette with exaggerated sexualized features. These mud flaps, in fact, are not those. They surprise me. Instead of the usual portrayal, the silhouette on the mud flaps holds out a book, an empowered counterpoint to the original version. Even the symbolism on mud flaps can challenge the objectification of women and serve as a tangible, if small, indicator of progress. My encounter is a welcome surprise as I drive to Costco to pick up donated catering.

"Thanks for contributing. I deeply appreciate your support," I tell the Costco manager.

"I've plucked the best-of-the-best Costco has to offer for your event. What you're doing is so valuable. Would've made a difference for me," she replies as she helps me lift the disc-shaped sandwich tray into the back of my tired-looking minivan. This attitude, too, like the mud flaps, reflects social change. Many people out working in the world covertly or overtly support the cause of girl justice and the mainstreaming of girls' empowerment groups. These hopeful encounters underscore the importance of transforming societal norms and representations across various platforms, including advertising billboards, mud flaps, and corporate corridors.

Arriving at the summit, hosted at a deluxe Girl Scouts facility south of Seattle, I make my way through a bustling, packed foyer.

The convening of over seventy-five representatives from various sectors such as government, education, health, nonprofit, philanthropy, and business is a significant achievement for the summit. The main objective of this gathering is to take a fresh look at data trends and develop a comprehensive understanding of the existing barriers and challenges that continue to affect girls' choices in various spheres of life. By collectively acknowledging and addressing these limitations, the summit participants can work toward devising targeted interventions and policy recommendations that can help overcome these challenges.

As I settle in, I notice the Nike Foundation's Girl Effect video playing overhead. The short film contrasts two outcomes for an eleven-year-old girl: one where she has access to education, safety, health, and leadership opportunities, allowing her to positively contribute to society, and another where these opportunities are limited, stifling her potential and impacting the broader community negatively.

This simple yet compelling portrayal emphasizes the pivotal role of investing in girls and their empowerment. It highlights how addressing the most pressing development problems hinges upon providing girls with the necessary resources and opportunities to thrive. By enabling girls to make choices and realize their potential, society as a whole can benefit.

As the video unfolds, it effectively engages the audience, leaving a lasting impression and setting the tone for the summit. It reinforces the importance of examining data trends, identifying successful approaches, and discussing the limitations that still exist in terms of choices available to girls across the state.

The video tapers off, and you could've heard a pin drop in the standing-room-only room. "As a region, academic, health, and leadership gains have not been shared equally by girls of color and/or those girls who grow up in poverty. Today is a day where we will showcase regional solutions that help to create opportunity for all girls," says our tall, White policy researcher in an authoritative voice as she stands beneath the blank screen.

Now on the big screen, our own state's complex data, pulled apart by gender, race and income, appears in bold font. Girls who are most marginalized in our state, those who are unhoused, involved in the child welfare system, or involved in the juvenile justice system—and frequently all three—face exponentially difficult mental health outcomes as a consequence of the violence they face.

"What do we do now?" another White academic poses as attendees offer ideas in popcorn fashion:

"Do more mentoring."

"Make sure people know the value of investing in girls' programs."

"Advocate for young women aged eighteen to twenty-five who aren't in college."

Chapter 6

"Secure funding to grow the girls' empowerment programs across the state."

I stand at the back and wrestle with an unpleasant feeling. Is it detachment? Overwhelm? Or is it cynicism? One too many times, I have had this conversation in this exact company of people. What the data tells us is we need to stop glossing over the girls who are most marginalized, or we will only end up expanding choices for girls who hold a great deal of privilege by comparison.

"I love the idea of mentoring," I hear a familiar voice say, "but how does taking the girl to the zoo address scoring an eight out of ten on the scale of adverse childhood experiences address the trauma she's experienced after enduring repeated acts of sexual violence from people close to her?" It's Lynn, a colleague and detention girls group facilitator. "Because of prior victimization and trauma, girls may not be comfortable sharing in a group setting. Consider individual counseling and working with them individually, too."

Lynn has named for us how heartbreakingly limited the choices are for some girls, for those whose experiences require a completely different type of mentoring and service palette. What does choice mean when a girl suffers abuse or physical violence at home? What does choice mean when her basic need to feel safe is repeatedly unmet? Confronting violence, as commonplace as it is for all girls and in all of its forms, is, we realize, ground zero to this broader vision of choice.

As mentors, until we go deeper with girls who have experienced profound levels of violence in these ways, until we commit to understanding how girls in violent relationships may believe their survival depends on staying in a violent relationship, the broader concept of choice will remain frustratingly elusive. Our role as a mentor is to acknowledge how hard it might be for a girl to walk away from an abusive relationship and help her to refocus on other, more positive relationships in her life. Recognizing the power girls can give to these relationships without judgment is a required skill set.

A young legislative aide takes Lynn's thread further through the needle. "Mentoring is one thing. But why are girls being arrested for running away and skipping school in the first place? Why are girls blamed for being victims? And these particular girls need services so far beyond what's being offered."

Now, we are talking about policy change, a move upstream to stop criminalizing these girls for the trauma they've experienced. This may be the gold nugget to come out of the day. The legislative aide agrees to set up a meeting with the state senator she works for, which eventually leads to a group of us—academics, advocates, and court administrators—providing legislative testimony on trends in the treatment of girls in the juvenile justice and child welfare systems. It's a start.

The summit's limits also glare at us. While the summit serves as a platform for raising awareness and catalyzing action, constraints in terms of the resources, influence, and reach necessary to implement comprehensive and long-lasting solutions are evident. Achieving meaningful progress requires not only commitment during the event but sustained efforts in the aftermath as well. It is becoming increasingly clear why progress often falls spectacularly short. The people making decisions about girls' lives (a) aren't girls anymore, (b) don't reflect the girls themselves, (c) make decisions based on their own values, and (d) don't bother to ask girls what works for them.

When policies and systems are developed without the input and perspectives of those directly affected, there is a risk of perpetuating existing power imbalances and reinforcing oppressive structures. The consequences of this can often impact girls disproportionately, limiting their opportunities and hindering their overall well-being.

To address this problem, it is crucial to prioritize inclusive and participatory processes in policymaking. This means actively involving girls themselves in shaping the decisions that affect their lives. By listening to their experiences, needs, and aspirations, policymakers can gain valuable insight into the realities on the ground and work toward developing more effective, equitable, and sustainable solutions.

POWER TOOL: A USING CHOICE, NOT CHANCE ACTIVITY YOU CAN DO WITH GIRLS

Introduction

A big part of the coming-of-age experience for a girl is battling a vague sense of powerlessness, of things feeling out of her control. Outwardly she may look like she is succeeding in school or elsewhere, but this can be deceiving. Psychologists and youth development researchers alike describe the power that comes from replacing a things-happen-to-me mindset with an I-make-things-happen-for-myself mindset as self-efficacy. Since a big part of developing confidence for a girl is learning to make choices for herself, this activity conveys how risky it is to not recognize your own ability to say yes or say no, essentially the control you do have to make decisions that reflect what you value.

Conversation Tips

Give some thought to your own triggers when it comes to words like choice and values. Stay conscious of the ways you may want to judge or control how a girl responds to the activity questions. Remind her that you are not judging her.

Goals
- Develop a deeper understanding of the concept of choice.
- Develop a fresh understanding of when she makes decisions from a place of choice.

Do This Together
1. Write up a few questions like these on slips of paper: Will I try out for basketball? Will I sign up for drama camp? When a girl is being bullied on social media, do I stop reading it, or

do I hit "like"? If I was asked to smoke pot to keep a friendship, would I do it? Others can be far-fetched, presenting a life-or-death ethical dilemma like "If there were people trying to escape a burning building, and the only option was to leave an elderly person behind so others could get out, what would I do?"

2. Pull up the online Magic 8 Ball (www.ask8ball.net), based off of the old-school Mattel toy used for fortune-telling or seeking advice. The online tool is a prop to be used in a game that conveys how arbitrary it is to not consider your own ability to say yes or say no. Then ask the girl to write up more questions. Play a few rounds using the questions you both wrote up. Once you are done playing, ask: When is a time you made decisions from a place of choice, not chance, or used personal not popular values as a guide?

3. Now read the definition of the power of using choice, not chance, out loud and the skills that it takes to build it. Ask the closing questions: What is a skill she needs to develop related to this power? Who can help her?

CHAPTER 7

Trusting Her Instincts, Voicing Consent

POWER #5

A girl who connects her emotions with decisions about her body reclaims control over it. Too often, girls are bombarded with societal messages that disconnect them from their intuition. As a result, choices about their bodies become driven by external pressures rather than internal desires. Developing this power means understanding the influences and norms that cause girls to disregard their emotional signals when making choices about their bodies. It involves learning to listen to one's desires, especially when making sexual decisions. With this self-awareness, a girl can make choices that reflect a healthier relationship with her body.

Everywhere girls turn, they're taught that their bodies should conform to harmful mainstream expectations. As Chimamanda Ngozi Adichie powerfully puts it, "Girls are socialized in ways that are harmful to their sense of self—to reduce themselves, to cater to the egos of men, to think of their bodies as repositories of shame."[1] Internalizing these messages is one of the reasons why girls disengage from trusting their intuition.

CHAPTER 7

This disconnect is further complicated by messages about sexuality. As Peggy Orenstein argues in *Don't Call Me Princess: Essays on Girls, Women, Sex, and Life*, "Young women today are sold the idea that sexiness is the same as sexuality, that being desirable is more important than understanding their own desires."[2] In response, girls often make decisions about their bodies, not from a place of self-trust but from a desperate need to maintain relationships—even broken ones—and avoid rejection.

The consequences of these pressures have created a crisis in girls' mental health and body image. Social media and stigma have fueled the problem, leaving astronomical numbers of girls struggling with depression, hopelessness, and even suicidal thoughts.[3] Meta's own research found that Instagram exacerbated body issues for one in three teen girls, and more than 40 percent of teen Instagram users in the United Kingdom and the United States said they felt "unattractive" and said the feeling began *while using the app*.[4]

At the root of these struggles lies a fundamental issue of control and agency. Research highlights how adolescent girls' lack of control over their bodies and sexuality is a key driver of poor mental health outcomes. It's a vicious cycle of objectification, shame, and loss of agency. Grabe et al. find that body objectification—being valued primarily for physical appearance—predicts higher levels of depression and shame in adolescent girls.[5] This finding is reinforced by Tolman et al. who identify how this lack of control over bodies and sexuality negatively impacts girls' mental health, proposing embodied selfhood as a protective factor.[6] Jacobs et al. argue for treatment approaches focused on fostering embodied respect, or respect for bodily autonomy, to counter mental health issues resulting from lack of body control.[7] These studies underscore the significant mental health challenges arising from objectification and lack of bodily agency for adolescent girls.

The impact of these experiences goes beyond mental health and becomes physically held in the body itself. In *The Body Keeps the Score*, Bessel van der Kolk illuminates how trauma literally gets coded into the mind and body, paving neural pathways to anxiety, depression, and more. His work points to an integrative, body-centered path to begin rewriting those traumatic imprints.[8] And this mind-body connection is where the science of neural plasticity becomes so relevant.

When we talk about developing girls' "gut power" and teaching them to trust their instincts, we're really delving into the realm of neural pathways. Our intuitive responses, habit patterns, and embodied experiences all trace back to how our brains are wired. Research shows that many of our default neural pathways are laid down from a young age, shaped by our epigenetics, family environments, and life experiences.[9] These are the well-trodden paths, the "can't teach an old dog new tricks" neural circuits.

Neuroplasticity refers to how the brain grows, how new connections, relationships, and habits can change our neural pathways. These "use or lose" neurons can be trained to "fire together *and* wire together," says Amy Banks, MD, director of advanced training and senior research scientist at the Jean Baker Miller Training Institute and the Wellesley Centers for Women. Banks encourages professionals and laypeople to help girls understand the quality of their relationships and strengthen their neural pathways for connection.[10]

Our health models tend to ignore these relational complexities, favoring assumptions of pure rational choice. As gender scholars argue, we must move beyond this limited view to contextualize the sociocultural forces and emotional undercurrents shaping girls' decision-making around sexuality and well-being. From this perspective, what preserves or maintains a relationship is a better litmus test for what sexual decisions a girl will make.

DEFINING POWER #5: TRUSTING HER INSTINCTS, VOICING CONSENT TO RECLAIM CONTROL

When a girl purposefully aligns her emotions with the decisions she makes about her body, she can reclaim control. A girl who uses this power makes choices about her body that reflect a healthier relationship with it. Advocates who teach girls about this power don't say things like, "You're being overly emotional or dramatic." Instead, they talk about trusting your instincts and taking responsibility for what your gut is telling you in your relationships. Teaching about consent and boundaries is a facet of this vitally important power. Advocates don't allow the word consent to be mysterious, and they don't forget to be clear in explaining about what consent to having sex is and is not.

Exploring this power, I saw girls push back when being shamed for an outfit they were wearing. Or alternatively, they felt unafraid to wear an outfit that wasn't "mainstream." I saw girls question "White, blue-eyed" standards of beauty that subtly influenced choices they made about makeup, contact lenses, or eating habits. I saw them push back on slut shaming, and girls began to stop blaming themselves for incidents of sexual harassment or assault. A few girls disclosed sexual victimization and chose to get support within their school system. By understanding the power of trusting one's gut and consent, a girl begins:

- seeing how decisions she makes about her body—for instance, what she eats or wears—are influenced by others.
- taking control of decisions she makes about her body.
- understanding what body shaming is and detecting when she's doing that to herself.
- being able to openly talk about or agree on what kind of sexual or physical activity she wants to engage in.
- naming what feelings of sexual desire in her body mean to her.
- understanding what sexual violence is and the circumstances that can surround it.

Visits to a sexual health and education class and a Paper Bag Fashion Show event offer unique insights into efforts aimed at developing this form of power. Used with groups to build a girl's understanding of what trusting her gut and consent mean in the context of her life, both activities spark a way for girls to feel greater ownership of their relationships with their bodies.

DEVELOPING THE POWER: COMPREHENSIVE SEXUAL HEALTH EDUCATION CLASS

Lulu, the life-size, anatomically correct doll we use in the program, lived in a brown burlap sack with black-corded drawstrings and was frequently stashed in the trunk of my car. She needed to be mobile. Lulu had tightly coiled brown hair, imperfectly shaped breasts attached with Velcro, poppy-red cording used to create her vulva, and a red velvet uterus. Her lady parts had earned her the nickname "jewel box."

Lulu escaped her bag at least once a week, and today was no different. Today, she was the main teaching tool of a ninety-minute workshop on sexual health and wellness at the county detention facility. The group, up and running for several years, was a collaborative effort between our nonprofit organization, public health professionals, and a sexual assault and trauma center. In addition to the health group, the team addresses the challenges of keeping girls who have court contact[11] safer in their day-to-day lives on the outside. So while Lulu was absolutely designed to help girls learn about the facts and risky behaviors associated with choices about sex, she was equally created to explore trust in intimate relationships and identify what sexual desire feels like in one's body. Lulu's job description included this broader scope, and on that day, the girls would be getting a dose of that.

For many of these girls, this day represented a pivotal moment. In a group where a staggering 85 percent had experienced sexual violence,[12] and some had been arrested on charges of "prostitution" stemming from commercial sexual exploitation,[13] it may have been the very first time they were told they have a right to make choices about their own bodies. It was likely their initial positive experience being surrounded by other girls in a supportive setting, an environment where they could feel safe, seen, and validated instead of judged or objectified.

Chapter 7

With others who have been in the group before, I am impressed by the level of leadership and initiative they take. They pass out snacks and hang up posters. We tended to see some of these girls, on average, three to four weeks in a row, and knew they needed to have leadership roles when they repeated the group.

"Good afternoon. Let's start with common ground today. Who'd like to lead it?" Lynn, our straight, White, middle-aged instructor asks. "I share common ground with anyone who has been in juvie before," says one of the girls when it is her turn to be in the middle. Every girl there moves to find a spot. It is something they can all relate to. We play a few more rounds, and the group starts to feel a little less icy.

"Girls, please welcome Lulu," says Jody, a Black public health nurse (also middle-aged and straight) as she shimmies Lulu out of the bag by her hair. Several girls walk over to help, holding the bottom of her bag. Tasha, a broad-shouldered Black girl with a small crescent-shaped scar on her chin, who has been to juvie a handful of times, is trained to help facilitate, since she has participated in past workshops. Tasha covers the basics of anatomy—three holes, normal for breasts to be two different sizes—while Jody debunks some of the myths girls have, like if your partner had an STD you would be able to see it, or you shouldn't get an IUD unless you've had kids already.

"I heard the pill makes you fat," chimes in one of the girls sitting in the amorphous circle. "And that you have to take it at the same time every day or it won't work," adds another.

Eventually, the Lulu activity sparks a conversation on how to look out for your needs in the heat of the moment or when you struggle to take care of yourself because you want to please your partner. "You may want to do whatever it takes to keep him, but you need to think twice about that," warns Jody. The group moves fast, and after forty-five minutes or so, Lynn transitions the group to the next activity. She pulls out a Magic 8 Ball from her oversized bag. Like in other girls' groups, the activity is a crowd favorite that provides an opportunity for a girl to explore what influences her choices and decisions. At today's workshop, they drill down on sexual choices and consent. Lynn passes around little sheets of paper with prewritten questions on them like "Should I have sex without a condom?" "Can you get pregnant when you have your period?" and "Will I say no if I am not in the mood to have sex?" These are the types of questions the girls will take turns asking the ball. When one of the last girls' turn comes up, she asks the Magic 8 Ball whether or not sexual desire is possible for girls. Jody shakes the ball, all eyes on her. "It is decidedly so," the magic ball foretells.

"Now I want to consider the idea that you can consent to your choices," Lynn adds, as girls continue to sit in the circle. "Consent means[14] you are being explicit and communicating what is or isn't okay with you when you are engaging in sexual activity. And just because you say yes to one thing, doesn't mean you have agreed to another. Periodically checking in with yourself and your partner by asking 'Is this still okay?' is important," she says as the girls listen and absorb the definition. For some of the girls today, who are victims of sex trafficking, the idea of consent will seem far-fetched and unrealistic. But the instructors are hoping that, if not today, one day it won't be.

Before the group can dive much deeper, the dinner cart shows up with a waft of starchy, overcooked food. The group ends a little too abruptly, but today feels like a good start. "Okay, girls. Thanks for your time today. We will be putting a special care package aside for you for when you get out. You will find a recap of what we talked about today, and some other goodies and resources. Harborview Center for Sexual Assault and Traumatic Stress is coming tomorrow," Lynn says as she closes the group. "They are going to talk about what sexual violence is. You know they'll be available if you need to talk with a counselor afterward."

CHAPTER 7

Walking down the long hall back to security, Lynn shares feelings of ambivalence. Sure, the program in juvenile detention is a start. Sure, developing the broader power of trusting one's gut and speaking the language of consent with girls begins by not blaming and punishing girls for their victimization. But it's not enough. Odds are one in a million a girl can survive the levels of violence and poverty *many of these particular girls* had and somehow escape a life of minimal choices after meeting Lulu, shaking a Magic 8 Ball, and learning about what consent means.

"Many of these particular girls have no choice about consent. They need to begin to understand their rights, and how violence and living in survival mode need not dictate their choices. They need consistent housing, consistent PTSD support, and counseling," she tells me. "If only we could have reached her sooner, upstream when she was younger, before the harm done to her left her with fewer choices," she says as her voice trails off.

KEEPING IT GOING: THE PAPER BAG FASHION SHOW

An example of a proactive activity called the Paper Bag Fashion Show is one I visit at a middle school. Offered to girls who are part of a longer-term girls' group, the activity happens after girls have experienced the values and media literacy workshops. Staging a fashion show, in which an outfit proxies for the choices a girl makes about her body, provides a way for a girl to consciously decide what happens to her body.

"I hope you all had some time to digest the media literacy workshop. I know it can be a lot to unpack. So we are going to explore what we discussed more deeply. Are you ready? We are gonna have a Paper Bag Fashion Show," announces Jill, a thirtysomething, White, pixie-haired instructor. "You will get to be both the fashion designer and the model. The fashion show will be an opportunity for you to express your creativity and push the boundaries of traditional clothing design. There is no first place, second place, or runner-up. Everyone's a winner. You are the judge of your design," she explains. Next Jill cracks open a duffle bag full of markers, ribbons, and scissors, and the designing begins. Emily, a White girl new to the group and somewhat reluctant, slowly migrates toward the duffle. She seems skeptical of participating and waits until the other girls take their materials and move into dyads together. Emily chooses to work alone. With scissors in hand, her bag transforms into a colorful checkered pattern of reds and oranges. Eventually, she drapes a sash that says "Miss Californication" across her shoulder, a riffed lyric from a concert she'd recently attended with her dad.

When all the girls have completed their designs and are ready for the show, Jill unfurls a red carpet. She asks the girls what they want their walk-up songs to be as she makes an impromptu playlist. When the girls begin to walk the carpet, one struts, one flexes her muscles like a pro wrestler, another marches like a soldier. The mood is playful. Once all the girls arrive at the front of the room, Jill asks them to take a bow. A tennis ball jammed into a cafeteria utensil serves as a faux microphone. "What colors, words, or ideas matter to you when you create something? What do you allow to be in your design? How do you choose what you want? and When were you influenced by the opinions of others in the choices you made?" are prompts that the girls enthusiastically respond to in popcorn style.

"I love red polka dots," one says.

"Sleeveless for me," says another.

"Not sure how I chose, but it felt good to wear what I wanted and not get in trouble from my mom." The designing and showing takes most of the ninety-minute group time.

Using a black Sharpie, Jill begins to close the group by writing a definition of consent on the red carpet: Consent is an ongoing process of discussing boundaries and what you're comfortable with. "We will be working to get more specific about how consent plays out in your life," she says as she tees up the content for their one-on-one time.

Chapter 7

"I loved the show," Emily tells Jill as she puts supplies away. "At first I thought it would be dumb. But it was actually really fun." Emily continues with the girls' group throughout middle school, and her one-on-one experiences with Jill become especially important. Emily has recently moved from a suburban middle school. Changing schools was not easy for her. She struggles to connect with teachers and other students. And after discussing choice and consent, Emily discloses a secret to Jill that has gnawed at her. A family friend had repeatedly sexually molested her. She hadn't told a soul about the abuse.

In their initial mentor meeting, Jill had informed Emily that she was a mandatory reporter. After the disclosure, Jill worked to ensure that Emily had as much choice as possible in how the investigation would happen by helping her plan details such as what time of day, where, and how they would undertake it. Jill also ensured that a trusted school representative engaged in a way that worked for Emily.

As the relationship between Jill and Emily strengthened, it was especially important to continue to describe and define the role Jill could play in Emily's life. Even though she developed what may have felt at the time like a friendship with Emily, it was in Emily's best interest to clearly communicate how her mentor role would translate into support. Working in the program meant Jill had to continually ask herself, "What's appropriate to share about myself?" and "What boundaries are important to maintain?" and "Have I communicated what I can and cannot do to support her?" These essential questions are in service of the well-being of a girl. As we were not case managers, therapists, or counselors, we worked hard to know the limits of our care and do "warm" handoffs to provide referrals so the girl could continue to heal. A girl so rarely feels safe to disclose sexual violence to anyone. It is an opportunity to upend the harm and guide her on a path toward healing.

POWER TOOL: PARENT/MENTOR TIPS FOR TRUSTING HER INSTINCTS, VOICING CONSENT
- Guiding Healthy Self-Disclosure

    In these conversations, a girl is encouraged to share personal information to understand her experience. However, to ensure a balanced and meaningful discussion, set the tone beforehand. Emphasize that personal stories and experiences are valued, while also considering the needs of the entire group. Say, "If you are uncomfortable bringing up a personal story or experience in front of others, please do not feel pressure to do so." And if a girl discloses too much personal information, don't cut her off mid-story. Gently guide her to a conclusion, thank her, and mention that you will follow up with her later.[15] These conversations can lead to disclosing a history or specific incidence of violence. You need to remind girls that you are a mandatory reporter. If they disclose that someone is hurting or has hurt them, or that they are considering hurting themselves, you are required by law to report this to your local Child Protective Services (CPS).

- Demystify the Consent Code

    Activities that help a girl learn about the facts and risky behaviors associated with sex and consent should go hand in hand with conversations that center on "What are you willing to do to preserve an intimate relationship? Does preserving the relationship or proving you trust your partner take precedence over the condom you had planned to use? How do you feel sexual desire in your body—pleasure, fear, vulnerability—and what do these mean to you?" Feeling entitled to desire and developing a language for what consent feels like is a crucial protective factor in combating the "it just happened" experiences for a girl. If you know what desire feels like, gender differences scholars suggest, you also know what it doesn't feel like.

- Her Relationships, Her Choices

Research suggests that girls prioritize their relationships when making decisions, often placing their own needs secondary. This need not be the case. You can honor a girl's commitment to her relationships as you support her in prioritizing her own needs. If a girl encounters difficulties aligning a choice with her values, or defaults to the views of others around her, you can prompt her with questions like "What is a clue that you are saying yes when you mean no?" and "What situations do you find yourself in when this happens?" Other questions to help a girl explore the pros and cons of relational decision-making are "When is a time you benefited from the advice of a friend and what was the impact?" and "When is a time you took terrible advice from a friend and what was the impact?" Girls will more intentionally learn to consider the ways they are influenced by others as they prioritize their own needs.

- Countering the Mainstream Culture

Providing an opportunity for a girl to consciously, creatively express what she puts on her body is a rare opportunity. Girls channel their preferences for clothes, hair, and overall appearance. By using creativity to directly change the choices they have, they discover that they can reject being defined by the dictates of popular culture. Giving girls opportunities to create what they like to wear is revolutionary—the start of seeing how they make choices in their lives more broadly.

My Solid Double Line Story

"Ann, we have your test results. Please come into my office," said the Planned Parenthood nurse. Before she could say anything, I glanced down on her desk. There it was. A solid double line on the pregnancy test. The only thing I recall hearing after that was, "Ann, do you have anyone to drive you home?"

Two days later, I unceremoniously traveled up to Chicago with my boyfriend to obtain an abortion. On the drive back, what can best be called a cocktail of shame, exhilaration, and relief floated in the air around me. Mostly, I was angry. Why was I in this position in the first place? Whose fault was it ultimately? Was it the dogma of Catholicism and its emphasis on no premarital sex and the holiness of virginity? Who was responsible for fogging up the belief that I had a choice about my body? No one at any point in my girlhood—not even once—had educated me about how to prevent a pregnancy. No one had told me that it was all right to have sexual feelings. No one had told me it was a natural thing to want to act on those feelings.

Before I arrived at the clinic that day, not a single person in my life had given an ounce of advice on birth control, much less sexual health, sexual pleasure, or consent. Not my mentor Claire from Pioneer Girls. Not my older sisters. Not my cheerleading coach. Not my mom.

Still, it was hard to place any blame at the feet of my mother, or really any other women in the generations before me. They were merely passing down what they'd been taught, their mothers passing down what they were taught. I was but one of the casualties in the next generation.

Personal childhood memories would continue to focus my building of the health curriculum, and these allowed me a solid-enough foundation. And at my workplace, a driving force for the on-the-ground girls' work was getting tools for conscious decision-making about girls' bodies out of the ivory tower debates and courtrooms and into their everyday lives.

One practical way to change the tools was by creating comprehensive sexual health education. That was easier said than done. There were roughly a thousand steps between starting a girls' program and opening the doors to one. Before Beijing, when I looked around for another who had successfully walked these steps—Girls Scouts or Planned Parenthood, say—I assumed that they continued to thrive because they had, well, been around for a century, which gave them critical resources like money, know-how, and committed members. Honestly, I wished for someone to come along and just tell me how to build the organization and the programming or, better yet, do it for me.

Chapter 7

When I started drafting a sexual health curriculum to offer to girls detained at King County detention, I quickly realized nobody was going to swoop in. Ideas, like popcorn, burst in my head—birth control, consent, and morning-after pills, for instance—only to remain half popped. Was I scattered? Yes. Did I yet have facility clearance or a background check to get into detention? No. Did I question my authority to instruct *other people's daughters* about sexual health education, especially those of color who had frequently suffered misinformation, judgment, and violence in systems? Yes. Did I fully trust my gut in how to run the program? No. Why not? I couldn't tell you. A handful of years later, gathered at our nonprofit office to brainstorm how to present on our comprehensive sexual health curriculum, I began to understand why I was struggling to trust my instincts.

My coworkers ranged in age from twenty to thirty; four of us were White, two were Black, one was mixed White and Latinx, and one was mixed White and Asian. The space where we worked, a two-story turn-of-the-century Craftsman-style home in the heart of the gentrifying central district, was a physical reminder of the racial tension we navigated every day at our workplace. "The girls and sexuality presentation is on Good Friday at the Girl Scouts," I said, aware of the gravy-like tension in the room. "This is a big opportunity to share the Lulu curriculum, possibly reaching hundreds more girls with our sexual health and wellness model," I said, trying to rally everybody behind the bigger meaning of what was at stake. "Who's in?" I asked. Silence. No eye contact. "Is something wrong?" I asked.

Truth is, in collaborating in this way, I learned about my motivations for girls' work every time. Broadly, I was learning about the complications of my power—owning my own authority while also acknowledging how I made assumptions about the needs of the girls I was serving. That was what the tension was about. Centering on the notion of "preventing pregnancy" as the high watermark a girl could achieve, given my own failure getting pregnant as a teen, was culture bound. In White girl Catholic culture, pregnancy was something to be hidden, aborted, or endured with shame. How would this judgment, unconscious or otherwise, feel to these girls, some of whom were already mothers or whose own mothers had decided to have and keep them, despite the barriers teen mothers face? And what about the stereotypes that teaching pregnancy prevention to girls of color implied? Centering choice on preventing pregnancy was a slap in the face, almost like we were choosing to prevent their pregnancy because it was a burden to us. We also needed to explore the broader context of a forced choice to prevent pregnancy. As advocates teaching about choice, we didn't have to travel too far back to find examples of places where women of color were denied choice. Black, Indigenous, and other girls of color had been coerced up until the mid-twentieth century into sterilization as part of an American experiment.

Then there was always my glaring, recurring blind spot: a high tolerance of violence and the way its denial implied that all girls, including, for example, those being sexually trafficked or sexually abused, had *any* choice about sex or pregnancy or agency over their bodies. They did not. Was I saying they should also be trying to prevent pregnancy on top of enduring the abuse? Here again, I had so much to unlearn about how I projected my experiences in places where they did not belong.

My experience related to developing the sexual health workshop was a rich site to mine. It improved the services we offered. In challenging the limits of teaching only pregnancy prevention in health education, we added a multipart workshop series for these girls. We brought in partners from public health, the homeless youth shelter, and the trauma and sexual assault center. We added spoken-word and arts expressions. We committed to supporting girls in accessing necessary referrals to social services. We put bus tokens and maps to these support services in their personal belongings. While all girls benefit from these types of supports, girls whose needs are frequently invisible especially did.

Chapter 7

Parent/Mentor Self-Reflection Power Tool

Recalling personal experiences of trusting your instincts and voicing consent provides valuable insights. By embracing personal insights, actively developing your skills, and addressing existing challenges, you can authentically support girls in developing their own power. Ask yourself:

1. What information about your own experiences of trusting your instincts and voicing consent is helpful to recall? Are there memories that you can unpack so that you are better prepared to support a girl in developing this power?
2. What do you need to do with what you've learned to develop your proficiency in supporting a girl in building this power?
3. What is your attitude toward changing your practice related to this power?
4. What existing habits might you need to unlearn?
5. What about your current environment prevents you from being successful in learning this practice with a girl?

Fostering Mind/Body Healing

Years later I see Emily on the steps of the Washington state capitol. Our connection comes full circle. We are both testifying in favor of youth development legislation that seeks to establish school-based health centers across the state. Emily is wearing her work badge, bright blue pants, a black shirt, and a keffiyeh draped casually around her neck. At thirty, she's recently moved back to the Pacific Northwest and now works in a supervisory position at a local nonprofit. "So great to see you, Ann," she chirps. "Let's grab coffee soon."

A few months later, Emily and I meet at a local café. When she arrives, she offers me a warm embrace and an apology for her tardiness as we order drinks and begin to pull the layers back from her experience in a girls' group. The butterflies I initially feel, the careful checklist I run through to ensure we had Emily's back to the best of our ability, quickly gives way to curiosity about where her life is now. It will be Emily's choice if she wants to revisit that part of her involvement with the girls' group and one-on-one experiences, her choice to guide the conversation where she wants to take it.

"One of the biggest things that stayed with me is talking about media, body image, and what you wear. It changed my perspective about myself and my choices. Just realizing everything you're fed isn't a huge thing," explains Emily as our drinks arrive. "When I realized I was different from the media creation, in fact that we are all different, I developed confidence and self-esteem. Creating my own standards, like we did in the fashion show, knowing that my experiences and how I felt, not what I looked like, were valid gave me such a boost," she continues. "That plays into everything. If you have peace about your own norm of what's beautiful, this allows you to feel in control. I can create a norm for how I'm supposed to be happy," she tells me.

As a light rain taps the window outside, Emily says, "And obviously building a relationship with Jill was life-changing. Jill was who I told," she calmly tells me. As the group facilitator to whom Emily disclosed the sexual molestation she had experienced at home, Jill became deeply involved in the school inquiry. Their relationship—the anchor of her girls' group experience—was forged in Emily's first year of middle school. Jill was a sounding board during one of the scariest choices Emily ever had to make: the decision to leave her home and live with her aunt hundreds of miles away so she could heal.

There are a few comfortable moments of silence, and the conversation moves on to other impacts of Emily's girls' group involvement. "What skill do you think a girl needs growing up, what mattered most to you?" I ask. Emily takes the conversation now in the direction of the powerful ways that girls can initiate other girls into a healthy girl culture. In her middle school hallways, she describes how her nonverbal communication shifted with other girls once she understood the precepts of how competition in girl culture led to relational aggression. Simple awareness of this changed her behavior. "I made a point of smiling at other girls in the hallway, you know, the smile effect really shifted girls out of feeling judged."

Emily explains that emotional intelligence is also incredibly important. Valuing how you feel, knowing how you feel, and communicating that effectively is how she sums it up. "If you can value the way you feel, you can effect change, and there is power that comes with that," she explains. Emily offers a telling example from her senior year of high school. "I was responsible for raising thousands of dollars to bring diversity workshops to my school. This was a direct result of being involved in a girls' group. 'I want to do this and I can do it' is how I think of taking action now." She continues, "The most powerful thing was speaking about my experience of sexual victimization. At least three girls came up to me afterward and told me the same thing had happened to them. The following year, they became leaders raising money for diversity workshops and used their experiences to make it easier for other girls to speak up. This was huge to me."

Our conversation winds down. Something Emily says to me stays with me. "I did not feel the burden of, 'I'm a woman, they won't listen to me.' I don't know what that burden is because I have always had a mentor or group or community telling me that I didn't need to feel it." Emily mentions that she is considering applying for a job leading a girls' group. She now feels a responsibility to lift up and give back to the next generation.

THE BIG PICTURE: CHANGE THE RULES, NOT THE GIRL

Hearing Emily's intention to become a part of a girl's broader social web makes me think that girls' work, which I think is so revolutionary, actually riffs off of the past. Feminist scholar Joan Jacobs Brumberg, in her seminal work *The Body Project*, underscores the historical context of the role Jill played in

Emily's life, and the role Emily hopes to play in the lives of others. Via Victorian-era diaries, Brumberg brings us into the lives of tens of thousands of working and middle-class girls between the 1880s and 1920s who dedicated time each week to being a part of single-sex groups intended to support and nurture girls' development. "Adult women were the most important part of the protective umbrella. Based on the need to protect all girls, not just one's own daughters, from premature sexuality and manipulation at the hands of men, this kind of guidance was based on a wide diversity of female mentors who reflected the social classes and religious backgrounds of the girls in the programs," she writes. Yet Brumberg also notes, "the protective umbrella" was more interested in keeping girlhood "wholesome and chaste" and providing a heap of religious morality.

Not anymore. Socializing girls in the ways suggested here takes its place in a long line of efforts, but with a new message. In state after state, comprehensive sexual health education is a powerful tool for helping girls understand how choice impacts them. Doing girls' work, the evolution as I described above, went from strictly focusing on pregnancy prevention, to supporting girls in understanding and respecting personal boundaries; developing healthy friendships and dating relationships; gaining a deeper understanding of human growth and development; developing skills to support choosing healthy behaviors and reduce health risks, including abstinence and other STD/pregnancy prevention methods, how to access valid health care, and prevention resources; and understanding the influence of family and society on healthy sexual relationships. Girls also received age-appropriate instruction on affirmative consent and bystander training.

Comprehensive sexual education has done more to bolster the efforts to address gender-based violence and protect girls from abuse than anything else could accomplish. In Washington state, for instance, 80 percent of women who experienced sexual assault were attacked before they turned eighteen.[16] Sex education serves as both prevention and intervention for sexual assault and rape. Young children being sexually abused don't understand what is happening until someone provides them with the tools and language to communicate it with a trusted adult. This education provides young people with information and resources about healthy relationships, so they are better able to respect personal boundaries, ask for consent, and learn how to say and receive a "no." It is a crucial bookend to Title IX's legal protections related to sexual harassment and assault.

Providing comprehensive sex education in public schools is also a powerful tool for promoting racial equity. Schools that teach disproportionately BIPOC students are more likely to use abstinence-only education, and students of color are more burdened with societal stigmas and stereotypes against them and their sexual freedom. Further, LGBTQIA+ youth deserve to see themselves reflected positively in sexual health education and experience acceptance by their teachers and peers.

Washington state provides a good policy road map when it comes to comprehensive sexual health education (CSHE). In 2020, a coalition of parents, educators, medical professionals, and advocates passed SB 5395, a law updating the 2007 Healthy Youth Act. Districts across the state are now required to teach age-appropriate, inclusive, comprehensive sexual health education to K–12 students. This law was backed by a massive statewide coalition and had strong support from most Washington voters. State-required curriculum content includes:

- HIV prevention (AOA)
- human growth/development
- abstinence
- other methods of prevention

- health care/prevention resources
- healthy/meaningful relationships
- avoidance of exploitative relationships
- interpersonal communication
- understanding of influences of family, peers, and media on healthy sexual relationships
- affirmative consent
- bystander intervention

State Senator Claire Wilson, a tenacious advocate for youth rights in our state, spoke from her heart on the day our state's CSHE bill was heard on the senate floor. "Some people hear the words 'sex education' and mistake the focus of the curriculum, which is health and safety and is age-appropriate for each grade level," Wilson stated following the bill's passage. "Students need a safe place to ask questions, to fully understand consent, and to have the information they need to make safe decisions," she emphasized. "There are children who will be targeted for molestation in the coming year. There are young women who may face sexual coercion or assault. They need access to information and lessons that will enable them to make decisions to ensure their health and safety."[17]

POWER TOOL: A TRUSTING HER INSTINCTS, VOICING CONSENT ACTIVITY YOU CAN DO WITH GIRLS
Introduction
We live in a culture in which a girl can end up with shame about, or fear for, her body, a culture of criticism, objectification, "locker room" talk, and more extreme forms of gender-based violence like rape, sexual assault, and femicide. No matter who you are or how you identify as a female, the media and society tell you a perfect girl or woman is "skinny, White, blond hair, blue eyes, sexy but innocent, childlike, and submissive." With so many contradictory messages, it's no wonder that a girl often chooses behaviors that are harmful to or that completely disconnect her from her body.

This activity opens the door to media literacy and how the media influences standards of beauty and self-image.

Conversation Tips
If strong emotions about body image come up for the girl her during the conversation, don't downplay these. Don't say things like "You're being hard on yourself." Instead, listen and let her express her feelings. If she talks about being strong in her body, praise her for the effort that goes into playing sports or eating healthy. And don't make body-shaming comments about yourself. Accept compliments about your own body size and—this is important—express that satisfaction within earshot.

Goals
- Develop a deeper understanding of how the media influences standards of beauty and self-image.
- Develop a fresh understanding of the messages a girl values about beauty and self-image.

Do This Together
1. Watch the "Evolution of a Model" commercial with a girl. Talk about what you saw in the video. Be sure to also emphasize that people of all sizes have body-image issues. While plus-size people may face more societal/institutionalized oppression and exclusion than straight-size people, it's important not to belittle someone's experience of body-image issues just because they are thin, etc.
2. Now reread the definition of the power of trusting one's instincts, voicing consent, and the skills that it takes to build this power. Ask her this closing question: What is a skill you need to develop related to this power? Who can help you?

Chapter 8

Celebrating Identity, Not Image

POWER #6

A girl who chooses experiences that encourage pride in her identities can confront negative assumptions about her communities and reject feelings of shame. This power allows her to establish healthy norms of belonging and develop resilience against discrimination. As she challenges stereotypes and authentically expresses herself, she becomes a source of inspiration for others to do the same. Developing this power means valuing different intersecting parts of her identities, promoting self-expression and authenticity within herself and her communities, and fostering inclusivity and acceptance instead of assimilation.

Thus far, we've journeyed to the outskirts of girls' experiences, exploring various aspects of their identity and supporting them in navigating healthy girl culture, racial awareness, conflict resolution, consent, and decision-making skills. However, we've yet to delve into the essence of who a girl is—the perspective she holds on herself and the aspects of her identity that she celebrates while navigating these boundaries.

CHAPTER 8

Just as no girl stumbles upon these powers by chance, pride in one's identity doesn't happen spontaneously. Cultivating identity as a source of strength may seem abstract, but it lies at the heart of a girl's power. As these powers converge, igniting different areas of development, we must recognize the guiding force at the core: identity itself. It's time to foster conversations about how our identities, shaped by our communities, impact our lives. It's time to nurture a deep sense of ownership and pride in a girl's multifaceted identities, recognizing them as wellsprings of power, vital sources fueling her ability to advocate for herself and those she cares about.

A girl might describe herself as, "I'm American, I'm a Midwesterner, I'm a girl, I'm short, I'm a youth, I'm Black, I'm Muslim, I'm a sister, I'm dyslexic, I'm a Taylor Swift fan, I'm a survivor of sexual violence." In her description of self, we might learn of her political views, moral attitudes, ethnicity, religion, interests, experiences, roles, and more. She may tell us of the relational roles she occupies—daughter, sister, friend, student—or family dynamics, socioeconomic status, and physical traits may be interwoven.

A girl's identity encompasses many strands, each carrying social significance that can spark a sense of pride and belonging or, at times, pain, shame, or ambivalence. As Sisneros et al. underscore, "A person's identity encompasses more than just the dimensions considered in models of individual development. Name, history, social status, gender and sex, ethnoracial identity, sexual orientation, ability, status, income/socioeconomic status, education, and religion all come into play."[1]

Over the past fifty-plus years, a wealth of groundbreaking scholarship has emerged, providing a substantial foundation for exploring girls' identity development. In doing girls' work, we stand on the shoulders of groundbreaking thinkers. Jean Baker Miller disrupted individualistic paradigms with her 1976 relational-cultural theory, underscoring how women's psychological hurdles often stem from relational disconnects and marginalization. Miller advocated for recognizing and addressing oppressive systems while amplifying the voices of marginalized populations as essential components of women's well-being.[2]

Shortly after, Carol Gilligan's *In a Different Voice* challenged male-centric moral development theories, illuminating girls' distinct "ethic of care" rooted in relationships and voices.[3] Her Harvard Project, on women's psychology and girls' development founded in 1997, spurred inquiries into girls' intersectional experiences across gender, race, class, and sexuality by Gilligan and fellow scholars including Michelle Fine, Niobe Way, Annie Rogers, Elizabeth Debold, and Lyn Mikel Brown, among others affiliated with the project. Their examinations of marginalized girls' resistances, friendships, and resilience against societal oppression have foregrounded the diversity of adolescent experiences.[4]

Kimberlé Crenshaw's pioneering intersectionality theory[5] examines how layered identities compound discrimination and inequality. Black women, for instance, face unique challenges in being both Black and female. Intersectionality highlights the need for supportive communities, especially for girls navigating multiple marginalized identities. Crenshaw's theory goes beyond questions of individual identity and is interested in deep structural and systemic issues around discrimination and inequality.

Maureen Walker and others continue Miller's relational-cultural work, emphasizing embracing community as a dynamic process of cocreating narratives and collective well-being through the power of belonging and relationships. Relational-cultural theory underscores nurturing girls' selfhood within communities while challenging internalized oppressive stereotypes.[6]

Researchers like Charmaraman and Damour have found that social media and online platforms exert significant pressures that can negatively shape girls' identities and self-perceptions during the critical adolescent years. Constant exposure to idealized images, societal pressures around appearance and sexuality, and the pervasive potential for cyberbullying and shaming can lead to poor body image, low self-esteem, and a distorted sense of self for many girls. However, these modern influences also provide opportunities for community building, self-expression, and redefining narratives around girlhood when navigated with guidance and resilience.[7]

Yet, despite all that we've learned over the past fifty years, girls' identities often remain unexplored. Instead, girls are frequently pigeonholed into a single identity marker within a given context: you are the Black student, or you are the female in this space. Those who feel a disconnect between their true selves and societal expectations may grapple with identity struggles in this way. And there is a significant, devastating consequence.

Members of marginalized or nondominant groups, defined by gender or race, often contend with societal stereotypes that undermine their abilities, leading to perceived underperformance relative to their peers. This phenomenon, known as "stereotype threat," permeates various settings, from classrooms to professional environments, as documented by psychologist Claude Steele.[8] In their seminal 1978 paper, Pauline R. Clance and Suzanne A. Imes introduced the concept of the "imposter phenomenon," which they studied among a sample of high-achieving women.[9] They described this inner experience of persistent self-doubt and feelings of inadequacy despite evident success.

More recently, researchers noted that imposter syndrome, often perpetuated by internalized sexism and racism, is particularly prevalent among high-achieving women and individuals of color.[10] It manifests as a persistent lack of self-confidence and sense of not deserving one's accomplishments, even in the face of external proof of competence and achievement.[11] Addressing these psychological barriers early on is crucial. By challenging negative assumptions about their communities, girls can reject shame and foster norms of healthy belonging, resilience against discrimination, and higher aspirations for themselves and their communities.

While some critics dismiss "identity politics" as divisive and promoting an "oppression Olympics," for girls, exploring identity is essential. From a young age, girls navigate rigid gender norms, stereotypes, and biases constraining their interests and self-expression. Media representation, dress codes, harassment—these issues are inextricably tied to the politics of female identity. Providing a framework to understand their intersectional experiences empowers girls to self-advocate across their diverse identities, rather than having narratives imposed. Nurturing identity pride equips them to claim their rights, dignity, and empowerment on their own terms.

DEFINING POWER #6: CELEBRATING IDENTITY, NOT IMAGE
Rae, aged twelve, a girls' group participant of mixed Black and Japanese heritage, was raised to cherish her cultures as she navigated living in an affluent, predominantly White community. Starting school burdened by academic insecurities, Rae grappled with the stereotypes imposed on Asian and Black girls. Through her involvement in the group, she connected how these stereotypes impacted how she saw herself and how membership in her communities shaped her. This knowledge helped her learn that individuality within a community was valuable and empowering and that she didn't have to assimilate. She could hold the tensions between her ambivalence about her intersecting identities and the unexamined stereotypes she experienced about her communities. You will learn more about Rae's story in this chapter.

Jean, twelve, a tall, strawberry-haired White girl, is another group participant whose involvement you will learn about as we explore the power of identity, not image. When she started the group, Jean had a largely undiagnosed case of dyslexia. Her family struggled to support her older sister, who had become involved in drugs and was slipping into trouble. In joining, Jean gained a set of ears, mentors that weren't judgmental and that stepped in for her so she could explore her identity from outside the box of her family.

Chapter 8

Rae and Jean's experiences in exploring identity mirror those of countless other girls I've had the privilege of working with. Whether confronting assumptions about laziness, loudness, or intellectual ability tied to their gender, racial, or ethnic identities, the girls understand how damaging and untrue these stereotypical beliefs can be. Their stories are powerful reminders that stereotypes aren't just harmless generalizations—they cut deep, constraining girls' authentic selves and forcing them to navigate undeserved prejudices. Yet in giving voice to these experiences, Rae, Jean, and their peers reclaim their narratives and their power.

Celebrating identity, not image, encourages pride in her identities so that a girl can confront negative assumptions about her communities and reject feelings of shame. This power allows her to establish healthy norms of belonging and develop resilience against discrimination. As she challenges stereotypes and authentically expresses herself, she becomes a source of inspiration for others to do the same. Developing this power means valuing different intersecting parts of her identities, promoting self-expression and authenticity within herself and her communities, and fostering inclusivity and acceptance instead of assimilation.

You can support a girl in fostering pride in identity when you:

- Encourage her to examine situations where she conceals her true self and presents a false image instead.
- Discuss the stereotypes she faces, recognizing them as discrimination.
- Provide platforms for voicing these experiences to challenge societal expectations.
- Guide her toward experiences facilitating growth of her genuine identities.
- Foster pride by celebrating community strengths/shared experiences she identifies with.

One class I've observed, Identity and Community, serves as a valuable starting point for initiating broader conversations surrounding identity. Another class, Gender Mending, offers a more in-depth exploration of specific aspects of identity, such as sexual orientation. However, this format can be adapted to delve into any facet of identity exploration. The structure typically involves providing definitions, debunking myths, and promoting inclusion and pride.

Developing the Power: A Visit to Identity and Community Class

On a damp, foggy day a month or so after the girls' group had started, still early days of the group and the formation of its culture, I return to see how Amina and Ty will teach Identity and Community class. Recall that you first met Amina, an Ethiopian immigrant, and Ty, who is White and transgender, when examining the power of engaging in conflict. Joining also today is Jenna, a biracial adult ally and master of social work student interning and mentoring girls as part of the program.

My visitor's badge awaits me in the school's main office. There is a note explaining a room switch. The girls' group is now occupying a new portable toward the back of the gym. "This happens a lot, unfortunately," the office assistant says as she shuffles a handful of school bulletins into an envelope. After roaming the labyrinthine halls for ten minutes, I arrive at the makeshift classroom with enough time to look around. As far as I can tell, the group is a success. The battery of hula hoops, beanbag chairs, the group's written agreement or functional constitution, and wall posters have all made the move to the portable.

The girls, ten strong, are sprawled and strewn about in the same manner as when I last visited. The biggest difference now? The walls display girls' drawings and writing. Among their completed works are posters delineating what constitutes healthy relationships and life-size supergirl posters, symbolic of the powers

Chapter 8

the girls deem necessary for safety and success. Additionally, there's a bin brimming with journals adorned with the girls' names. Ty gestures for me to join the circle, and I settle between two girls, Rae and Jean, for whom this activity will hold significant meaning.

Rae struggles with the stereotypes imposed on Asian and Black girls. She was recently taunted with a racial slur about "being mixed" in the schoolyard, which exacerbated her struggles with belonging. Despite a strong bond rooted in empathy, Rae and her mother occasionally clash. Her mother, a fifth-generation Japanese American, established a thriving insurance business despite the significant barriers she faced, but has a hard time understanding what Rae's day-to-day life at school is like, such as her discontent with school norms, cliques, and the pressure to fit in. Rae's unhappiness caught the attention of the school counselor, who recommended the after-school girls' group. Initially reluctant, Rae now engages eagerly with the group.

Amina wastes no time diving into the discussion. "What does community mean to you, and what is one example of a community you are part of?" she asks, prompting the girls to reflect. The group consists of both mature but new to the school sixth graders and somewhat self-assured seventh graders. One girl tentatively asks, "Do you mean, like, where I live?" Ty points to a bright yellow piece of paper adorned with text. "Community is a group of people any size that share common values, identities, location (neighborhood, city, school), culture, religion, or historical background," they explain.

As the conversation progresses, another girl chimes in, "I am part of the band community, my Mount Zion church community, and the Black Achievers community." The ice is now broken, and the sharing continues. "Saint Gebriel's Ethiopian Church and the basketball team," one girl calls out, while another, a mixed-race girl, shares, "My family is really involved with the Mexican community here."

Each girl takes a turn to express her affiliations, but there's a noticeable tension when they discuss their school community in comparison to their racial or religious communities. "Why does coming to school make me feel like I want to hide who my parents and my family are?" Rae whispers to Jenna, her mentor, as other girls nod in agreement. Sensing the need to move the discussion forward, Amina redirects the group to the next activity.

"We are going to do an activity called Step in the Circle," she announces. "Let's explore what the words identity and stereotypes mean, how you view your identities, and the ways in which you experience shame, discrimination, or limitations as a result of your identities." With that, she unveils a poster board with a definition, ready to delve deeper into the topic.

Identity is:

- The ways we define who we are, the way we think about ourselves, and often the way the world sees us.
- Pieces of ourselves that we feel pride in.
- Communities and groups that we have chosen, and some that have been assigned to us.
- Pieces of ourselves that are intersecting and complex.

Amina proceeds with the activity, instructing the girls, "Without saying anything, please step into the circle if you identify with the statement I make." She emphasizes the importance of respecting each girl's individual experience and refrains from calling out experiences of others in the group. As the girls participate, Amina carefully tallies the results, noting the responses of the ten girls present that day.

- I wish I were someone else. 10/10 step in.
- People assume things about who I am because of what I wear. 10/10 step in.
- I have specific responsibilities because I am a girl. 10/10 step in.

- I have been left out of activities because I am a girl. 10/10 step in.
- I have been followed around in a grocery store. 7/10, all girls of color step in.
- People assume that I ate certain things because of my race. 7/10, all girls of color step in.
- I have been categorized as having a race I do not identify with. 7/10, all girls of color step in.
- People assume I do or do not do certain things because of my religion. 2/10, both Muslim girls, step in.
- One or more of my parents are immigrants. 2/10, both Muslim girls, step in.
- I have a disability. 1/10, a White girl steps in.
- I have questioned my sexual orientation. 0/10 nobody steps in.
- I am proud of my sexual orientation. 0/10, nobody steps in.
- I feel confused about my gender identity. 0/10, nobody steps in.

For some girls, these also might be entirely new concepts, or they may not know what these terms mean, depending on where they have grown up. Amina notices that sexual orientation and gender identity didn't prompt any movement into the circle. She reflects on whether this aspect of identity might feel risky to disclose in the newly forming group. Sexual orientation and gender identity are often deeply personal and can carry significant social stigma or the risk of marginalization. Amina recognizes that until the girls feel genuinely safe and supported, they may be hesitant to openly share or explore these aspects of their identity. She acknowledges the importance of creating an inclusive and affirming environment where all identities are respected and valued.

When the question about disability is asked, Jean steps into the circle. Jean has recently transferred to the school. She loves the literary arts and does exceptionally well on oral presentations in class, but feels angst as a girl who doesn't really fit in. She does not have a particularly open relationship with her mother and often feels they are emotionally hurtful to each other. Her family struggles to support her older sister, who has become involved in drugs and is slipping into trouble. Jean joined the group after noticing a flier up at school.

The girls' engagement in the discussion about stereotypes demonstrates their readiness to confront and discuss challenging topics. Despite the potentially sensitive nature of the conversation, they participate without fear.

As they discuss specific stereotypes they've encountered, such as assumptions about laziness, loudness, or mathematical ability based on racial or ethnic identity, the girls demonstrate a critical awareness of the harmful impact of such beliefs. They recognize that stereotypes are often negative and untrue, and they share personal experiences of feeling stereotyped, highlighting the emotional toll it can take.

The sidebar conversation between two girls of color about White people moving into their neighborhood illustrates the complexity of racial dynamics and the girls' willingness to openly discuss their experiences and perspectives. Amina and Ty's unfazed reaction suggests that they are accustomed to facilitating discussions about race and identity, and they create a supportive environment where the girls feel comfortable expressing themselves. Overall, the girls' engagement in the activity reflects their maturity and willingness to challenge stereotypes and engage in meaningful dialogue about identity and discrimination.

"Okay, circle up. Let's everybody come back together," prompts Amina. "What is wrong with stereotypes? How do they impact how you imagine other people think about your community or groups you are a part of?" she asks. The room falls silent.

Jean, silent in the larger conversation so far, takes a risk and says: "They make other people think you are stuck up or snobby. They keep us separate."

Now Rae leans in and says, "It makes them think I better show up as a model Asian or a troublemaking, stupid Black student, so they don't expect anything from me."

The girls are next invited to do an activity that uses a worksheet with a drawing of an iceberg, a metaphor that effectively prompts them to reflect on both the visible and invisible aspects of their identities. The iceberg metaphor for identity, developed by social psychologist Andrew Hall in 1976, likens an individual's identity to an iceberg.[12] The visible portion above the water represents the more obvious aspects of one's identity that are readily seen by others, such as race, age, gender expression, and so on. These visible "tip of the iceberg" identities we ascribe to people are just a small part of their full, multidimensional sense of selfhood. Below the surface lies a larger portion of the iceberg, representing the many complex and nuanced layers of identity that are not immediately apparent. This can include things like ethnicity, cultural background, values, beliefs, lived experiences, sexual orientation, and other components that shape how one views themselves and the world.

Because of the complexity of identity and the challenge of reconciling internal and external perceptions, the facilitators intentionally do not ask the girls which part of the iceberg represents their "true" selves. This allows space for, and highlights, the ongoing process of self-discovery and self-acceptance that the girls are navigating. Overall, the activity fosters introspection, empathy, and a deeper understanding of the layers of identity, contributing to a supportive and reflective environment within the group.

"Now it is time to do a community mapping activity," invites Ty. "Think back to our definition of community. What communities, like clubs or drill teams, are you a part of? Think of communities you have chosen, and those you have been assigned to that you don't get to choose," they explain. The girls take a few minutes to shout out their responses. Ty brings up an observation shared by the girls: those of color tend to identify with ethnic, religious, or cultural communities they were born into, while the few White girls mention their neighborhood or extracurricular activity communities.

"That's an interesting pattern I'm noticing too," Ty says thoughtfully. "It seems like for many of you, your racial, ethnic, or cultural backgrounds are a core part of how you define your community and identity. While for some others, communities like your neighborhood or hobby groups feel most salient." They pause, letting that observation sink in. "I'm curious to explore that more—why do you think there might be that difference in how we relate to or prioritize different types of communities based on our backgrounds? What makes ethnic, cultural, and religious communities so central for some but not others? I'd be really interested to hear your perspectives on this. How about you take time to think on that before the next group. We can talk about it then," Ty tells the group.

"All right, now we're going to do an activity focused on exploring our identities and communities," Amina explains as she passes out large tangerine-colored poster papers to each girl. "On your paper, you'll see four concentric circles."

Amina pauses to make sure everyone has their paper ready. The girls lean in, listening intently.

"In the center circle, I want you to write your name or draw something that represents you as an individual," she instructs. "In the second ring circling that, choose a specific community you belong to—it could be your family, school, neighborhood, or any other group. Draw or write what that community is and the different people or elements that make it up."

The girls start jotting down notes and sketching little doodles on their circles, nodding along as Amina continues.

"For the third ring, I want you to draw or describe some of the challenges or difficulties that community faces and how those impact the people within it. And finally, in the outer fourth ring, illustrate or write about that community's strengths—the positive qualities, resources, or ways it has overcome those challenges." Amina scans the room, making eye contact with each girl. "The idea is to visually capture your sense of identity, the communities that shape you, the obstacles they deal with, and the power they possess to persevere. Don't overthink it. Just let your ideas flow!"

The room fills with the scratch of markers and pencils as the girls dive into the introspective activity. Amina circulates, offering encouragement. By the time they've all finished their concentric circle posters, there's a kaleidoscope of vibrant imagery reflecting their diverse identities and communities.

Amina sees that the time for today's group is up. She concludes by asking the girls to share one thing they could do this week to challenge any judgments or stereotypes they may make about people. The girls have a lot of thoughts and feelings about this subject that will spill over into the next group or their one-on-one mentoring session.

Keeping It Going: Exploring Gender Identity and Sexual Orientation

"Thank you for the invitation! I'll be sure to join the Gender Mending activity tomorrow," I express to Rose with enthusiasm. Rose, a dedicated girls' group instructor and single mother of Black and Filipina heritage, has been instrumental in providing support and guidance to girls at risk of dropping out of school. Gender Mending is an activity designed to facilitate exploration and reflection on key concepts related to sex, gender identity, sexual orientation, and societal norms surrounding these identities. Through this activity, girls are encouraged to delve into the meaning of these terms and critically examine their own perspectives and experiences.

I arrive at the group that day as Rose poses the opening activity. "Today's activity is called Gender Boxes. Start by drawing a line down the middle of the paper you have and across to make four squares. Title the two squares on the upper half of the paper positive female characteristics/labels and positive male characteristics/labels. Then on the bottom half, title those squares negative male characteristics/labels and negative female characteristics/labels," Rose instructs. "Fill in each section with the positive and negative labels that we associate with males and females."

Girls write furiously, and after about ten minutes, Rose asks them to turn to a partner and share similarities they notice in the boxes and what they think this says about how women are considered in our culture. "It's sort of depressing that my list of negatives for girls is so long," one girl says. Her list of female negatives says things like slut, ho, gold digger, does the housework, and not an athlete, while a concise list of negative male labels includes things like simp, gay, pussy, bitch boy, stupid jock, man whore, and perverted. Rose relays a theme she notices, that so many pejoratives for boys are based on association with femininity, and most negative female characteristics are considered positive for men.

As the girls share their experiences of being labeled with derogatory terms, the atmosphere in the room becomes heavy, and Rose names this before redirecting the group. By next presenting clear definitions of the difference between sex and gender, she provides an opportunity to shift the focus toward education and understanding, allowing the girls to engage with the topic in a different way.

> **Sex** is biological: females are born with a vagina; males are born with a penis.
> **Gender** is constructed by society. For example, women should be nurses and school teachers/men should work in construction; women can wear dresses/men wear suits; women can have short and long hair/men have only short hair.
> **Binary** is system of categorization that divides groups into two oppositional parts, valuing one over the other.

Chapter 8

Gender nonconforming refers to a person whose behavior or appearance does not conform to prevailing cultural and social expectations about what is appropriate to their gender.

Sexual orientation refers to individuals' romantic and sexual attraction to others or lack of attraction (asexual identity).

Heteronormativity communicates a worldview that promotes heterosexuality as the normal or preferred sexual orientation.

After presenting these definitions, Rose digs deeper, "How does valuing one group over the other, categorizing in a binary way, hurt people?" Girls share these insights.

"You close yourself off if society doesn't agree. I hide who I am. And then, in the long run, I would feel very ashamed of myself," offers a willowy girl wearing a baseball cap.

"You feel controlled," suggests another.

"Right now, though, I think people are becoming more aware, more people are willing to be who they are, there's greater acceptance, less judgment," counters a curly-haired girl in a quiet voice.

Rose summarizes the conversational terrain and asks the girls to think over the discussion. "Today I asked you to think about the difference between the words sex and gender. I asked you to think about stereotypes about gender. Why do you think that was important?"

"Not everyone feels like the body they are born in. But people assume they do," offers the same willowy girl.

"People bully you if you act too far from the gender you appear to be. If you're a boy, you are supposed to act like the stereotypes of a boy. You get called nasty words if you act like a girl," calls another.

"People assume your gender identity and sexual orientation are the same thing. You can't support someone to feel good about who they are as a whole unless you let people come out of the box and unless you understand these are two different parts of yourself," surmises another.

Rose acknowledges that schools can *still* be one of the most homophobic and transphobic social contexts, where girls or students who do not conform to gender and sexuality norms are at high risk of stigma and discrimination. She acknowledges that, for many students, fear of being misgendered, outed without consent, and subsequently invalidated, marginalized, and psychologically damaged by a lack of awareness surrounding their gender identity and/or sexual orientation is ever present.

In light of the school context, Rose closes the group by reminding girls of the importance of the community norms they've created for the culture they aim to have in the girls' group. "If you are willing, feel free to share the gender pronouns you are most comfortable using. I hope moving forward we can use gender pronouns as a way of creating a more inclusive space. Again, this is totally voluntary."

Power Tool: Parent and Mentor Tips for Celebrating Identity, Not Image

- Define and Disrupt Shame

  Supporting girls in understanding the definitions of shame versus guilt is important when building the power of identity. Girls often internalize societal messages that undermine their self-worth, leading to self-criticism and disparaging language. While our instinct might be to directly challenge these negative beliefs, it is more effective to acknowledge their feelings and gently guide them toward new perspectives. You can inquire about a girl's reasons for the shame she expresses and explore the underlying narratives she has absorbed. Instead of merely negating her self-perception, you can also provide specific observations, such as her resilience in gameplay or her passion for reading, fostering tangible reflections that validate her strengths and encourage further growth.

- Give Voice, Don't Let Language Lapse

CHAPTER 8

Language constantly evolves, and you must stay current to serve the needs of the girls you are working with. Creating a gender-inclusive classroom means understanding various gender identity and expression concepts. Promoting an inclusive environment requires raising awareness and providing learning opportunities for students and teachers. Activities like the one discussed can help establish a shared vocabulary by introducing key distinctions between sex, gender, and sexual orientation.

MY BOOKSTORE MOMENT: AN IDENTITY WAKE UP CALL

One memorable period of exploring my identities occurred during my college years at the University of Illinois in Champaign, Illinois. I resided in a wedge-shaped, hastily constructed apartment building on the outskirts of campus, where I came to terms with my own identities. The apartment, with its paper-thin walls and lack of privacy, housed myself and my three sorority sisters, all second-generation Serbian, Greek, and Polish immigrants.

Most evenings, we gathered to cook dinner and watch popular TV shows like *Moonlighting* and *Who's the Boss*. Despite our shared suburban Chicago roots, my roommates conversed in their parents' native languages, while I struggled to connect with my own cultural heritage. My understanding was limited to classroom lessons from studying abroad in Italy and stories of my immigrant grandparents' contributions to building the Santa Fe railroads.

Living alongside these diverse backgrounds, my cultural identity felt shrouded in mystery, concealed behind the facade of White suburbia. Despite our shared continuum of European immigrant cultural identity just one or two generations removed, my roommates and I were still subject to societal expectations that shaped our gender identity and sexual orientation. As young women in the 1980s, these expectations were firmly entrenched:

- We were supposed to identify as heterosexual and be attracted to individuals of the "opposite" sex.
- Dating outside our racial identity was discouraged, with little consideration given to our Whiteness except in relation to dating.
- Our behavior, speech, dress, grooming, and overall conduct were expected to align with traditional feminine norms, reflecting our assigned female gender at birth. This included being polite, accommodating, and nurturing.
- Advancing to the next economic level, whatever that might be, was highly valued and anticipated, primarily through marriage.

Despite our different ethnic cultural backgrounds, these were the societal expectations that heavily influenced our identities and experiences as young women navigating the complexities of the eighties era.

At the University of Illinois, my roommates and I, like many others, upheld the binary expectations of female gender roles. Shortly after I arrived in Champaign, the hallways of Hopkins Hall buzzed with activity as girls participated in sorority rush, a prominent event in one of the nation's largest Greek letter systems. I decided to join Delta Gamma, where traditional female gender roles were enthusiastically reinforced. Our chants, like "I know a girl, and she is a DG," reflected this commitment. While I was aware of the gender fluidity and sexual freedom depicted by pop icons like Cyndi Lauper and Madonna, I clung to the expectations ingrained in me during my restrictive Catholic suburban upbringing. Delta Gamma's adherence to traditional norms provided me with a sense of acceptance and social survival, despite the allure of alternative expressions of femininity and sexuality.

That balancing act of "What happens when identity is defined for you?" and "What happens when identity is disrupted?" came most fully into view my senior year. I would soon graduate as a business major, head to Chicago, and put on my pinstripes.

Chapter 8

My identity at that moment felt solid. That is, until I made an unscripted trip to the Illini Bookstore a few weeks before graduation.

In retrospect, I am hard-pressed to think of a day when my identity as a girl was disrupted more than that day. It was the first time I had gone to the university bookstore without a directive. Instead, I was left to wander the rows of books. I walked past Keynes's *Tract on Monetary Reform*, and near the end of the ordered aisles was a one-shelf section called Women's Studies. It was not uncommon to make it through business school in the 1980s without noticing such a field, but I found myself stuck in place. The range of topics and books on the shelf had a resonance I had not felt from the other shelves.

Simone de Beauvoir's *Second Sex* captured my attention in the bookstore that day. If I were to chart the journey from my identity as a Delta Gamma sorority girl to the one I embraced after finishing de Beauvoir's tome, it would be a straight line, a trajectory aimed at challenging the gender expectations I had once adhered to. De Beauvoir's book profoundly influenced my life by deepening my understanding of my female gender role. She adeptly pinpointed the issue of gendered identities being socially constructed, along with the internalization of powerlessness, shame, and self-blame that often accompanies this construction. After completing the book during the summer following my college graduation, I found myself eager to challenge various gender expressions. I stopped conforming to societal expectations for feminine appearance, such as shaving my armpits, wearing makeup, and tight clothing.

This shift also prompted a profound change in my people-pleasing tendencies, leading me to let go of relationships that confined me to gendered expectations. Instead, I began gravitating toward individuals who shared my values. My behavior evolved as well; I began prioritizing my own pleasure, took up hiking, and embraced activities traditionally associated with masculinity. Keeping my last name after marriage and finding a partner who embodies feminist values further solidified my commitment to challenging gender expectations and embracing a more authentic identity.

This newfound understanding of my gender identity served as a gateway to exploring all aspects of my identity. It enabled me to recognize and confront various forms of oppression, not only related to gender but also intersecting with other societal issues. It prompted me to take the first step in understanding the broader struggle against violence targeting women. It illuminated how patterns of violence against women and girls manifest in relationships, families, streets, and workplaces globally. With this expanded perspective, I was motivated to advocate for others and contribute to efforts aimed at addressing and combating gender-based violence.

Reflecting on my gender identity experiences in the Greek system, in particular, in comparison to those of girls in our programs and my coworkers, has also been illuminating. The Divine Nine historically Black fraternities and sororities served as a core support system for girls and instructors alike who attended predominantly White collegiate institutions. This aspect of identity development was instrumental for them, providing a space to embrace both their racial and gender identities. For these girls and instructors, Whiteness and other socially accepted identities operated as an inherent default, rarely requiring conscious consideration. These spaces for identity affirmation contrasted starkly with their experience of having identities that aligned with the dominant culture. For me, as a White woman, this points to the privilege of having parts of one's identity accepted and validated by the mainstream, never having to grapple with the weight of societal marginalization. I check myself by asking: What does it mean to hold identities that are so seamlessly woven into society's fabric that we need not be acutely aware of them?

CHAPTER 8

Parent/Mentor Self-Reflection Power Tool

Recalling and reflecting on your own experiences of identity sparks valuable insights to support girls in developing their power. Unpacking memories and understanding how your day-to-day life has been influenced by these experiences can enhance your ability to guide and support them. To develop your skills in supporting a girl in building her power, first ask yourself:

1. What information about your own experiences of celebrating identity is helpful to recall? Are there memories that you can unpack so that you are better prepared to support a girl in developing this power?
2. What do you need to do with what you've learned to develop your proficiency in supporting a girl to build this power?
3. What is your attitude toward changing your practice related to this power?
4. What existing habits might you need to unlearn?
5. What about your current environment prevents you from being successful in learning this practice with a girl?

Celebrating Identity

Ten years after we first met, Rae, a senior at the University of Washington, sits near the window of a tony coffee shop in South Lake Union, not far from her part-time job at a sandwich shop. At twenty two, she lives by herself, balancing work and college. She greets me with a big smile.

"At my age, I want that girls' group experience again. I am still searching to repeat it." She explains that she loved having one-on-one mentors, not mother figures but objective listeners. Rae recalls Jenna. "Jenna was part Japanese, and I had never been connected to an older, wiser woman of color like her." Rae describes the mutual understanding that developed and feeling connected to her. "She related to me because she's been through what I have. I could tell her all my insecurities, because if anyone can relate to them, she can. She was patient with me." At that age, having that one-to-one moment to say what she wanted, talk about her goals and aspirations, and reflect on it when it was over was transformative for Rae.

I ask, "What skills did you learn? How do you use these now?"

"As girls, we were often confined by societal expectations," she reflects. "Learning that individuality within a community is valuable was empowering. Every girl deserves this insight." She then shifts the conversation to her hair. "As an Asian, I faced pressure to maintain long, flowing locks. So, just before my twenty-first birthday, I declared to my friends, 'I'm tired of this look.'" Without disclosing her plans, she had her mom drop her off at the salon. "Initially, it was just a few chunks, but gradually, more went. It was incredibly liberating," she says, her eyes glistening.

Curious, I ask about the reactions from her family and colleagues. "My coworkers were shocked initially, but now they see it as a part of who I am," she replies. "After shaving my head, I felt empowered by taking control of my body," Rae asserts. Many girls approached her, expressing admiration for her bold choice, which encouraged them to consider it too.

"I owe a lot to Jenna," Rae offers. "I never fully conveyed how much her mentorship meant to me." She then opens up about her struggle to integrate aspects of her identity rather than assimilate into mainstream expectations. "For my psychology project, I explored my upbringing as an Asian in a predominantly White community. I realized I was deeply confused," she tells me. "People stereotyped Asians, assuming we were 'fresh off the boat.' I felt restricted; I couldn't diverge from expectations." Joining a supportive community aided Rae in connecting with younger individuals. "Having mentors during formative years sparks a chain reaction of inspiration," she muses.

Chapter 8

Jean is another girl I reconnect with. A national slam poetry contest winner and published writer, she has returned from an East Coast tour. "I'm back living with my parents between gigs," she explains as she takes a seat at the café where we've agreed to meet. She immediately tells me about her next opportunity, teaching do-it-yourself promotion workshops at an East Coast college. "Like in music, you used to have to wait for a label, but in my generation, we just get out and do it." Jean gets animated and tells me about a breakthrough moment. "I started going into stores and putting my little books on the poetry shelf. I didn't tell anyone, I just put them on the shelf. I walked in there and felt so sad thinking, 'I'm never going to be the next Maya Angelou, not alphabetically, not anything. So I made space, put my books next to hers, and left.'"

Jean frequently revisits the theme of cultivating an artistic identity throughout our discussions. She reflects on the valuable lesson she learned in healthy girl culture: the power of transcending gender labels. "People don't have to see me as a female artist or poet," she asserts, emphasizing her desire to be recognized simply as an artist, free from gender constraints.

This acceptance of ambiguity in artistic identity resonates with broader feminist issues, positioning Jean as a writer navigating the middle ground. She articulates her belief that the evolution of healthy girl culture hinges on striking a balance between extremes. Referencing Beyoncé's song "Bow Down," Jean critiques the appropriation of Beyoncé's style by White feminists and the ensuing debates within feminist discourse. She highlights the complexities of race and gender, noting the importance of acknowledging diverse perspectives within feminist movements. She challenges the notion of feminism as a battleground, advocating for a more nuanced and inclusive approach.

Unable to pursue college due to struggles with standardized tests stemming from a rare form of dyslexia, Jean initially grappled with feelings of inadequacy and embarrassment. However, she's since reframed these challenges as unique strengths that distinguish her. "Despite bypassing traditional higher education, I embarked on a journey of self-discovery through work experiences." She began with a position at a film company shortly after high school, then immersed herself in screenwriting and producing. Subsequently, an internship at a magazine led her to journalism, where her passion for music writing flourished. "Music holds a special place in my heart, serving as a gateway to connect with different times and cultures," she continues. "Being embraced by a supportive community of artists, friends, and family, I've cultivated a path that allows me to pursue my passions while maintaining a livelihood."

"So, what's next? Any big plans?" I ask.

"My goal has always been to become successful enough to work in LA but live in Seattle. So if you know anyone interested in hiring a hella dope writer who's also super useful, I'm your girl. Aside from that, I'll keep living life. I'll keep going on random adventures, sparking conversations with strangers, eavesdropping in coffee shops, trying to stress less about money, reading everything I can, and continuing to write more stories that need to be told."

During our formative adolescent years, Jean, Rae, and I each grappled with our intersecting identities in distinct ways, shaping our understanding of ourselves. Delving into questions like "Who am I?" and "Who do I want to become?" propelled us toward profound developmental growth. Untangling internalized stereotypes from our sense of self proved crucial early on. Embracing and finding pride in our identities, particularly as girls, shattered self-hatred and empowered us to advocate for ourselves and others. It allowed us to confront various oppressions and define our own sense of pride.

What if every girl experienced this liberating power of celebrating her identity? What if pride in one's identities granted agency and freedom? Imagine a world in which girls freely express

CHAPTER 8

their gender identities without fear, where they're spared from microaggressions in educational settings. Picture a girl thriving in her racial identity, unimpeded by stereotypes. Envision a world where disabilities aren't hidden. How different would the world be if every girl embraced her true self, shaping a future brimming with authenticity?

Two Steps Forward, One Step Back

In the late summer of 2022, the advocates who filled the small conference room in Jacksonville, Florida, are in a mood of excitement and anxiety, but mostly excitement. For two years, many of us have refrained from travel to avoid catching a deadly COVID-19 strain. The ever-present news stations remind us, like a vice grip, that attending the inaugural Georgetown and Delores Barr Weaver Policy Center Girl-Centered Practices Certification Training means our human rights might not be observed; a false step, even unintended, could be dangerous.

Still, there is plenty of excitement. The enthusiasm is due to being in the company of caring, like-minded advocates, away from the heavy political landscape outside. That these two venerable organizations could host us was never a given. Pandemic turmoil and a growing list of Florida laws like Don't Say Gay had all put the training and our attendance at risk. But here we are. Advocates, attorneys, police officers, judges, clinicians, and artists gathered to create change in how we did girls' work.

The twenty-minute opening video, called "See the Girl Monologues," in which girls bravely tell their stories of solitary confinement, of being bounced between five foster homes, of being trafficked and then blamed for it, go by lightning fast, a closing punch line delivered with a haunting crescendo: "See me for who I am, not for who you think I am. See me for who I am and who I can become." For the narrator, an LGBTQIA+ Black woman, asking to be seen as she truly was —a LGBTQIA+ Black woman—required immense courage, especially considering the additional risks of bias, violence, and punishment.

If books are a place where girls get to "see" themselves, then in recent years, the state of Florida has made that increasingly challenging. The state's book banning efforts, particularly targeting books with LGBTQIA+ themes or characters, as well as books addressing race and racism, have led to the removal of numerous titles from school libraries across the state. Books like *Gender Queer* by Maia Kobabe, *Lawn Boy* by Jonathan Evison, and *The Hate U Give* by Angie Thomas have been frequently targeted. The book bans have ignited protests from students, educators, and free speech advocates, who argue that these measures amount to censorship and deprive students of access to diverse perspectives and experiences. At the school where the policy center offers programming, there was no choice but to remove illustrated children's books about Rosa Parks and other activists from the girls' program space due to the pervasive fear that staff could face arrest or risk losing funding by keeping such materials available.

During my visit to Florida, Ronny, the policy advocate at the Delores Barr Weaver Center, remarks, "Do y'all feel like you've gone back to the dark ages?"

Attempting to maintain graciousness, I respond, "Not a chance! There's always so much to learn from each other."

However, Ronny countered in a warm Florida drawl, "Ann, we can't say gay here." This exchange referred to the controversial bill, dubbed "Don't Say Gay," which prohibits classroom instruction on sexual orientation or gender identity in kindergarten through third grade, or in any manner deemed inappropriate by state standards. Its proponents argue it grants parents control over LGBTQIA+ topics and permits them to sue schools for noncompliance. The "Don't Say Gay" bill, officially titled the Parental Rights in Education Act, was signed into law by Florida Governor Ron DeSantis on March 28, 2022, and went into

CHAPTER 8

effect on July 1, 2022. The law has faced numerous legal challenges from LGBTQIA+ advocacy groups, parents, and students, arguing that it discriminates against LGBTQIA+ individuals and violates free speech rights. In May 2023, a federal judge temporarily blocked the law's enforcement, ruling that it was unconstitutionally vague and discriminatory. However, the state of Florida appealed the decision, and the law's future remains uncertain as legal battles continue.

Sadly, similar bills emerged in other states: Alabama passed its version, which broadly limits discussion on LGBTQIA+ topics, including gender identity and sexual orientation, aiming to marginalize LGBTQIA+ individuals and families. In Texas, there were a staggering number of anti-LGBTQIA+ bills in the legislature, the highest in the country. These included sports restrictions, bans on gender-affirming healthcare for transgender youth, threats to revoke medical licenses for providers treating trans youth, HIV criminalization, and bills enabling anti-LGBTQIA+ discrimination in housing. An example was Governor Greg Abbott's directive for child welfare agencies to investigate parents aiding their transgender children in medical transition.

Seeking a glimmer of hope, a member of the policy center's Girl-Centered Practices Certification Training's workgroup inquired about positive developments in Washington state. In recent years, we have celebrated numerous legislative victories, embracing a girl-centered race equity lens in policymaking. These victories encompass measures to safeguard and uplift unique aspects of girls' identities. For example, starting from the 2022–2023 school year, menstrual hygiene products must be provided free of charge in all gender-neutral and female-designated bathrooms in K–12 schools and higher education institutions. Additionally, school and district staff are mandated to undergo cultural competency training focusing on equity, diversity, inclusion, and antiracism, with one professional learning day dedicated to such training each year.

Celebrating Identity, Not Image

While Washington state may not have established protections for young people of various sexual orientations or gender identities to the same extent as Colorado and California, our achievements are commendable. Washington boasts robust safeguards for LGBTQIA+ youth, as outlined in the Human Rights Campaign's 2021 State Equality Index. These are:

- explicitly protecting LGBTQIA+ youth from bullying and harassment
- prohibiting discrimination based on sexual orientation or gender identity in public schools
- banning licensed mental health providers from conducting conversion therapy on minors
- addressing LGBTQIA+ youth homelessness through training requirements and nondiscrimination policies for service providers
- mandating inclusive sex education that encompasses LGBTQIA+ topics
- ensuring that LGBTQIA+ young people are shielded from discrimination in the juvenile justice system

Sharing the legislative landscape with my colleagues in girl justice evokes both sorrow and tenacity. Their unwavering determination to pursue progress in such hostile environments fills me with hope. Together, we can find solace in our shared values and continue the fight for comprehensive legislative support for all aspects of a girl's identity.

Power Tool: A Celebrating Identity Not Image Activity You Can Do with Girls

Introduction

When a girl digests the stereotypes she encounters in the world around her, she can develop a false image of self that diminishes her aspirations and limits her potential. Pride in one's identity is a potent antidote. When a girl unburdens herself of the (often subconscious) shame she has internalized because of the lower status assigned to her by her gender, race, class, or pressure to assimilate, she develops resilience and a feeling of self-worth. This activity is a firsthand way of beginning to explore history and identity in the face of culture-bound expectations.

Conversation Tips
Be careful *not* to assume that your experiences of discrimination or the stereotypes you encountered growing up are the same. Avoid projecting your experiences onto a girl. Try to stop saying things like, "I know exactly how you feel" and "That happened to me." Even if there are similarities, you likely don't really "know" what she feels. Let her tell you.

Goals
- Develop a deeper understanding of what truly makes her who she is: her history, beliefs, and identities.
- Develop an understanding of stereotypes she has experienced as discriminatory and harmful and those experiences and people that help her gain pride in her true identities.

Do This Together
1. Inspired by George Ella Lyon's "Where I'm From" poem, print out a template from Freeology (https://freeology.com/wp-content/files/iamfrompoem.pdf) and fill in the blanks accordingly.
2. Share your poems. Ask her: What did you like and value about the activity? What was difficult or challenging?
3. Explore the idea of building an image versus building an identity. Ask her: Are there times when you tend to put up a front or false image for others? What are the circumstances? Why do you want to project that image? Can you name a time where you experienced a stereotype as discriminatory

Celebrating Identity, Not Image

and harmful? What are experiences or settings where you show your brightest, most honest self? When's a time you felt pride because you shared belonging with others based on your values or identities?

4. Now reread the definition of the power of celebrating identity, not image, and the skills that it takes to build it. Ask the girl this closing question: What is a skill you need to develop related to this power? Who can help you?

CHAPTER 9

Deciphering the Codes of Dominant Culture

POWER #7

A girl who can code switch has the power to navigate different cultural norms and behavioral expectations with confidence. By learning to "read" and adapt to the unwritten rules within the dominant culture, she gains the ability to access greater opportunities as she grows up. Developing this skill means understanding how exclusionary norms limit her opportunities, embracing her own leadership style while code-switching when she chooses. By linking her values, identities, and decision-making, she can cultivate a personal leadership style that rings true for her.

In today's American culture, girls, especially BIPOC girls, frequently find themselves needing to "code switch" or change their behavior to match the unspoken expectations of those around them. The ability to code switch is a crucial skill for girls. It empowers them to adapt to, influence, and reshape their environments. Decoding these social codes is vital for girls as they navigate the complexities of accessing opportunities in the world all around them.

Chapter 9

Mikki Kendall, author of *Hood Feminism: Notes from the Women That a Movement Forgot*, explains the importance of this form of power for BIPOC girls: "Code-switching in these spaces is a key skill that not everyone can or will acquire. And the toll of not being adept at this skill plays out not only in how girls are treated by their peers, but also in how they are treated by the systems they encounter."[1] Those who are unable to navigate these spaces effectively may face discrimination and exclusion, both socially and within institutional systems. When you don't feel like you fit, you often don't show up at all.

Until the broader cultural landscape and the rules for accessing opportunity are shaped by a wider group that reflects this generation of racially diverse girls, framing code-switching and skill development in terms of what education researcher Dr. Lisa Delpit (1988) calls "the codes of power" is a vitally important approach we use in doing girls' work.[2] In her influential 1988 article "The Silenced Dialogue: Power and Pedagogy in Educating Other People's Children," Delpit explains that young people of color need an explicit understanding of classroom rules that are often implicit and unstated. Further, she suggests these expectations and the language we use to communicate them are the "codes of power" that young people need to learn how to use. Our work with BIPOC girls clearly involves highlighting the arbitrary nature of these codes and the power dynamics they embody.

For girls of all racial backgrounds, the codes of dominant culture across various social settings are ingrained early, and it is important for them to understand the ways they get silenced from the start. As girls grow into adulthood, phrases like *wearing the pants*, *bossy*, or *the glass ceiling* signal the gender bias that awaits them in the workplace, in getting elected to public office, or in owning a business. The power to confidently navigate the cultural norms that prescribe women's roles equips girls to confront the codes of bias head-on. Instead of blaming themselves for not fitting into a culture that glorifies a hierarchical leadership mold, they can name norms that girls experience as exclusionary.

The phenomenon of women being interrupted and silenced in professional settings, often referred to as "speaking while female" (SWF), is well documented in various research studies and publications.[3] A study published in the *Journal of Language and Social Psychology* in 2015 found that men interrupt women significantly more often than they interrupt other men, and that women are more likely to be interrupted when they are in a position of authority or when they are the primary speakers in a group setting. The study also suggests that this pattern of interruption can undermine a woman's credibility and influence in professional settings, potentially hindering their career advancement.[4] These situations, though seemingly extreme, are not uncommon, and reflect the cultural norms, expectations, and biases of White, male-dominant cultures that devalue women's voices.

The issue of women being silenced and underrepresented in decision-making processes matters greatly because it has far-reaching consequences for both women and society as a whole.[5] In their book *The Spirit Level: Why Greater Equality Makes Societies Stronger*, Richard Wilkinson and Kate Pickett present evidence that more equal societies fare better on a range of health, social, and economic outcomes, arguing that reducing inequalities leads to societal benefits. When women opt out or are not equally represented due to exclusionary spaces and sexist attitudes and behaviors, it perpetuates a costly problem. Without inclusive and equitable representation of women in decision-making processes and a concerted effort to combat these biases in all aspects of society, girls' rights and opportunities will continue to be compromised.

Still, for a good reason, many ask: Does code-switching put authenticity at risk? Why should a girl be pressured to conform to White cultural practices, as it may feel inconsistent with maintaining a sense of personal authenticity? The need to constantly adjust one's behavior to fit into predominantly White spaces can lead to a sense of disconnection from one's true identity and values. While some may argue that code-switching is a necessary adaptation strategy for navigating institutionalized racism and achieving success in mainstream environments, others may view it as a form of cultural assimilation that erodes personal authenticity and perpetuates systemic inequalities. Ultimately, the debate surrounding code-switching underscores the importance of creating inclusive spaces where individuals feel empowered to express their authentic selves without fear of judgment or discrimination. It also highlights the need for broader societal changes to address systemic racism and promote diversity, equity, and inclusion in all aspects of life.

DEFINING POWER #7: DECIPHERING THE CODES OF DOMINANT CULTURE TO ACCESS OPPORTUNITY

Code-switching teaches girls the power of alternating between two or more sets of cultural norms for behavior, giving them more confidence to access opportunities as they grow up. Developing an understanding of cultural codes and their contexts is powerful. When combined with a personal definition of leadership, this understanding becomes an antidote. It allows a girl to adapt to dominant cultural codes when she chooses, or rewrite them entirely, without blaming herself for not fitting in. Offering girls an opportunity to explore code-switching as a skill and a means for navigating exclusionary norms is a first step.

Code-switching, defined as the changes a girl makes to her language, appearance, and behavior as she moves back and forth between White and other cultural environments, shows up in everyday encounters, such as:

- the language she uses to talk to her teacher vs. talking to her best friend.
- the language and tone of voice she uses to talk on the phone to her boss vs. talking to her mom.

- changing how she pronounces her name on the phone with the doctor's office or insurance company vs. how she introduces herself to others in her community.

Using code-switching to her benefit is about helping her first see the places she is doing it. Then it is helping her develop leadership tools for authentically adapting and, when possible, blending her leadership style to stay true to her values while being able to function within mainstream culture. Girls' work is about authentically keeping space to support girls to consider:

- Who are the people that have to code switch the most to navigate this world? Why?
- Why do folks who are not White males have to code switch? How do institutions (schools, jobs, hospitals, legal systems, the criminal justice system, etc.) enforce this and punish those who don't?
- What are the pros and cons of code-switching?
- How do you think code-switching/mixing impacts your sense of opportunity?
- What situations make you change or adjust yourself? What things cause you to feel more powerful as a leader? What things don't?

Visiting a code-switching and leadership authenticity workshop provides a firsthand opportunity to witness how girls engage with and apply the understanding of code-switching and leadership authenticity in their lives. These workshops serve as on-ramps for girls to explore and develop this power within the context of their experiences.

During the workshop, participants may engage in various activities and discussions aimed at fostering an understanding of code-switching, leadership authenticity, and their intersection. Girls may reflect on their own experiences of code-switching and how code-switching impacts their sense of identity and belonging in different social contexts. They may also explore alternative forms of leadership that go beyond traditional norms, recognizing their unique strengths and capabilities.

Workshop leaders guide girls through exercises designed to build confidence in navigating diverse social environments while staying true to oneself. Through roleplaying, group discussions, and self-reflection exercises, girls can develop the skills and insights needed to navigate complex social dynamics with authenticity.

Developing the Power Part 1: The Code-Switching Workshop

Angela, a biracial instructor who will facilitate the code-switching workshop, meets me at the school. Angela is known for her wry humor and legendary kindness, qualities that both instructors and girls appreciate. The day's plan is discussed as we lug sectional furniture from a staff lounge into a music room. We recognize that sparking conversations on code-switching can be messy and ambiguous, much like the process of rearranging this furniture. However, we embrace the challenge, aiming to create a space where discomfort can coexist with safety.

Our goal today is to help the girls understand the power of deciphering the unwritten codes of dominant culture while exploring their own definitions of leadership. Despite girls' potential feelings of being imposters in certain spaces, we aim to support them in navigating these challenges with confidence and authenticity. The group today consists of six racially diverse girls from different Seattle middle and high schools, ranging in age from fourteen to eighteen. This gathering is part of a five-part model workshop series rather than a yearlong girls' group. Two of the girls, Betelhem and Lena, have a unique connection to me: they are my daughters, and I had recommended that they join the group.

Betelhem is the middle child, recognized in all realms of her life as a peacemaker. Orphaned by AIDS, she joined our family at the age of six. Remarkably, she remembered her village's shared phone line, enabling her to bid farewell to her remaining family before departing for the United States. Betelhem appeared to thrive despite profound loss, excelling academically and embracing her Ethiopian heritage through regular attendance at one of Seattle's Ethiopian Orthodox churches. All through middle and high school, she'd navigated classrooms where her skin color stood out, and her smaller stature had caused her to be the target of harsh remarks. In the last couple of high school years, she'd surprised herself and others by joining wrestling and gaining a lot of self-confidence and strength.

She began to challenge herself by taking leadership roles, such as at the Congress of Racial Equality (CORE), where she facilitated conversations revolving around various social issues. Coming to the United States at a young age and figuring out family and school as an Ethiopian girl often in White spaces exposed her early on to code-switching. At the workshop today, she could more deeply explore her feelings about these experiences and consider the form of leadership she brought to engaging with these various codes.

"Today, we are going to think about ways we communicate, dress, or act the same or differently, depending on who we are around. And the first activity we are doing is called Crack the Code," Angela explains as the girls sit in a circle and munch on popcorn. Angela then asks them to use their purple stickies to write down three to six ways they've communicated, dressed, or acted with teachers or authority figures. "It can be a statement, a word, or a symbol," she explains. Then on the yellow stickies, she asks the girls to answer the same question—three to six ways that they've communicated, dressed, or acted—with friends. "The idea is to explore 'acceptable' codes in different settings. How do you talk, behave, and show up differently depending on who you are talking to? For instance, friends vs. adults, boys vs. girls. Notice if anything surprises you," she adds before leaving the girls to pair share.

Chapter 9

"For me, the one that is the same is how I dress," shares one of the girls, a mixed-race high school senior who identifies as Black and Filipina. "I have a pretty big spectrum of outfits I can wear, which depends on how I feel that day or how the weather is. Sometimes I will wear something a bit more like, you know, I wouldn't wear it to an interview. For how I act around people, though, um, it's different. For friends, I put it more as fun because I am sort of a goofy person out there. But with higher authority, I act more professionally or put together. More kindly if I want to be a butt kisser. You know how that goes," she concludes before inviting her partner to share her thoughts on the topic.

"For communication, I am overly nice and quiet with adult figures. With professionals, I proofread and make sure everything I say is polished. With friends, I text and I'm more straight up. I would use slang. I do dress pretty differently. It's always pretty comfortable, but sometimes it's more conservative. Talking with friends, I am cheery and upbeat, but with adults I follow the rules more. I am like, 'yes, I will do that' if an adult figure asked me to," her partner, a White high school freshman, remarks.

Another girl comments, "With friends, I feel calm, happy, playful. I have a spectrum of ways I can act and places I can go inside myself. I dress casually and comfy, sometimes I dress up, wear makeup. There's no opinion going against me. I am more myself. How I act around my teachers depends on how they treat me or how they treat other people who look like me. I will give my opinion on big problems because teachers like opinionated people. I will talk and act like I know things, especially politics. I am not as interested as I pretend I am. I keep my back straight. I try to be more innocent. I try to be grammatically correct. Because if you are, their perception of you goes higher. But I dress the same around adults and friends. I don't think my dressing should take away from their opinion of me," she adds.

As the workshop progresses, Angela gathers the pairs back into a small group, prompting them to delve deeper into the concept of code-switching. She tells the girls that code-switching involves adapting one's language or expression based on the audience, emphasizing that understanding it empowers individuals to navigate it consciously rather than feeling inauthentic. Angela then challenges the group with thought-provoking questions.

- Why do non-White and non-male individuals often find themselves compelled to code-switch? How do institutions enforce this behavior and penalize those who deviate from it?
- What are the advantages and disadvantages of code-switching or code-mixing?
- How does code-switching or code-mixing influence your perception of opportunities? Your willingness to explore new avenues? Your ability to succeed or handle failure? How does it impact others within your social circle?

The girls engage in a twenty-minute discussion, reflecting on what they found acceptable or unacceptable, what surprised them, and what did not.

Betelhem raises her hand to share her perspective. "For me, code-switching is almost second nature at this point," she began. "Coming from Ethiopia and then being adopted into an American family, I quickly learned to adapt how I communicated and presented myself in different contexts." "With my Ethiopian community and at church, I could be more expressive, using our native language and following cultural norms," Betelhem explains. "But at school or in other predominantly White spaces, I had to tone things down, speak more formally, and be cautious about behaviors that might be perceived as too different."

She paused for a moment, reflecting. "I remember in middle school, some of the other kids would make fun of my name or ask ignorant questions about my background. So I was willing to go by 'Beth' at times, just to avoid drawing unwanted attention to myself. It was a way of code-switching to fit in."

Betelhem shakes her head. "Looking back, I wish I hadn't felt the need to downplay that part of my identity. But you learn pretty quickly which codes are expected in different environments when you're a person of color."

"At the same time," she continues, "I do see the advantages of being able to adapt and make others feel comfortable. It helps me navigate various social and professional situations successfully. But it's exhausting always having to monitor yourself like that." The other girls nodded in understanding, some sharing similar experiences of modifying their language, appearance, or behaviors based on the context. Angela made a note about exploring ways to create more inclusive spaces where code-switching isn't a necessity.

Observing how the girls seamlessly transition between various cultural and linguistic contexts and navigate different parts of their identities within a single interaction impresses me. I note the significance of "cracking the code" and emphasizing the power girls have to "reset the code" themselves. The point is to support them in recognizing their agency, highlighting that they possess the ability to choose whether to adhere to established norms if they prove advantageous or to challenge and redefine them according to their own preferences.

Keeping It Going Part 2: A Workshop on Leadership Authenticity

In the next workshop, Angela shifts the focus from code-switching to exploring authentic leadership. Today's group will allow girls to examine ways that their leadership style could be authentically expressed given the depth and complexity of the content the girls have digested over the past month. This workshop prompts me to reflect on Lena, my younger daughter and one of the younger members of the group, who had struggled for years to express herself as a leader as she mixed and switched codes in various settings.

While Lena may have appeared confident on paper, her journey through middle and high school years was not without its challenges. As we delve into discussions about authentic leadership, Lena's experiences and perspective serve as a poignant reminder of the importance of inviting younger girls into the dialogue to define and embody leadership in ways that resonate with their beliefs, values, and strengths.

During her childhood, Lena grappled with self-consciousness regarding her family dynamics and her role within the family. Anxiety plagued her throughout adolescence, exacerbated by the constant comparisons made between her and her close-in-age adopted sisters by others in the community. The stark differences between Lena and her adopted sisters proved bewildering for her to comprehend. At the age of five, she found herself perplexed by the need for assistance in tying her shoes, while her sisters, Betelhem and Adanech, nearly her exact age, had mastered the task independently years prior. This dissonance underscored Lena's struggle to reconcile her own experiences with those of her siblings, deepening her feelings of uncertainty about her place within the family.

Though her reasons for agreeing to join the group sprang from snags with her family, she was also feeling like she did not belong at school. Attempting to be bold and direct at school came with a price. She wasn't finding "her people" at her school. This insecurity was met with a tendency to be extremely hard on herself. Still, Lena consistently demonstrated a willingness to be direct, honest, and caring, given all the contradictions and setbacks she experienced. She thrived in circumstances that put her on the edge of her comfort zone. Conversations, such as the ones that the five-part group offered on healthy girl culture, identity, code-switching, and leadership among racially different girls, deeply interested her.

Angela opens the group by noting, "You may or may not consider yourself a leader. But since we've been talking about power for the past few weeks, I want us to think about what the world would look like if we used that power from knowing our bodies, identities, and choice making to become leaders. How can we be leaders who can navigate the world/code switch and still hold our integrity and identities intact?"

Then she explains they will do an activity called Power Lines. Angela puts up a sign that says "agree" on one side of the room and "disagree" on the other and instructs the girls to line up and asks them different questions. The girls place themselves wherever they want on the spectrum when viewing the following statements.

Agree or Disagree:

- I am a powerful leader.
- I see people that share my identities as leaders in the world.
- I feel confident using my voice to express my opinions.
- I have to shape-shift or compromise pieces of myself to be seen or heard sometimes.
- My skills, opinions, and work often go overlooked.

As girls line up in different areas, Angela asks them why they placed themselves where they did. "I disagree. I don't really see myself as a leader. I don't really like to draw any attention to myself or take center stage. I will speak out in class, but I don't really ever feel confident," Lena offers, which, full disclosure, made me incredibly sad to hear as her mother. "And I agree that my skills, opinions, and work often go overlooked. I think people use me at school so they can have my notes," she adds. "But I do see people that reflect my identities as leaders in the world. I have teachers at school and other adults who I truly admire. Being around these people is a life raft for me," she concludes.

At that moment, Lena notices how she stood on the opposite side of the Power Lines for most of this activity. Not only is she one of the youngest girls there, but she is also the only White girl involved in this group.

The others, Black, Asian, and mixed race, stand on the opposite side of the spectrum when asked the questions about seeing people that reflect their identities as leaders in the world and having to shape-shift or compromise pieces of themselves to be seen or heard sometimes. Lena observes this and comments, "I am at a high school where there are very few students of color in my classes, despite it being a racially diverse high school. We never really talk about the impact; we just go along like it's normal. I see more clearly now what that impact is."

But what also stands out, and is consistent with studies in the field, is when the Power Line is about agreeing that they are a powerful leader, each of the group members of color stands by the "Agree" sign. And the same is true for using their voice to express their opinions. All agree. The entire group ends up standing huddled by the "Agree" sign together—across age and race lines—because they all agree that their skills, opinions, and work often go overlooked. That is tough to see, honestly. Does having these conversations add salt to the wound, or does it build solidarity among girls to surface these shared experiences? Angela lets an unwelcome but necessary silence sit as we all digest what we see, a Power Line that is down for each of the girls present.

"Now we are going to do an activity together called Leadership Statement," Angela instructs. "I am going to give you a giant piece of paper because I know your vision is big and bold," she says, handing them out. "And you need a lot of space to think about it. The guidelines are simple. Just write one sentence in the present tense about yourself." She provides an example, "For instance, 'I am a confident and trustworthy leader' or 'bold even in the face of big setbacks.'

"Then write three steps you can take in consistent practice to support being that bold and confident leader. For example, pushing yourself to speak your mind when presented with an opportunity, when tempted to be quiet. Or for me, sometimes, as a leader, I try to take on too much," Angela says. "Being a powerful leader doesn't mean you are out there on the front line by yourself. It's about bringing in community and collaborating with others. Then I am exhausted, which compromises my ability to show up. So my action steps are committing to self-care twice a month. Or saying no," she quips with a smile.

"And lastly, at the bottom, write the strengths or values you can bring to this leadership statement. You've brought up so many strengths throughout these workshops. Sometimes when we are moving toward something big, we need to ground into our strength," she concludes, before asking if the girls had any questions.

Girls jot down things like, "don't put too much on your plate, do not back down, know what you say is important, don't react, and educate people." Under strengths and values, one girl writes, "Empathetic and able to connect with people, wanting to make a difference in people's and children's lives, understand myself, my values and how to be happy and how to appreciate people in my life." After about twenty minutes or so, the girls huddle back up. Angela recaps, "one way to be a powerful leader is to be able to express ourselves, and today we are going to practice by presenting these leadership statements. Many of us can get shy, so let's practice how to do a 'power stance' in our bodies." Angela demonstrates by making a double fist with a serious face. "One at a time, you are going to do your power stance and say your leadership statement," she instructs.

A girl who wears a Smith College hoodie, with her hair pulled back, offers, "My statement is I am an expressive and inspiring leader. But I am nervous about doing the same things in my new East Coast life. So I am going to push myself to engage. Even if I am out of my element. My strengths are that I am consistent, understanding, and analytical. My values are love and community." The girls fist bump her as she triumphantly sits back down.

Another adds, "My leadership statement is I am a confident and direct leader who creates space for growth. My action steps— I made boxes because I like checking stuff off—are to speak out three times a week when I don't want to. I'm lazy sometimes. Also, I want to do something I feel confident in to build my confidence. And find a leader I can relate to. My strengths are that I am kind, observant, and strong. I value truth, honesty, and integrity." The girls applaud her as she takes her seat.

Finally, Lena strikes a sturdy stance. In her measured way, she states, "I am a determined, self-motivated, and genuine leader. My steps are to set my own goals and timeline, be firm with myself, not let things go too long, and not give up when presented with a no. I can do self-scans and check how I want to react and how I feel versus how I am reacting and feeling. My strengths are that I am compassionate, positive, dedicated, and intelligent." The girls offer her snaps as she rejoins the circle.

Angela reflects on her experience of listening to the girls' statements. "I felt moved to hear your statements. How about you?" she asks.

"Listening to all of us and realizing you don't have to be an adult or older to be opinionated and able to speak up. Even as freshmen to seniors, we are educated and know what's happening. The stereotype that teens don't know what they are saying or doing was disproved during these workshops," says one of the girls.

"Listening to everyone, I thought it was just me when it came to things I needed to improve on, like, oh my god, this is only me who needs to fix this. We are all brilliant, younger and older, and hearing people's leadership statements makes me think how much we have in common," adds another.

"There was such a diversity and abundance in terms of what leadership can look like," notes Angela. "And in closing, let's share a word or two on how you feel. What can you do to support your leadership goals this week?"

The girls christen the room with their insights.

"Happy because we got to meet new people. I will try to do one of my action steps.

"Empowered and inspired by all of you. I will do one of the things I wrote down. Talk to my friends about all this. We can talk about political power and racism."

"Impressed and proud of the girls in this group and the girl culture we created here. It's cool how we've connected this week. I want to work on remembering when I feel down on myself that there isn't one thing that defines a person. Not letting things blow up in my brain."

"Contemplative. Is that the word? This week I will try and speak out more in my classes and with my friends."

"Relieved to know more people, specifically females, who I have all this stuff in common with and who think like me."

"Blown away. You don't know that other people are thinking like you, knowing there are others who have the same opinions or can help you form and make more opinions. What I will work on is being more confident in my opinions. Being able to voice it to get it across to people in power is something I want to work on."

Angela closes the group on a high. "These are so powerful. I hope you put them above your bed or by your mirror so they are in a place where you can see them every day. I feel grateful I got to spend time with you and witness all of you in your power."

POWER TOOL: PARENT AND MENTOR TIPS FOR DECIPHERING THE CODES OF DOMINANT CULTURE

- Check Your Leadership Bias

    Girls in our circle reflect a wide developmental range and have not all had equal access to opportunities for their leadership development. Discussing leadership styles and code-switching can inadvertently reinforce what we are trying to undo. We make this mistake by showing (often unconsciously) bias in favor of girls who show up as leaders the way we do.

We make this mistake by showing (often unconsciously) bias in favor of girls who more easily adopt our own "standards" or "codes" for behavior, language, and attitudes. Emphasize that there are many forms of leadership, each valuable in its own right. Name and own yours. Don't overpraise girls who have greater comprehension or are more experienced in a leadership style you relate to.

- Hold Space for Persistence not Perfection

Often, girls create their leadership styles and develop confidence inside the group. Yet when they are in the world, they still face the same barriers and dismissive attitudes from adults. The feeling can be incongruent and frustrating for girls. Honor the frustration and stories of girls when they face roadblocks in their leadership. Remind them that the path to social change is long and that we need allies and support from people around us. We often raise girls to be self-reliant and seek perfection in their leadership, which can lead to isolation and self-criticism. However, remind them that they can seek allies in all areas of their life. Leadership is more powerful and effective when you have people that support you, and when you are persistent—not perfect— as you pursue leadership.[6]

- Notice the Quiet and the Loud

It is okay for a group to be quiet and reserved as long as you feel girls are participating—which might look different from group to group. And some girls are more outspoken than others—which is fine—except when the equity in the conversation goes off balance and other participants get shut down. For overly quiet groups, challenge them to speak up and get involved. If the girls continue to be radio silent, do an icebreaker with movement or an extra creative, art-based activity in which they share out. Don't act disappointed or make participants feel bad though. We also utilize small groups and pairs so that shyer girls have an opportunity to practice taking up space in a low-stakes situation. For overly dominant participants, those who talk over others or don't share the space in conversation, community agreements are very helpful. Bring girls back to the idea of "step up, step back."

MY CODE SWITCH STORY: CONTINENTAL BANK

Although I did not know it at the time, deciphering unwritten codes of dominant culture began during my pivotal college years. First, there was a delayed spring break flight, on which I found myself engaged in a conversation with a confident, much older, White male who questioned my professional aspirations and influenced my decision to pursue a major in finance upon returning to the University of Illinois. "Why do you want to count other people's money instead of making your own?" he'd quipped as the plane was finally about to take off.

Influential figures like my father, the man on the plane, and a friend's dad provided mentorship and guidance and inadvertently steered me toward a career path in business. Lacking a network of women to offer guidance, I relied on their advice and insights.

Landing a finance internship at Continental Bank, I recall feeling grateful for the chance to explore new horizons beyond the traditional gendered professions of my mother's generation. On my first day at the new job, the sticky autumn air embraced me as I stepped out in a fresh wool suit of laurel green. The taupe Coach handbag, a gift from my mother, complemented the outfit perfectly. To complete the look of a confident young career woman in her early twenties, I slipped into a pair of sky-high snakeskin pumps.

During that time, like many of us seeking a new vision of womanhood, I looked to Hollywood for cues on the societal codes I was expected to follow. However, one vivid memory stands out from those heady days: the heel of my shoes snapped off as I stepped onto the elevator grate. Mortified, I opted to skip joining my internship class for lunch that day, fearing judgment for my footwear mishap. Instead, I spent the afternoon hungry and preoccupied with concealing my damaged shoes from my peers. The repercussions of my absence from the networking opportunity became apparent the following Monday.

Months went by. I genuinely liked other members of my internship class. It was a fifty-fifty split between males and females, and we shared the camaraderie of being early twenties Chicagoans newly graduated from a good university. We regularly hit happy hour, occasionally invited one another into other social circles we were part of, and some even ended up dating for a time. On the professional front, under the guise of "you can't manage what you can't measure," we had ongoing training and workshops. This curriculum taught us all about solving business problems using managerial and cost accounting principles and vocabulary.

In the hidden curriculum of male networking, despite the gender balance of our internship class, there was a whole other layer of turoring going on. There was golfing for males. There were fist bumps and congratulatory remarks when the football bets were made. There were lewd comments about the bodies of female interns when they left for a minute to go to the restroom. There was no equity, diversity, and inclusion officer to go to when this type of exclusionary behavior created a culture that tolerated sexism and racism.

By then, I had finished reading *The Second Sex*, and I began to talk about it with my cubicle mate, Nena, a Black woman in her forties who eagerly supported my assessment of what was happening around us. "How do you do it, Nena? This place is just totally exhausting," I put out to her one day.

Despite being there for five years, she hadn't progressed to a manager position or beyond her station. She was in an "offshore accounting coordinator" purgatory that paid the bills. "Get out while you can," she said, taking a drag off her menthol Virginia Slim. "I can't. Got kids to get through high school."

Chapter 9

Nena's advice bobbed at the surface of my thoughts for a short while. I quit Continental Bank a few weeks later.

Not then, or until many years later, would the concepts of code-switching and/or having a language or latitude for understanding my leadership style be on any radar. Without a language for naming microaggressions, I easily blamed myself for not fitting in. Without a personal exploration into the ways my leadership style actually mattered to the overall success of an effort, I assumed it didn't. Without sharing indignant "that happened to you, too?" moments with others where the rewriting of the codes could commence, they didn't. Many of us in the internship simply moved on or opted out.

Understanding *the impact of the lack* of skill I possessed to code switch and to explore my personal leadership development as a girl has benefited my work with girls in countless ways. Again, this exemplifies the importance of knowing what you don't know. I am more skilled at noticing when a girl blames herself for not fitting in and able to openly challenge that blame. I provide language to a girl to explain why her contributions matter, even if she isn't the loudest voice in the room or hers wasn't the most popular opinion offered. I believe her when she tells me she has experienced a microaggression and help her develop a way to address it in the moment. I support a girl when she reaches higher than she imagined she could because she is traveling "out of her league."

My connection to girls as a mentor and a mother calls me to remember what I hadn't had myself: permission to be a leader as I defined it, in a nontraditional way. I want them to have that experience. Naming and improving upon *my limitations*—say, my minimal authentic leadership development as a girl and lack of relevant experience with code-switching to draw upon as a White girl that was relevant to girls of color—girds my ability to be effective in supporting girls. In mapping my experiences and using these as a point of connection, I help girls to develop the power to think about how they get stripped of the confidence to express themselves as leaders; how they are impacted historically, racially, and culturally to have no control over the "codes of power"; and how they can instead develop the power to rewrite the codes.

Developing this power *in myself* is something I never really learned until I was older. This always motivated me, imagining that things would be better for the next generation and that they could rewrite the codes of the dominant culture once they held the reins. As a White woman, so much of my identity already matched when considering the way I code switched. But what does it mean to speak with an accent or a nondominant language structure? In what ways might code-switching also act as an opportunity for people, especially people of color, to keep a piece of themselves to just their personal life? What does it mean for some of us to want to bring our "full selves" to workplaces, and for others to not want that?

Parent/Mentor Self-Reflection Power Tool

Recalling and reflecting on your own experiences of code-switching sparks valuable insights to support girls in developing their power. Unpacking memories and understanding how your day-to-day life has been influenced by these experiences can enhance your ability to guide and support them. To develop your skills in supporting a girl in building her power, first ask yourself:

1. What information about your own experiences (or lack thereof) with code-switching is helpful to recall? Are there memories that you can unpack so that you are better prepared to support a girl in developing this power?
2. What is your attitude toward changing your practice related to this power?
3. What existing habits might you need to unlearn?

4. What about your current environment prevents you from being successful in learning this practice with a girl?

THE RIPPLE EFFECT OF REWRITING THE CODES

A handful of years after their girls' group, as a wintry day unfolds and their school breaks come to a close, Betelhem, Lena, and I prepare to take a wooded walk together near our home to talk about their experiences of code-switching and leadership. Betelhem has returned for the weekend from graduate school and is dressed comfortably, with her black hair braided and tucked into a silk scarf. Lena, a senior in college, is visiting for a long weekend. Her brownish-red hair sits in a bun on top of her head.

I feel nervous as we layer our rain gear over down jackets, pocket Clif bars, and leash up the dog. The relationships I had wished for with my own sisters so long ago, the ones that felt irreparably disrupted by the trauma of surviving the murder of our oldest sister, are possible and within reach for my own daughters. There has always been a deep level of respect between these two sisters, and I love how they always had each other's best interests at heart. They are one grade apart in school and had even attended college together. Over the years, they had had difficult conversations about race on occasion. Betelhem had experienced feelings of deep frustration at the impact of racial bias all around her. As much as she wanted to be a support, Lena had never had to deal with this as a White girl, and this chasm of understanding could never really be bridged.

The conversation I hope we have on our walk—given our complex family blend of racial and cultural identities—is one that reflects the healthy girl culture we strove to create in our family, a respect for anger and skills for confronting it, efforts to resolve conflict among sisters, an openness to talking about race and the context around code-switching, and the digging deeply into values and identity as they relate to leadership. I have my years of girls' work to thank. And our conversation will no doubt be challenging in the ways that all conversations about racial and cultural identities and the codes that go with them are. The stakes feel so incredibly high; the potential harm I always worried about doing in my girls' work had all the same potential at home.

Betelhem jumps in first. "The main thing that impacted my confidence was how people treated me because I was a shorter person, where often other students would belittle me because I was smaller than them," Betelhem tells us this as we walk under a large canopy of towering Douglas firs. The wounds to her psyche are deep ones. "And growing up, I didn't know how to exist as a Black girl in White spaces or Black spaces, as I didn't feel like I fit either group. Girls' groups gave me a space to start getting the language to express myself and made me not feel like I was alone. I was also connecting with mentors that took me seriously."

I probe, "How did having no control over the 'codes of power' impact you? Did the girls' groups help you understand or navigate this?"

Betelhem's eyes shine with a characteristic pensive look, and she offers, "I think this speaks to my self-blame over things I couldn't control without understanding at the time that I couldn't control them. For example, where I attended high school. The isolation I felt wasn't exclusively due to my interactions with other students, but was also due to how the school was segregated, how the advanced placement programs were regarded and funded, and who they were accessible to.

"My experience as a Black girl in the AP program was influenced by how the schools were constructed and who had access to the different programs. Again, the girls' groups were more of a space of connection without judgment compared to what I was experiencing in my school. As far as rewriting the codes, I think going to college and making friends with other students of color (specifically Black students) helped me see that I didn't have to center or accept the White male dominant culture. While it is still prevalent structurally, within my personal life and my spheres of influence I try to center Black voices and create a culture where we're pushing back against dominant cultures. I want to rewrite how we view success and value different people's lives, among other things. The girls' groups contributed to opening this line of questioning of what we consider normal, what is accepted, whose narrative we accept as truth, etc. I try to do that in my work, personal life, and school," she concludes.

I look away as I listen to Betelhem's analysis of her experiences. Trying hard not to make this moment about my own experience of watching her grow into this place of self-confidence, vulnerability, and authenticity, I think about Alemitu, Betelhem's Ethiopian mother. As Betelhem speaks, I look up with a smile (and a hidden trickle of tears) and signal to Alemitu that *our* girl, despite so many odds against her, has solidly grown into herself, after many, many years of struggling to do so.

Betelhem says matter-of-factly, "I think it's essential to incorporate girls' advocacy work with the work I want to do in public health, especially as it pertains to structural racism, patriarchy, and capitalism." In her master of public health application essay, Betelhem put it this way, "I am a Black woman. I am an Ethiopian adoptee. I am an immigrant from Ethiopia. I have learned to balance and pay attention to my converging realities and multiple identities. I have critically analyzed the root causes of my health, state of mind, and the ways that I exist. I always consider my own positionality and its limitations, but also the abundance of connections and opportunities it provides in working in systems. This intersectional perspective I hold led me to take a range of classes and experiences that uplifted the health needs of Black people and, specifically, Black women. For the past two consecutive summers, I created two five-week programs that unpacked the factors that influence the sexual health and reproductive health of Eritrean and Ethiopian women and girls. The program has provided ways to incorporate more open dialogues about reproductive health and sexual health issues to shift the culture around this subject within our own lives and communities. This program has created a foundation for the work I want to continue in the future."

Betelhem became adept at code-switching to access the resources she needed to ensure she could bring these things back to her community. Like she was on a seesaw, she balanced converging realities and multiple identities alongside an ability to critique but not assimilate to the dominant culture as she was accessing its resources.

As we wind our way through the winter garden, I notice the splashes of color, sweet fragrances, and striking bark on some trees. It is fitting that we had made it to the halfway point of our walk and that Lena is ready to contribute to the conversation.

"Feeling as though my voice wasn't appreciated in school and that speaking up or taking the lead marked me as 'bossy' or a 'know-it-all' really limited my willingness to express myself as a leader. I think that I felt much safer in girls' leadership groups and began to see taking leadership as a more positive thing in this context," she tells us. "My willingness to silence myself stemmed from wanting to make sure that I was viewed by others, particularly men, in a positive and nonthreatening way. I now know that it's important for me to take leadership and speak up regardless of whether or not it fits within a socially acceptable view of women for those around me."

As Lena speaks, my mind reluctantly rewinds to elementary, then middle, then high school. All held socially difficult transitions for her. When she shared her intellect with confidence and sought to buck the codes for White girls—of compliance, deference, and being nonthreatening—she was punished by peers *of both genders*. This came to a head when, during her eighth-grade year, a boy she had known since elementary school circulated a sexually harassing "poem" about her. In a textbook ending, she had also been cast out by many of the girls in her grade, who sided with the boys over the incident, saying Lena was "overly sensitive" and "took things too seriously."

Chapter 9

To cope, she had gravitated toward adults to hold on to her willingness to speak up. But by her sophomore year, there simply wasn't enough cover to duck under. Her social anxiety and the social pressure around her proved debilitating. She was depressed, so she started working with a psychiatrist and taking medications. The medication helped her get to higher ground, where she could see that the codes of high school she was experiencing were not the only ones. Eventually, she had taken courses at the community college, meeting older and more mature students, many of them immigrants. She graduated a semester early after being accepted to the college her sisters were attending. The day before she left home, she'd given us a plaque that read, "Thank you for seeing me before I could see myself."

Lena continues to speak about being involved in girls' groups as we head up a hill toward Azalea Way, one of our favorite trails in the arboretum. "The most important thing is that I can better tell when a situation will lead to a toxic outcome or relationship. I also more consistently seek the positive, safe, and open feeling I found in girls' groups in other relationships. I don't feel the need to settle for relationships that I know are unhealthy because I have experienced the joy and warmth of healthy and positive communities of girls and women. It was a place that held the whole of me, grounded me, and allowed to me to seek other experiences that made me feel that way."

One place where Lena found that was on Sundays working at a local farm. The women who ran the farm were irreverent and devoted and radiated warmth. "They taught me how to be brave and quick thinking in moments of pressure, set boundaries, stand my ground, and be fully present in a moment. Mucking paddocks one Sunday morning, I recognized the most spiritual moments of my life—my true codes—were outside of the walls of my parish."

Lena also shares how her experiences led to a lasting commitment to upending the codes of power as they exist in the world around her. In the summer of 2020, while attention was fixated on mounting deaths and infection rates, Lena learned about a parallel health crisis through an internship. There, she researched the impacts of COVID-19 on youth of color, analyzed racially disaggregated health statistics from a state youth survey, read public health reports, and listened to professionals talk about what they saw on the ground.

"This experience was an important foundation for the work I would do that summer with youth in crisis at the Seattle Indian Health Board. I led discussions with youth about their health and identities; many of these students recounted stories of violence within their homes and communities. Beyond the initial difficulty of helping these youth receive necessary medical support, what struck me most deeply were the limits of the support that I could provide. Outside of calling the authorities and actively listening during discussions, I could not help these youth secure the resources for recovery that they needed because *they do not exist*," she shares.

It was clear from talking to her that, on both a personal and structural level, these experiences were illuminating and discordant for her. "These observations helped me understand the entrenched cycles that limit access to basic human needs and how significant this access is for health and fulfillment. The goal of being able to rewrite these codes of power and do more than hope for changed systems and protocols is what makes me feel most inspired to work on health policy and create community-based and trauma-informed protocols for recovery that children affected by violence need and deserve."

In Betelhem and Lena, we see girls with the power to navigate cultural norms traditionally seen as male or White middle-class dominant. With this under their belts, they can consider how to value their leadership styles alongside it.

What about the girls you are raising and mentoring? How do they get stripped of feeling the confidence to express themselves as leaders? How has having little or no control over the codes of power impacted them in historically, racially, and culturally specific ways? How are you supporting them to rewrite these codes of power?

POWER TOOL: A REWRITING THE CODES OF DOMINANT CULTURE ACTIVITY YOU CAN DO WITH GIRLS

Introduction

"Speaking While Female" (SWF) diagnoses the problem of women being interrupted and silenced in corporate environments. Whether a woman is being constantly interrupted or has a fear of being perceived as too aggressive, being silenced comes at a cost. This cost can be missed opportunities to share promotion-landing ideas or feeling chronically excluded in a workplace culture. For many girls, long before they encounter being silenced in the workplace, a fear of speaking up takes root. Speaking up in class becomes problematic for many. But a girl needs to understand that speaking out—in public or in a small-group setting—gives her valuable cultural currency, a tool for being able to help alternate between differing cultural norms for behavior. This activity prompts practice in speaking up with confidence and provides context for ways the broader culture can make it challenging for a girl to do so.

Conversation Tips

Tell her about a time where you felt great about speaking in public—a small group counts. Tell her about a time where you felt lousy about speaking in public. Explain what helps you overcome your fear or hesitance in speaking up. Teach her about phenomena such as speaking while female and imposter syndrome.

Goals
- Develop a deeper understanding of the importance of public speaking as cultural currency.
- Develop a fresh understanding of ways to practice public speaking so she's less likely to silence herself.

Deciphering the Codes of Dominant Culture

Do This Together

1. Ask, what is an issue she cares deeply about? Why? It's helpful to ask open-ended questions; you are aiming for deeper responses and explanations instead of yes or no answers. Draw on a past conversation in which she expressed a passion to get her thinking about issues she'd want to speak up about.
2. Ask her to develop a two-to-three-minute personal story that sums the issue. Teach her to tell a simple, personally meaningful story—one that is concrete and personal—before she inserts data she knows. If she struggles, model this by sharing your own story.
3. Challenge her to practice it in front of you. For many girls, a huge part of confidence comes from speaking truths to a friendly, even possibly like-minded audience first. Developing confidence in her idea will make her less concerned with likability. A huge part of practice is working through the emotions—the fears—that diminish her confidence and teaching her to name her fears as she moves through them.
5. Listen actively and give feedback. Stay focused on what she is saying. Bookend praise—"your point about the rainforest was crystal clear"—with critique—"next time shorten the part about China's role in climate change, because you lost me."
6. Now read about the definition of deciphering the codes of dominant culture and the skills that it takes to build this power. Closing question: What is a skill she needs to develop related to this power? Who can help her?

CHAPTER 10

Embracing Horizontal Leadership

POWER #8

A girl who recognizes the significance of horizontal leadership actively confronts hierarchical structures that often perpetuate inequality and limit opportunities. Proactively, she challenges societal norms around traditional vertical leadership models and redefines what is considered valuable in leadership. Developing this power means engaging in open and honest dialogues about the consequences of unequal distributions of power and responsibility, practicing skills to speak up on issues she cares about, and fostering an awareness of self-care practices when taking on leadership roles.

We can't expect a girl to rewrite the rules of leadership until she can navigate the dominant culture's codes. Research shows as girls get older, their confidence to lead often takes a nosedive. So step one, helping her find her voice within the prevailing cultural norms and power structures, lays crucial groundwork for leadership that prepares her to challenge and reinvent systems, ensuring they function more equitably, in communities, in institutions, or within her own home. This is the essence of embracing horizontal leadership. With this power, girls learn to reject hierarchical, top-down models in favor of inclusive decision-making and shared authority. It's an approach that prioritizes collaboration over competition, uplift over domination.

This power can be developed as the others are in process. It's important to remember that nothing about girls' work necessarily happens in a linear or sequential manner. Of all the powers, this embrace of a leadership style feels like the one that stretches girls to share power, weaves their developing skills together, and maps their actions and selfhood out into the future.

Upending a traditional notion of leadership isn't a huge stretch for most girls. One seminal work, *The New Girls' Movement: Charting the Path* (2000),[1] suggests that girls routinely challenge traditional top-down notions of leadership prevalent in the culture at large. Rather than seeing leadership as taking charge, girls see leadership as being "charged with taking a stand and having a vision." The study identified five leadership types girls demonstrate in informal single-gender settings. These are:

1. Cascading: Older girls serve as supporters and role models for younger girls.
2. Collective: Leadership is built on the development of group power and solidarity.
3. Survival: Girls utilize skills developed in response to adversity as tools for leadership development.
4. Culture: Leadership that involves reclaiming values and customs to help girls assert their place in the world.
5. Roving: Leadership that is grasped intermittently and organically by girls in informal group settings.

A Girl Scouts Research Institute study noted that girls described "boy" leadership as being about authority, control, and ego, while "girl" leadership focused on being a good listener, building consensus, and ensuring others' happiness. Leadership was seen as both having admirable qualities and taking actions to help others achieve dreams. However, many girls were ambivalent about leadership itself due to a lack of self-confidence and awareness of gender biases, setting a high bar for women leaders. While race and income correlated with leadership aspirations indirectly through self-perception and attitude, other influential factors included family (especially mothers), peers playing both positive and negative roles, and participation in organized activities and leadership opportunities.[2]

This scholarship suggests that the issue lies not in girls' inability to share power, but rather in the widespread devaluation of the forms of leadership they typically exhibit in broader societal contexts. It is therefore crucial to support girls in recognizing this devaluation of the leadership styles they often aspire to and in cultivating a more nuanced understanding of leadership beyond traditional hierarchical models. By embracing the alternative forms of leadership that they genuinely value, girls can work to normalize these approaches, challenging prevailing norms and contributing meaningfully at home, at work, and in their communities.

As younger generations of girls enter the workforce, there is an increasing preference for more participative and egalitarian leadership styles that align with their values of autonomy, transparency, and shared responsibility. Adrienne Mari Brown's *Emergent Strategy: Shaping Change, Changing Worlds* discusses how emergent strategy at work requires shared power and a collective vision among those involved. In shared, nonhierarchical leadership, power is distributed rather than concentrated at the top.[3] Teaching girls to value and pursue horizontal leadership is an integral aspect of social justice work in particular, what Edwards describes as "moving from working OVER others, to working FOR others, and finally working WITH those who are impacted by the injustice."[4]

Valuing new leadership models is crucial; however, it does not diminish the value of the ability to speak up effectively in public and small group settings. Long before encountering workplace silencing, many girls grapple with a fear of speaking up, which can hinder their participation in class discussions. These patterns can persist into adulthood, contributing to a workplace landscape characterized by a leadership gap, promotion gap, and support gap, alongside women shouldering three times the unpaid care work compared to men.[5]

Phenomena like speaking while female—describing women being interrupted and silenced in corporate environments—and mansplaining—a condescending explanation by a man typically to a woman—have their roots in girlhood experiences and are commonplace in the workplaces girls will enter. It's important to acknowledge that women are often pushed out of leadership roles in the workplace. Whether it comes from continual interruption or a fear of being perceived as overly aggressive, being silenced exacts a toll. This can result in missed opportunities to share promotion-worthy ideas or a persistent feeling of exclusion from workplace dynamics.[6] Girls who value horizontal leadership enter adulthood equipped to challenge such microaggressions, reshape cultural norms around leadership values, and champion diverse perspectives. They advocate for policies that address the discomfort of not fitting into homogenous settings and strive to transform the culture itself.

Horizontal leadership is a key to unlocking girls' potential as changemakers in the political arena as well. The traditional model of leadership often seen in politics is one that many girls find alienating—the classic "good old boys" club mentality that requires conforming to a particular male-dominated style. This paradigm frequently leads girls to feel pushed out or disenchanted, causing them to disengage from the political process entirely. Many feel their voices aren't adequately represented by the current political establishment and its leadership norms.

Data shows young female voters across racial lines consistently demonstrate a commitment to voting for policies that uplift themselves and other women and people of color.[7] When girls see horizontal leadership in action—policies crafted through inclusive processes, campaigns built on mutual upliftment—they recognize the potential to create genuine, lasting change. By teaching girls to value a new model of leadership and supporting them to recognize their collective power, we can cultivate a generation of politically engaged girls who actively shape the future of their communities and our nation.

DEFINING POWER #8: EMBRACING HORIZONTAL LEADERSHIP

Embracing horizontal leadership is the power to value leadership as a balance and blend of what a girl wants for herself and what she gives to others as she engages as a leader in the world around her. Recognizing the significance of horizontal leadership, girls understand the importance of equitable sharing of responsibilities both at home and in professional environments.

By embracing horizontal leadership, girls challenge societal norms and redefine what is considered valuable. They encourage a more equal distribution of responsibilities, both within their immediate environments and on a broader societal scale. By cultivating this power, a girl discovers that her desire to effect change in the world can coexist with her aspirations for leadership, empowering her to confidently pursue progress she sees as meaningful. With this power, she becomes a catalyst for positive transformation within her family, community, and society at large. A girl who possesses this power:

- understands the significance of a shared leadership style and its impact on shaping environments.
- has the ability to assertively say yes or no when distributing workload within groups.
- appreciates her unique expression of leadership and values her individual contributions.

- has tools for speaking confidently in public and prioritizes self-care to sustain her efforts.
- utilizes her power to effect change collaboratively, recognizing the collective strength in working together toward common goals.

People literate in teaching girls about power don't deny the glass ceiling or dismiss an egalitarian leadership style. They remind girls about the role women play in movements for change and the shoulders on which they stand. They acknowledge that past injustices make for present challenges for women in the workplace. They don't gloss over or downplay the importance of speaking up. Instead, they teach that even though the larger culture rewards a more male style of speaking and banter, practicing speaking up (even if it terrifies the girl) primes her to speak up later. The importance of public speaking and sharing their opinions publicly is a learned skill that girls need to bring with them into womanhood.

Teaching about this form of power is also about underscoring the importance of taking care of oneself as a revolutionary act when doing community organizing. We teach girls to upend the larger cultural notion of self-sacrifice for girls and women and the stunted, limited notion of self-care as a commodity only available for purchase. Burnout is an epidemic in organizing spaces, yet we rely on an outdated understanding of self-care. You can support a girl in developing new practices rooted in what gives her joy, strategies that sustain her as she practices leadership in the world—what Black feminist Audre Lorde has named "joy as an act of resistance." By upholding self-care as a revolutionary act and empowering a girl to prioritize her well-being, you can help her cultivate the resilience, sustainability, and joy necessary to thrive as a leader in her community and beyond.

Working with girls, I've observed numerous positive changes as they develop this form of power. A girl can:

- verbalize different forms of leadership and be less ambivalent about identifying herself as a leader.
- embrace her authentic leadership style, shedding the pressure to feign niceness.
- reject barriers to expressing leadership such as stress, fear of talking in front of others, seeming bossy, and peer pressure.
- stop idealizing leadership and set expectations and leadership skill development goals at a reasonable and attainable level.
- undertake and complete homegrown projects she deeply believes in her local community and beyond.

Developing the Power: Public Voice and Self-Preservation

Adanech, my youngest daughter, is in high spirits as I drive her across town to attend a workshop on public speaking and self-care. Her renewed participation in a girls' group is the source of her exuberance. For the next ten weeks, she and other program alums will continue to unpack the conditions that allow girls to cultivate collective power by stewarding the group's culture, building their skills as facilitators, and exploring ways to engage in social change.

For Adanech, the experience will culminate in an opportunity to emcee the organization's fundraising event. "Can you believe they've asked me to do it?" she says with a wide grin as she exits the car.

"Yep. I can," I call back to her as she opens the door to the community center where they will host the girls. Her self-confidence is evident, but it was never a given.

As she races toward the door to the center, I think back to the first time we met, at Toukol Orphanage in Addis Ababa. When she saw me and Kevin, my husband, Adanech, five, clung to her older sister, Betelhem, and cried. Understandably, she struggled to adapt to a perennially changing landscape. Her first step on an

Chapter 10

airport escalator would lead her to a world of unknowns. There were no escalators in Gondar, Ethiopia, where she was born. The compound she had lived in was shared with two other families. When their family learned that both their father and mother had contracted AIDS, and that medications were unavailable, she and her siblings were split up between relatives who took them in for care. Within a year, both parents had passed and their grandfather decided that the best hope for them was going to the orphanage.

Months later, she and her sister Betelhem left with us from there for life in Seattle. Three flights and two continents later, we arrived on Christmas Eve for them to meet the rest of our family, including their new sisters. Throughout her childhood, Adanech would easily attach to people she did not know well, even strangers. She struggled with food insecurity and would frequently become dysregulated in family settings.

When we worked with a specialist, we learned that these are all common attachment issues that come from instability, loss, and living in institutional or foster care settings. During middle school, she encountered difficulties fitting in and navigating social issues with other girls. This stemmed partially from Adanech's difficulty focusing in class and partially from her struggle to find a sense of belonging within any particular group. Additionally, being a transracial adoptee left her with numerous unanswered questions about her identity. She grappled with whether she identified as Ethiopian, a Black girl, or both. She was boisterous and fun-loving by nature, but the tween years had zapped her of confidence.

The girls' program was a godsend, a place of belonging and identity exploration. Joining the alum group as a council member was like coming home. Iman, a first-generation Ethiopian immigrant, is the group's facilitator for today's workshop and has mentored these girls through several other programs. She comes to youth empowerment work from a background of supporting youth mental health in schools. Iman's skill as a facilitator is keen.

Whatever magic she's done to create such a caring community and get the girls reconnected so quickly is something to behold. Tanisha, a twentysomething Black woman, is volunteering her time to assist Iman.

"Who is a leader whose values you admire, and what is something you notice about their public speaking style?" asks Iman. "Let's start with that question today."

"This is kind of random, but Emma Watson is someone I think of," says one girl. "If you think back to her story, how she wanted to go to school, an Ivy, and is fearless. She did what she wanted and wasn't afraid of what people thought of her. What I like about her speaking style is she isn't afraid to be vulnerable, you know, she's relatable."

"I think of a girl at my school. She is sure of what she believes in and is not going to be persuaded away," adds another.

"The first person that comes to my mind is Michelle Obama. One thing we have in common is I want to make that difference with people," says Adanech. "I like how she uses metaphors in her speeches like, 'When they go low, we go high.'"

Finally, another offers, "I look up to my grandma. She's the type of person who is always kind to the people at her senior home. When she sees something wrong, she doesn't let it rest. She hates public speaking, though, so I am not sure of how she does it."

With the ice broken, Iman and Tanisha lead the girls through an activity called Speak UP, which helps them practice speaking up with confidence and provides context for understanding how the broader culture can present challenges for girls in doing so. Iman asks the group to think back on phrases they've encountered in previous workshops: speaking while female (SWF), imposter syndrome, and mansplaining, which all highlight phenomena that originate in girlhood experiences.

Next, she asks the girls to revisit their values definition worksheets from a previous group and to consider any issues they have identified that align with their values. This encourages them to reflect on the issues they'd like to speak up about. It signals to them that what they have to say matters to the rest of us, a belief that, once it goes missing for a girl, can shut her down.

"One powerful way to be a leader is to practice speaking out loud in front of others, speaking about our needs and intentions in the world," explains Tanisha. "One way to do that is to develop a personal story that sums up the issue you want to speak about. I want you to tell a simple, personally meaningful story, one that is concrete and unique." In a popcorn-style format, the girls share brainstormed stories that they might like to explore further. Topics range from making sure more girls have a girls' program and girls' safety on public transportation to animal protection, food justice, and affordable housing for people in the community.

"I first got involved in the program when I was very young. My sister was in programming and I looked up to her. I saw how much it meant to my sister and I wanted that," Adanech explains to her partner. "I think more girls should have this same opportunity even if they don't have a sister to tell them about it. That's the change I want to see in the world. More girls getting this kind of programming." As Adanech shares her story with a partner, Iman provides guidance to the group. "Each person should listen actively and give feedback. Stay focused on what your partner is saying. Bookend praise—'your point about the lack of access to girls' programming was crystal clear'—with critique—'next time, shorten the part about your big sister's role in getting you involved because you lost me in the details.'"

A significant aspect of the practice involves addressing and navigating the emotions—particularly the fear—that can diminish a girl's confidence. It's essential to teach her to identify and articulate her fears as she progresses through them. "You may notice that your confidence kicks in more when you are expressing truths in your story to a like-minded audience like the girls here," Tanisha tells the group.

"Developing confidence in your ideas with a supportive audience first can help reduce your concerns about likability or appeal to a group you don't feel comfortable with." Iman and Tanisha give homework to the girls to write up and practice speaking a two-minute story and prepare to deliver their presentation next time.

Now it's time for the second part of the workshop. Tanisha posts a quote by Black self-care activist Sonya Renee Taylor from her book *The Body Is Not an Apology: The Power of Radical Self-Love*. The quote is a grounding segue. "Radical self-love necessitates changed hearts, beginning with our own. Quite simply, we cannot build in the world that which we have not built in ourselves." Tanisha next invites the girls to brainstorm self-care strategies for their mind, body, and spirit and set a goal. Tanisha incorporates movement, having them share while dancing when music plays, and then stopping to discuss with new partners.

As they wrap up, the girls tuck away their speaking notes and self-care plans. They understand societal factors suppressing girls' leadership, have tools to refine their voices, and see self-care's importance in sustaining themselves. Sharing power counteracts the helplessness their generation often feels.

Six weeks later, Adanech stands backstage, steadying her nerves before emceeing the organization's gala. The journey of getting here flashes through her mind. Adanech smooths the deep green dress she has picked out specially for tonight. The confidence she has built over the past months is simultaneously empowering and terrifying her in this moment. She goes over her opening lines again under her breath.

"You've got this," Bella whispers, giving her hand an affirming squeeze before rejoining the other youth ambassadors. Adanech takes a deep breath as the event coordinator cues her. She strides out on stage, chin up, shoulders back. The applause rings in her ears as she approaches the microphone.

"Good evening everyone, and welcome to the annual gala!" Her voice projects clearly across the hall. "My name is Adanech, and I'm honored to be your host tonight . . . "

As she continues speaking, her initial jitters fade away. The storytelling exercises have prepared her well. She weaves together humor, startling statistics on issues facing girls globally, and uplifting accounts of the organization's local impact. Adanech ensures that the crowd feels both the gravity of the challenges and the urgency of the mission.

When she reaches her closing, she pauses briefly, locking eyes with Iman, who gives her an encouraging nod. "Each of us has a story that sparked us into action for girls' empowerment. My story began an ocean away . . . ." Adanech shares her truth about her childhood and her struggles with identity, yet finding her voice through the girls' community here in Seattle. "This organization showed me that embracing *all* my identities—as an Ethiopian, as a Black girl, as a leader—is a radical act of self-love. They gave me the skills to speak up with confidence about the change I wish to see." When Adanech was in kindergarten, her teacher said she had the "courage of a lion." After a challenging adolescence, it was beautiful to see her find her power again.

Adanech would take this regained confidence to Whittier College, where she would major in sociology with a concentration in Black studies. As an excellent student and dynamic dancer on the Afro-fusion dance team, she still found time to focus her energies on addressing social inequities. She was an active organizer and supporter for the campus food-service union when they were on strike in her senior year. The strike was ultimately a success. The union leaders attended Adanech's Black graduation celebration to "express our love for her commitment."

KEEPING IT GOING: STEM TRAILBLAZING

On a damp Pacific Northwest day in springtime, I visit the suburban five-hundred-plus-acre Microsoft headquarters, about ten miles from my home, which feels a bit like a college campus set in a small town. Retail shops, restaurants, running and walking trails, sports facilities, and green spaces. One of the first walls you see when you enter the main building's lobby is a live plant wall. Automatic watering and lighting ensure the plants are healthy. There are sofas all around, vending machines, refrigerators, and open pantries. I am told there is even a huge gym, cricket grounds, and pool tables, all promoting community among the tech workforce. In theory, these workspaces are a key to supporting greater creativity and collaboration for their workforce.

That day, myself and staff from the nonprofit where I work had been asked to become instructors at the new weeklong Microsoft DigiGirlz boot camp. "The camp is an effort to show high-school-age girls what the technology industry is all about, what careers are available, and to let them see how exciting it is to create something that can truly impact a large number of people," says Mylene Padolina, a Microsoft senior diversity consultant who is the brains behind the DigiGirlz efforts. "We try to give them a broad view of the technology and the products we create, along with the different kinds of positions it takes to make all that happen."

Infiltrating the corporate world with the seeds of horizontal leadership is on our agenda. Together, we will offer girls activities aimed at immersing girls in elements of a healthy girl culture as they learn about tech—a culture not commonly found in the world I've walked into. By incorporating basic trust-earning games and exercises like Common Ground and creating community agreements, the program challenges the exclusion and lack of belonging that many women in tech report, factors that ultimately contribute to their departure from the field.

"We want these girls to know that IT's not just for boys. IT's not just for geeks. Technology innovation is for everyone," says Padolina. Over time, the program evolves and morphs into a one-day DigiGirlz Day at Microsoft offices all around the world.

CHAPTER 10

AAUW research[8] highlights several important aspects related to horizontal leadership as an integral part of a girl's pathway and the workplace dynamics she may encounter if she continues on this path:

1. Change how classes are taught by connecting STEM experiences to girls' lives; promoting active, hands-on learning; and emphasizing collaborative and community-oriented approaches to STEM education.
2. Teach girls of color mathematics through open-ended and cocreated problem-posing and discovery.
3. Promote welcoming work environments, including ensuring pay equity; offering flexibility; implementing strong family and medical leave policies; providing inclusion and antibias training; facilitating mentorship, networking, and allyship opportunities; and enforcing robust antidiscrimination and antiharassment policies.

The importance of horizontal leadership emphasized in the AAUW research extends beyond STEM fields to the corporate world at large. A 2022 McKinsey report reinforces that promoting collaborative, inclusive leadership models is critical for organizational success and employee well-being. The report found that companies exhibiting more caring, participative, and inclusive leadership styles had higher satisfaction rates and lower levels of burnout among employees.[9]

Developing these horizontal leadership abilities from an early age, as the AAUW advocates for girls, can better prepare the next generation to challenge top-down hierarchies and bring more voices to decision-making tables once they enter professional environments. By fostering girls' skills in collaborative problem-solving, community building, and cocreation, programs like DigiGirlz equip them to enact positive change through shared power dynamics in their future workplaces. On the leading edge of STEM programming, many of Microsoft's innovative ideas and strategies have caught fire in our region.

When my daughter Bella was sixteen years old, she was a beneficiary of one such initiative. On a Saturday early in her sophomore year, Bella joins hundreds of attendees at STEM Exploration Day at the very Microsoft campus where Powerful Voices staff and I worked to upend off-putting cultural aspects of tech. The event features a keynote panel with women working in STEM fields who share insights and inspiration about their careers, and girls are awestruck. Hands-on activities using hardware and software further demystify the tech world. College and career readiness for tech are presented in a way that suggests there are ways girls can use technology to make a difference in their world.

Workshops cover a range of topics, including "Virtual Reality, Young Engineers," and "How Do Scientists Monitor the Health of Our Local Waters?" The workshops engage participants not only in traditional hands-on activities with hardware and software but also prompt critical reflection on the meaning of college readiness and who benefits from it. Social change and the history of women and femmes in technology are also on the agenda.

The timing could not be better for Bella. At the start of the school year, she had walked into her high school engineering class, and every student stopped what they were doing and looked at her. She was the sole girl in the room.

Bella was identified early on as "academically very capable." She did not readily fit in at her school with other students and stood on the outskirts of many group activities. At home, Bella's status as the eldest sister had saddled her with many unspoken responsibilities. Uneven power dynamics inherent in being the eldest further shaped her young life. She spent hours with her three younger sisters playing the Sims video game. In the game, she created and controlled virtual people called Sims, managing their daily lives in various settings.

Chapter 10

When she was in her teens, I prodded her to take the computer science classes and engineering classes offered at her high school. I wondered if it was doing more harm than good. Would she feel forced into enrolling? One more pressure-filled expectation? Would it breed resentment and a greater reluctance to participate? The classes were initially daunting, and she had to construct a completely new toolbox to cope with the shame that began to surface simply because of her gender. She got stuck taking notes at the meetings, doing more of the "detail work," or bringing snacks. But she quickly learned to push back.

Bella learned to directly confront a boy when interrupted, looking him straight in the eye and continuing what she was saying. In some situations, a boy would make negative or taunting comments. She found herself choosing to ignore it, laugh it off, or respond, depending on the circumstance. However, she also encountered boys who acted as allies and spoke up for her, especially when she felt cornered. Fortunately, she had not experienced any situation where her technical inputs were doubted solely because she was a girl. Bella tells me, "I had to really learn to be confident in what I said. I don't open sentences saying things like, 'I guess I am wrong but . . . ' or 'You may not think this is right . . . ' but instead say, 'I think' or 'We should consider this approach.'" One thing she found to be extremely helpful was keeping up on highlights from Seahawks and Huskies games from the day before so she could participate in small talk with her peers.

Nine months after attending the STEM Exploration Day and walking into Mr. Fell's period 5 engineering class, one of Bella's Instagram posts paints a telling picture. The room is filled with boys, and Bella is seen laughing with her arms around them. Throughout the year, barriers slowly broke down as they developed an appreciation for each other's humor and differences, fostering mutual respect. This hands-on class also became Bella's favorite.

Years later, when Bella attended her first computer science lecture at Haverford College, she strode in confidently, giving friendly nods to the handful of other women scattered among the hundreds of men. Her experiences had prepared her for this male-dominated arena. Having pushed past the initial isolation of being the only girl in her high school engineering classes, Bella learned to assert her voice, exchange humorous banter with male peers, and find allies. The STEM Exploration Day and other girl-centered programming awakened her to the immense possibilities a tech career could offer for driving social impact.

Now a double major in computer science and economics, Bella was determined to create an ecosystem of inclusion and empowerment. She joined a program to catalyze creative and entrepreneurial thinking around a problem, need, or question, with the goal of fostering new solutions and opportunities. As a result of her involvement, she and two other young women developed a start-up—a program called Gradual—as part of its incubator.

In her junior year, she was able to fly to Detroit and attend the *Forbes* Women under Thirty Summit for three days of conversations, learning, and connecting. The summit featured more than two hundred speakers and nine thousand attendees. "The conversations I got to hear while there ranged from reenvisioning large-scale transportation to the underinvestment in women-founded (and particularly women-of-color-founded) start-ups to the importance of mitigating climate change. The speakers conveyed a common theme: businesses have the potential to drive positive social change with the right leadership. Every day brought new information that reframed the way I think about innovation," she shares. "All of this ties to my own work with a website I worked on this past summer with two fellow women computer science majors, which allows students to map their major and graduation requirements to ensure they are on track to graduate. In particular, it gives me a blueprint for how we can emphasize Gradual's social impact while also operating as a business."

In her partnership with her Gradual cocreators, Bella made sure to incorporate the horizontal leadership principles she'd been steeped in: fostering collaborative problem-solving, ensuring all voices were heard, and creating a supportive judgment-free zone. She advocated for rotating leadership roles and creating inclusive team charters upfront. If anyone exhibited biased behavior, she addressed it head-on through direct feedback.

Bella's dedication to cultivating female tech talent and horizontally led environments didn't go unnoticed. She had many job offers when graduation came around. Whichever path she chose postgraduation, Bella knew she would be championing the principles that allowed her to thrive: creating space for all technologists to show up wholly and lead boldly.

Power Tool: Parent and Mentor Tips for Embracing Horizontal Leadership

- Discuss the "Why"

  As girls enter adolescence, they often face increasing societal pressures that can diminish their confidence and leadership aspirations. Share examples of how gender and race stereotypes, media portrayals, and peer dynamics can subtly discourage girls from embracing their full potential as leaders. Help them understand why girls' leadership ambition fades. For instance, highlight how leadership qualities like assertiveness are sometimes labeled as "bossy" or "aggressive" when displayed by girls. Or discuss how narrow beauty standards and emphasis on physical appearance can distract from girls' intellectual and leadership capabilities. Framing these external forces helps girls understand the systemic factors behind any wavering desire to lead, empowering them to overcome such barriers.

- Encourage Her to Occupy Space

  One of our best tips is encouraging girls that take up a lot of space to utilize their gift as a leader. We have worked with girls that can overpower or build cliques. Try having a strength-based conversation with them, for example, "I notice you are a powerful leader and the group really listens and is swayed by your opinion. Can you use that talent to help me lead the next activity? Or could you help encourage _____ who is a bit shy to talk more?" We want to reframe qualities that girls are often penalized for into strengths they can use in their lives.

- Amplify Her Public Voice

    One powerful way for a girl to be a leader is to practice speaking out loud in front of others, speaking her needs and intentions in the world. Standing up, presenting her ideas with conviction, intention, and care are all essential tools for her to learn. Ask her to consider things like: How does positioning her body help her feel confident, strong, powerful? What helps her manage and hold onto her confidence as she speaks? Providing feedback to her on what she does well and what she can improve, and inviting her to keep practicing speaking up, are important ways to help her grow in this skill.

- Prioritize Self-Care for Sustainable Leadership

    When a girl feels overwhelmed or burnt out, her motivation to lead can wane. Encourage her to prioritize self-care practices that replenish her energy and confidence. Suggest activities like journaling, meditation, exercise, or simply taking breaks to recharge. Frame self-care not as an indulgence but as an essential component of sustainable leadership. For example: "Great leaders know when to pause and refuel. What's one small self-care routine you can try this week to avoid burnout? Even ten minutes of quiet reflection can work wonders for staying motivated and clearheaded as a leader." By modeling self-care as a leadership strength, a girl can maintain her drive and passion while avoiding the physical and emotional exhaustion that drains her will to lead.

CHAPTER 10

My Horizontal Leadership Arc at Home and Work

It was a dizzying, disorienting, summer, the summer I moved to Seattle, and I met Kevin Alexander. The year was 1990. Though we'd attended Illinois high schools just five miles apart, our paths unexpectedly crossed on the other side of the country. A mutual friend shared my landline number and the rest, as they say, was history. Kevin won my heart by introducing me to Pacific Northwest hikes, something I had never done before. When a bout of homesickness took hold, he placed sandwiches from the café where he worked by my front door. His nerdy encyclopedic knowledge of history and social movements dazzled me. Most of all, Kevin shared my social justice values, and we fostered integration of our Catholic, suburban White upbringing with the growing awareness of the conflicts these identities created within us.

Despite being utter and complete opposites in many ways, we moved in together. Within a short few months, I unceremoniously popped the question. "Hey, Kev, my mom says there is a cancellation at the Riviera Ballroom in Lake Geneva for next summer. Do you want to get married?"

Power sharing and horizontal leadership are afoot in many aspects of our life, especially our professional decision-making and support of one another. "You should really go to Beijing," emphasized Kevin, after we'd been married for two years. "It will be an amazing experience." Beijing wasn't the first time he had encouraged me to jump headfirst into the pieces of my professional life that would fill in the blanks of my learning. Only the year before, when I was a second-year MSW graduate student, he'd encouraged me to head east when the chance arose to intern at the Center for Ventures in Girls' Education, a newly forming nonprofit near Cambridge, Massachusetts. The effervescent founder, an instructor at the Harvard School of Education, had agreed to take me on as an intern for the final spring semester. Newly married and shy of twenty-seven, I hopped an Amtrak train across the Rockies, northern plains, through the Midwestern states of Illinois and Ohio, and into Boston. For the train ride from Seattle to Boston, Kevin gave me a copy of psychologists Lyn Mikel Brown and Carol Gilligan's *Meeting at the Crossroads* (1992), the first of many thought leaders he would share with me as I began my professional journey.

Last year, more than thirty years later, he would encourage and accompany me on a different aspect of my professional journey, a work sabbatical in which I walked the Via Francigena pilgrimage from Canterbury to Rome. Kevin walked through unrelenting rain for the first three hundred miles. An avowed agnostic, Kevin somehow put aside his ambivalence about the church and pep talked me through the blisters, leg cramps, and general discomfort. When we parted ways after a month of walking side by side, he softened the blow by downloading a new map program for me and wiping my tears. "You got this, Ann. I will be your number-one pilgrim support from home," he told me as I left him at the Gare d'Nord so he could make his way to the airport and back to Seattle.

Kevin's professional pursuits matter deeply to me as well. In 1995, early in his time as an educator and school administrator, Kevin and I had the opportunity to work together at a school. He was a dean of students, and I was an administrative assistant. We commuted together every day, swapping stories of our interactions with staff and students. Kevin's humor, integrity, and ability to deeply listen to the needs of students are legendary. Going almost anywhere in Seattle I bump into someone who knows him through his work. "You're Kevin's wife?" a parent asks bemusedly at a restaurant where we await a table. "Did he tell you about the time when all the kids dressed up like him for Halloween?" Kevin is a beloved fixture at the school where he works. His practical jokes break down a whole host of power dynamics between adults and students.

What I see as Kevin's greatest strength lies in his efforts to connect students more deeply to the social justice values we share. Our values align in pushing students to confront harsh historical truths and reflect on the systemic oppression and abuse of power that enabled such injustices. This commitment is exemplified in the annual Civil Rights Summit trip that Kevin developed and coleads each spring. The summit looks at civil rights past, present, and future. It also incorporates the understanding that personal growth strengthens your ability to effect change.

Power sharing, importantly, is on display not only in how we support each other at work, but at home as well. When considering what last name to give our children, for instance, we agreed that girls would get my last name, and boys would get his. We ended up with four daughters who have my last name. Day-to-day domestic chores are shared. Kevin cooks, I clean. Kevin launders the clothes, I put them away.

But traditional gender roles are still definitely at play at times, like when we blow a tire on the car or it needs an oil change. Kevin is the one who takes care of it. When the house needs maintenance, he gets the tools. Gendered norms are most glaringly on display in our conflict-resolution styles. If we get into a conflict or argument, he wants to completely avoid processing it. I am typically the one to try to engage in some form of conflict resolution, though I have used more passive tactics like the silent treatment more times than I care to admit. Improving in our power sharing related to conflict resolution, as we grow older, begins with first acknowledging these ingrained patterns and working to upend them.

Outside of my marriage and home, gravitating toward models and experiences of power sharing is something I have done at work and continue to do. One recognizes one can never arrive at perfection or a finished state to the work. The gains and growth happens as you "strive to arrive."

One concept that has helped me think more deeply about power sharing with youth is encapsulated by the term "adultism."

In the last two decades or so, the term has been resurrected by John Bell. In 1995, he defined adultism as "behaviors and attitudes based on the assumptions that adults are better than young people, and entitled to act upon young people without agreement."[10] More recently, and closer to home, in 2016, Adam Fletcher called it "an addiction to the attitudes, ideas, beliefs, and actions of adults."[11] The concept of adultism wraps up all the reflective questions you have considered over the course of the book. It is one more conceptual bridge over the generation gap that allows us to shift the narrative.

Youth voice[12] is another. This refers to the "distinct ideas, opinions, attitudes, knowledge, and actions of young people as a collective body, and application of a variety of youth development activities, including service learning, youth research, and leadership training.

Where I work, our Girls Advocacy and Impact Network (GAIN) program provides an excellent example of how we structure our programs to build youth voices. Girls learn about and practice different types of advocacy to address the issues that affect their lives and upend who is advocating for the systemic change they need. Instead of being led by adults, groups are led by girls who teach new members how to amplify their collective voices and effectively influence the policies that directly impact them and that they care about.

Girls participate in interactive activities and data-driven discussions in order to build advocacy skills, connect with each other, gain confidence, and develop solutions for problems in their communities. They identify target legislative advocacy goals and have the opportunity to speak at events, testify at public hearings, and attend our monthly coalition advocacy meetings to educate our members and advance their vision. For example, there is a GAIN group at Echo Glen, a state residential juvenile rehabilitation facility. Girls have testified remotely in favor of legislation that would impact them in the juvenile justice system. Our GAIN groups are also active in advocating for ending the use of detention for status offenses, for mandatory sexual education in schools, for ensuring access to menstrual hygiene products, and for establishing school-based health centers, providing issue briefs and testimony in partnership with adult members of the coalition.

Power sharing with funders and community partners is leaning in a more egalitarian direction as well. In 2018, I was part of an interdisciplinary fellowship that requires power sharing at all levels. "We have been learning from you all," says Beth Toner, Robert Wood Johnson (RWJ) Foundation's chief communication officer. "RWJ has been supporting leadership since the 1970s, but only recently have we challenged the single discipline focus on traditional leadership styles."

The "we" Beth is talking to includes me and an eclectic group of interdisciplinary advocates, activists, and researchers from all across the United States, who were selected for a three-year fellowship to advance public health and upend the traditional power dynamics that surface when doing health equity work. "The narratives about leadership we came to use are not the same ones we have now. We have gone way beyond the hero narrative. Leaders are not exceptionally charismatic people; rather, social change happens, in movements and communities, when, regardless of stature, people come together to solve problems."

While the concept of horizontal, shared leadership that RWJ has come around to may seem novel in Western discourse, it's crucial to recognize that many non-Western, primarily noncolonial communities have long-standing traditions of such power structures. The idea of horizontal leadership is not new, nor does it have to be in relation to gender. Many communities across the world, primarily communities in noncolonial areas, have a history of shared power.

Parent/Mentor Self-Reflection Power Tool

Your background and experiences have likely played a significant role in shaping your views on embracing horizontal leadership, particularly in how you approach collaboration, empowerment, and inclusivity within a team or community setting. Perhaps you have memories of instances in which traditional hierarchical structures stifled creativity or hindered effective communication. Maybe you've experienced firsthand the power dynamics that can arise within groups, where certain voices are elevated while others are silenced or overlooked. Whether you are a parent figure or you are wearing the hat of a trusted teacher, mentor, or counselor, be an adult who puts aside an agenda of expectations and instead creates a space for an open exchange of ideas centered on what accessing this form of power means in a girl's world. Ask yourself:

1. How have your background and experiences shaped your views of embracing horizontal leadership? Are there memories that you can unpack so that you are better prepared to support a girl in developing this power?
2. How have you educated yourself about the impact of traditional hierarchical structures at home and work? What do you need to do with what you've learned to develop your proficiency in supporting a girl in building this power?
3. What are the ways you can transfer this knowledge and understanding to develop skills and proficiency to support a girl in building this power? How do you support your growth alongside their development?
4. How can you keep open to feedback and hold yourself accountable when you make mistakes or act in ways that perpetuate top-down leadership?
5. What can you do to create and support spaces that are both inclusive and supportive? What actions do you take to foster equity and contribute to an inclusive environment?

EQUALIZING POWER, SHARING THE WEIGHT

A pilgrim's backpack sometimes feels inexplicably lighter. One can almost forget the weight of what one carries. My "professional backpack," unbearably heavy, got a break when the organization where I work approved my sabbatical to walk the Via Francigena, a time for me to care for my soul. I took it. And so, much to my surprise, did my daughters.

Bella and Adanech, each joining me for a week on the Way, are navigating new roles and responsibilities within the family dynamic and society at large, and the miles of walking are a perfect undivided opportunity to reflect on how power sharing has evolved as they pursue professional lives postcollege, and between them and in our family. What, if any, is the impact of being exposed to girls' programs and other opportunities to consider horizontal leadership at home and out in the world? I hope the Way can be the first of many discussions that normalize the changing dynamics of their relationship with one another as well.

A pilgrimage ideally brings you closer to your heart's deepest purpose, and after a week of walking together, Adanech tells me, "To find joy in a job, place, and people around me is my purpose." The stages and the one-hundred-plus miles we share from Besancon to Lausanne covered the route of the Absinth, the astounding castle of Joux, mystical Marian prayer shrines all along the Way, Swiss countryside, and a mercifully shady Orbes Gorges and, finally, deposited us at the shores of Lake Geneva. This gal greeted every person on the Way with such genuine love and openheartedness.

My week with Adanech held insights into the role power sharing and being in a girls' group had in shaping her. "Older sisters create a road map, so this is an interesting topic. If she [Bella] did it, we did. I mean, I joined Young Women Empowered (Y-WE) because Bella loved it. It was a special place for our family because it was a place for me and all my sisters to find and to be around powerful women. We were met with strong people to support us and love us and give us opportunities."

We walk alongside one another in the heat of the late afternoon as she continues her reflection. "My new life had me moving between various worlds. On Sundays, Betelhem and I would attend St. Gebriel's [the Ethiopian Orthodox church]. On the walk home, we would pass by the familiar smells of injera. Between the Ethiopian restaurants, you could get tamales and fried catfish. My high school was really diverse. Living amongst many cultures opened me up. I developed the ability to understand a variety of perspectives. I'm not going to lie. Sometimes all this was really confusing."

Adanech offers a number of reasons why it was hard moving through all these different worlds. Going to a historically Black high school, being socialized at an Ethiopian church, and having White parents and siblings and friends from all different backgrounds caused her to feel confused about who she was. "I began to seek out spaces where I could explore my identity like Young Women Empowered (Y-WE) and Y-Scholars (YMCA program for Black scholars). Y-WE gave me a platform for discussion, leadership, and exploration. Y-Scholars gave me confidence, discipline, and determination. And the best thing about Y-WE is that I could be all of my identities, not just only one."

As the youngest sister, Adanech initially followed in her older sisters' footsteps, emulating their actions and gravitating towards their way of navigating the world. "I felt like I was always trying to catch up, to do things the way they did," Adanech recalls. However, she soon realized that mimicking them did not achieve the same positive outcomes, partly due to her own trauma and the need to adapt to a new environment with different social norms. "I started to understand that their path wasn't necessarily the right one for me," she says. Despite the challenges, her sisters demonstrated how to present herself in this newfound world, and Adanech grasped these lessons by closely observing their every move.

Over time, this hyperfocus on following others' lead brought more anxiety into Adanech's life. "I was so caught up in trying to be like them that I lost sight of who I really was," she admits.

Chapter 10

It was through her involvement with Y-WE that she found a space to genuinely be herself, where her leadership skills and self-confidence flourished.

As she matured, Adanech learned to embrace and wield her power confidently, while also witnessing her sisters' own journeys of career growth and newfound leadership abilities. "I started to see that we could all be leaders in our own way," she reflects. Her collective Y-WE experiences fostered an ongoing commitment to shared leadership, consistently striving to dismantle age-based hierarchies and celebrate each other's unique styles. Today, while still turning to her sisters as trusted confidants, Adanech asserts her own voice. "They know I've got this," she says with a smile. This shift allows her to share the burden of leadership, fostering a deeper sense of sisterhood with increased mutual support and respect.

At the end of our time walking, over one hundred miles later, we are headed to the train station in Geneva, Switzerland. From there Adanech will fly back to Seattle and return to her new job as a Head Start teacher at Neighborhood House, a nonprofit. She will be working with young children as a classroom teacher and conducting home visits with families. Seeing her hop on the train that day, I can't help but think back to several summers ago, when we all went back to Ethiopia as a family. At Bole Airport, I watched Adanech as she watched that same escalator that had seemed so intimidating to her. She hopped on and didn't look back. Today, she had that same expression on her face.

A week later my next walking companion, Bella, arrives for the next beautiful September stretch of the Via Francigena. With her by my side, my pack feels lighter. We drink in some dazzling scenery along the Way: hugging Lake Geneva's shore out of Lausanne, climbing into the Lavaux vineyards and elegant, art-thriving Montreaux, onto mystical Saint Maurice, and then climbing up, up, and over the Great St. Bernard Pass, only to lose most of the 6,500 feet of elevation gain the next day, descending into the Aosta Valley.

"Be careful, momma, the rock is slippery," Bella tells me, each day, always from a few feet ahead of me on the trail. She scopes out the danger, a role reversal I am humbled by. This powerful girl has turned into a powerful woman. Perennially wise beyond her years, she has not only been navigating the Via Francigena for us this week, her positivity will literally carry us over the Great St. Bernard Pass. "The beauty, momma, can't believe it," she says every now and then, peppering our fatigue. We refer to her state of appreciation and wonder as "Bell-Awe."

Bella's segment of the walk, her choice to accompany me over the technically hardest part, the Alps sections, reflects the internalized expectations and the many shades of gray she has learned to hold growing up as an oldest daughter. Bella's experience resonates with many who understand the often unspoken responsibilities that come with that role. The dynamic she shares with her younger sisters embodies not only the nurturing and protective instincts ingrained in her from a young age but also the weight of emotional responsibility that she carries within our family. From a tender age, Bella took on tasks beyond her years, stepping into the role of a caregiver and helper within our family unit. Whether it was looking after her siblings or supporting her parents during challenging times, she became accustomed to shouldering these burdens, often without recognition or acknowledgment.

"Up until grade school, my thinking was more binary: something was either good or bad, black or white, true or false. Inevitably, this type of thinking experiences disruption. Gray is what follows. For me, gray became more apparent when my own family became Black and White. This came after our family grew from four to six." She tells me that initially she'd attempted to categorize our family, but struggled because we didn't fit conventional standards. This prompted her to seek her own definitions at places like girls' groups. "This shifting of reality didn't fog my perceptions; instead, it increased my capacity for growth. I used this knowledge as empowerment, becoming comfortable with a life that didn't fit simple definitions."

Chapter 10

The concept of "gray in family" reflects Bella's journey from simply fulfilling duties to understanding how these experiences shape her identity and capabilities. Bella now finds herself navigating the complexities of her role within the family dynamic as a mid-twenties tech professional, questioning her own limits and boundaries, and discovering the depth of her capacity to provide support and care.

The "gray" now is also a symbol of her opportunity to learn to upend the power dynamics as an older sister and practice a less hierarchical collaboration with her sisters. "The more I learn, the more that reality redefines my black-and-white world. Maturity and evolution requires discerning the truth with all its shades and complexities. The result is a perspective that reflects reality far more accurately than black or white ever will. Sometimes, nostalgia surfaces for the past, the binaries. But this is fleeting because this in-between, this gray, is dynamic."

Months later, our dinner table is set for four. Kevin has several pans ablaze with fish taco fixings. All of our daughters have graduated from college, and two, Adanech and Bella, are living at home for the time being. From the start, tensions have existed between these two. They are polar opposites. Where Bella keeps her cards close to her chest, Adanech jumps headfirst into the deep end. Where Adanech succeeded in sociology courses in her academic settings, Bella was an excellent math and science student. Adanech finds joy in salsa dancing, and Bella would rather not dance at all. Beloved by our family and their wide circles of friends, they share being known for their generosity and bigheartedness.

Watching my daughters shift and share power, and fight for a mutual relationship where power is distributed, gives me hope. It also inspires and pushes me to reflect on my own sibling dynamics. The compassion Bella and Adanech show makes me think about my relationships with my sisters, the disruptions after our eldest sister—the arbiter of our healthy girl culture—was so tragically taken from us. How can I, many years past my own girlhood, embody horizontal leadership with my own sisters as we age?

I don't have all the answers, but one meaningful memory stands out: after my older sister Janice received a heart transplant at thirty, I called her to the stage during my wedding and presented her with my bouquet. "This is for all the grace you've shown in your life in the face of all the struggles you've held," I said. A small gesture, but one that spoke volumes about the truth of Janice's experiences growing up in the aftermath of our family's profound loss.

The weight of stepping into the role of oldest sister fell squarely on Janice's shoulders. At times, that weight weighed so heavily that I fear it quite literally hardened, if not broke, her heart. The burdens she carried shaped her in ways my other sisters and I could never fully grasp.

My path back to Janice, and to all my surviving sisters, lies in extending that same compassion, a hallmark of great leadership. Despite our political differences, conflicts, and divergent values, I strive to show up with compassion, love, and forgiveness. It is through this openhearted approach that I hope to share power equitably with the very women who helped shape my identity.

THE BIGGER PICTURE: REPRESENTATION

Each year, the Center for American Women and Politics at Rutgers University sends a children's book about inclusive leadership to every female legislator, member of Congress, and governor in the United States. They ask that these leaders visit a local elementary school, read the book, talk about their experiences as elected officials, and donate the book to the school library. The goal of TAG, the Teach a Girl to Lead program, is simple: by being present and visible in the classroom, even for a day, women elected officials can encourage young girls to follow in their footsteps. Sustaining a will to lead in this and other arenas is all about them having the aha moment: "It's not just me?"

Programs like Teach a Girl to Lead are vital for countering the socialization that often discourages girls from aspiring to leadership roles, especially in traditionally male-dominated arenas like politics.

Interventions that expose girls to women occupying positions of power can help shift mindsets from an early age. A 2019 study by scholars at Harvard and Brigham Young University found that among girls with virtually no prior experience with women in leadership roles, meeting a woman working in local politics increased their expectations for pursuing leadership by 20 percent. The effect was particularly pronounced for Black girls and Latinas.[13] Researchers concluded that achieving gender parity in leadership across sectors hinges on "disrupting stereotypical notions of what a leader looks like."[14]

On a policy level, advocacy groups are championing legislation to embed leadership development into school curricula and extracurriculars. In 2021, Illinois became the first state to pass a law requiring public schools to incorporate a unit on women's suffrage and modern leadership into history classes, including instruction on the significant advancements, discoveries, and contributions made by women in science, technology, engineering, and mathematics (STEM). The bill's sponsor, Rep. Mary Edly-Allen, cited alarming statistics on girls' leadership ambitions plummeting by middle school.

Ultimately, the goal of such grassroots and policy efforts is to create a culture shift in which girls don't see female political leaders as exceptions, but as the norm across all fields. By intentionally cultivating their leadership identities and giving them relatable role models, we equip the next generation with enduring confidence in their ability to shape our civic and political landscape. Only then can we level the playing field and realize the full scope of what societies stand to gain from girls unleashed into their power.

In terms of the policy impact, studies show that increasing gender and racial diversity in legislatures leads to more progressive and family-friendly policies getting passed. Research from Rice University found that as more women join state legislatures, those states are more likely to approve policies supporting women's economic rights, reproductive rights, and family leave programs.[15]

An analysis from the Center for American Women and Politics determined that congresswomen of color are significantly more likely than White men to prioritize and introduce legislation focused on civil rights, gender equity, and social welfare policies. Having more women and BIPOC women at the decision-making table reshapes systems of power. If we want more of them, we need to rethink how we are currently teaching girls to play with power.

POWER TOOL: AN EMBRACING HORIZONTAL LEADERSHIP ACTIVITY YOU CAN DO WITH GIRLS

Introduction

Talking about power doesn't come easily or naturally for most girls and women. Yet, whether a girl talks to you about it or not, she is digesting ideas about the power she possesses—or lacks—every day. This activity provides a way to have a thoughtful conversation about what she's digesting, be it the traditional, media-driven notions of power; more next-generation, progressive ideas about power; or both.

Conversation Tips

Please note, almost any discussions of power can be emotionally heavy for you, the adult. But strong opinions or "telling" a girl what to think defeats the purpose here. Let a girl go first in sharing opinions and use a three-to-one rule. For every three things she says, you say one.

Goals
- Develop a deeper understanding of how mainstream culture defines power.

- Develop a fresh perspective for how to define power in life as a girl.

Do This Together
1. Together, decide on a definition of power.
2. Fold a piece of paper into thirds. On the tops of the page write the words "power-over," "power-under," and "powerful."
3. Flip through magazines to pull images that represent these words.
4. After you've both finished your collages, ask some open-ended questions.
    - What did you notice about their collage?
    - Are there any themes?
    - Who did they mark as powerful and why?
    - Do certain groups of people have more power in our society or community? (i.e., men, White folks, rich people, police officers, etc.). If so, why do they think that is?
5 Now reread the definition of the power of embracing horizontal leadership you've explored in this chapter. Ask her these closing questions: How do these definitions of power support or defy more traditional ones? What do you think is powerful about you?

Closing

Visioning a Better World

"You have been practicing for months. Trust all the hard work you've put into this," Meg, the young, White program leader, tells the group of ten girls who will lead workshops at Girlvolution, the one-day social justice conference they have created. "Remember, the people in the audience want to hear what you are saying," she reassures.

Standing in the newly floored, freshly painted gym, five feet or so outside of their huddle, I can see the girls are nervous. Two have their arms draped around each other like pretzels, while one swings her braids from side to side. Another twists her earring; others silently stare at the shiny gym floor. Above us, the bright lights are a welcome contrast to the gloomy gray filtering through the huge windows. None of today's three-hundred-plus expected participants have arrived yet. Meg's pep talk is well timed, letting the girls know they're not alone in feeling anxious.

My heart is full watching these courageous young women preparing to take center stage and lead this groundbreaking conference. Girlvolution is the culmination of their eight-month leadership journey: envisioning, organizing, and now facilitating a space for girls to explore critical social issues through a lens of empowerment.

It all started back in the fall, when this passionate group of high school students from diverse backgrounds first came together. What united them was a shared frustration at seeing their gender, race, and other identities being undermined or marginalized at every turn. In school, in their communities, even within their own families, they felt their voices weren't being heard or valued.

But rather than sitting back and accepting the status quo, they boldly decided to create their own platform to drive change. With the support of Meg and other interns, they spent months engaged in workshops and training to build their knowledge, confidence, and leadership skills.

They learned about systems of oppression and how to analyze issues through an intersectional lens that considers how different identities like race, class, and gender overlap and compound. They studied the history of social movements, grassroots organizing tactics, and principles of youth-adult partnership. But most importantly, the girls supported each other in getting clear about their visions for a more just and equitable world.

At Girlvolution, these visions will finally take center stage as the girls lead a full slate of workshops and activism sessions for their peers. It's a radical rethinking of the traditional youth conference model—rather than adults calling the shots, these girls drive every aspect from inception to facilitation, embodying the horizontal leadership model they've learned. Rather than a traditional top-down approach, they practice collaboration, equal participation, and shared responsibility. This rejects hierarchical structures that often perpetuate inequality and limit opportunities. By embracing horizontal leadership, they challenge societal norms and redefine what is considered valuable. By distributing roles and decision-making authority equitably among themselves, the girls model how disrupting ingrained dynamics of gender, age, and authority encourages a more inclusive society where all perspectives are uplifted. It's an inspiring contrast to the tokenization they've experienced in so many other spaces.

As the doors open, throngs of participants line up at the registration table, abuzz with anticipation. Among them is my oldest daughter Bella, attending her first Girlvolution. "You know, I was actually pregnant with you when I started Powerful Voices," I share as we head toward the workshop rooms. Bella rolls her eyes gamely. "How many times are you going to tell me that, Mom?" But I catch the hint of a smile playing at the corners of her mouth.

The conference is a redundant hive of activity. In one room, fourteen-year-old Maria speaks powerfully about the devastation of having her father deported when she was just eight years old. Down the hall, Delesha, seventeen, educates a riveted crowd on "period poverty": the lack of access to affordable menstrual products that keeps so many girls out of school. Another workshop, "False Images of Beauty," led by Monica, explores the detrimental impacts of the narrow representations of women propagated in media and advertising. In "Beautiful Disaster," Shea courageously shares her story of her mom's struggle with addiction and the youth center program that provided her family support. At lunch, I reconnect with Lynn, the public health nurse I worked with years ago at the county juvenile detention center. A local all-girl pop-punk trio provides an energetic soundtrack as community organizations host a resource fair.

"Lynn, it's so good to see you!" I exclaim, pulling her into a warm hug. "We've been doing girls' work for a long time, haven't we?" She nods, sweeping her eyes across the lively scene.

It's this grassroots thrust, this organizing and agitating led by girls themselves, that gives us hope to keep fighting.

As Lynn and I reflect on the power of grassroots organizing and the legacy it has in communities, I'm reminded of a powerful example from my own community, the enduring legacy of my sister Kim.

Hope, Healing, and Community: A Girl's Legacy

The auditorium at Libertyville High School has come a long way in the nearly half a century since my sister Kim's time. I soak up the stunningly renovated performing arts space. Comfortable seats, a state-of-the-art sound shell, and even an art gallery. What I've always loved about Libertyville, my hometown, is the community. Each spring since 1977, on Honors Day at Libertyville High School, a student, typically a girl, walks up on the stage to receive what I think of as a love note from my sister Kim. The Kim Muno Scholarship is awarded to a graduating senior who shows great interest and promise in pursuing a career in healthcare.

Only recently did I learn that it was my dad and mom who started the scholarship fund. It was Kim's classmates who kept the scholarship legacy going. "I will always remember the day I called your dad from a cubicle at my workplace to tell him we were taking it over from him and planned to continue the scholarship. He started sobbing. I started sobbing. We went on like that for quite a while. It was the most beautiful moment and I will never forget it," says Steve Lichter, Kim's classmate and the person behind keeping her scholarship legacy going. "Kim was a very special human and she just brought so many people together. She was such a well-rounded, loving human being. Student council, cheerleading, and athletics, and Penwasciz."

My parents wanted to honor Kim's legacy and her passion for healthcare in a lasting way. With contributions from our extended family and friends, they were able to establish the Kim Muno Scholarship to be awarded each year to a Libertyville High student pursuing medical studies. For years, my parents managed the scholarship selection process and awarded the funds themselves. But as they grew older, keeping it going became difficult. That's when Kim's friends, now accomplished professionals themselves, stepped in to take over the operations.

"She was just such a light," Steve continues, his voice thick with emotion. "We couldn't let that light go out. Continuing this scholarship in her name was the least we could do to pay tribute to the beautiful soul she was." Steve and Kim's other classmates now run the scholarship, raising funds, vetting applications, and determining recipients. I'm deeply moved that Kim's positivity, empathy, and caregiving spirit have inspired so many and created a legacy that will persist for generations of Libertyville students to come.

I had forgotten about Kim's commitment to volunteering at the local hospital through the Penwasciz program. Remembering this has me imagining, for only a few minutes, what her life might have looked like if it wasn't cut short at sixteen. Though heartbroken, I felt proud knowing what an incredible person my sister was.

Nothing will ever replace my sister, whose life was lost to violence. But there is a great comfort in knowing Kim is not forgotten, and that in her death, this scholarship supports the dreams of young women who are pursuing careers centered on healing, hope, and community.

I imagine a world where all girls are nurtured in an environment of hope and healing, as described in *Powerful Girls*, rather than facing discrimination, violence, marginalization, and oppression. In such a community, we would see:

- confident and self-assured girls who truly believe in their ability to achieve their dreams and make a positive impact in the world.
- girls encouraged to pursue their passions and interests without gender- and race-based limitations or societal expectations.
- abundant supportive networks and mentorship programs that provide girls with role models, guidance, and resources to navigate challenges and overcome adversities.
- educational institutions and community organizations prioritizing girls' mental health, emotional well-being, and overall personal growth.
- a culture that unapologetically celebrates and uplifts girls' diverse identities, backgrounds, and perspectives, fostering a sense of belonging and inclusivity.

Closing

Let's stop telling ourselves, "This is the way it was when I was growing up." Let's stop expecting girls to do it on their own. Instead:

- Start imagining how you can use your power to change things.
- Start saying, "I can make a difference."
- Start ensuring girls don't develop the powers by accident or not at all.

Let's create a world worthy of them. How can you use your own experience and the activities in the book to change the world with girls? Powerful girls are not born; they are raised in environments that nurture their potential, instill confidence, and provide them with the tools and opportunities to thrive.

Notes

Introduction

1. Throughout the book "girl" refers to any person who identifies as one, including cis girls, trans girls, nonbinary youth, gender nonconforming youth, genderqueer youth, and any girl-identified youth.

2. The racially disaggregated, groundbreaking report *Shortchanging Girls, Shortchanging America* focused on how gender bias adversely affects girls' self-esteem, school achievement, and career aspirations. Journalist Peggy Orenstein's bestseller, *Schoolgirls*, reported real-life experiences of Bay Area girls aligning with the data in *Shortchanging Girls*. Psychologists Lyn Mikel Brown and Carol Gilligan found that many girls silenced their needs to conform to gender-based expectations. Other studies explored how girls influence each other's health, sexual choices, and overall safety, shedding light on aggression among girls and the resulting emotional and social harm.

3. American Association of University Women, *Shortchanging Girls, Shortchanging America* (American Association of University Women, 1991), http://www.aauw.org/files/2013/02/shortchanging-girls-shortchanging-america-executive-summary.pdf.

4. Peggy Orenstein, *Schoolgirls: Young Women, Self-Esteem, and the Confidence Gap* (New York: Anchor, 1995).

5. Lyn Mikel Brown and Carol Gilligan, *Meeting at the Crossroads* (Cambridge, MA: Harvard University Press, 1992).

6. Deborah L. Tolman, "Female Adolescent Sexuality in Relational Contexts: Beyond Sexual Decision Making," in *Beyond Appearance: A New Look at Adolescent Girls*, ed. Norine G. Johnson, Michael C. Roberts, and Judith Worell (Washington, DC: American Psychological Association, 1999).

7. Mary Pipher, *Reviving Ophelia: Saving the Selves of Adolescent Girls* (New York: Putnam, 1994).

8. Throughout the book, I use both the terms "girls of color" and "Black, Indigenous, and people of color" (BIPOC) girls. I use BIPOC to center the unique experiences of Black and Indigenous communities and to avoid generalizing all people of color. While many people are widely using the term

NOTES

"BIPOC," others don't. Since what people want to be called is a personal preference, I aim to respect both.

9. Ibram X. Kendi, *How to Be an Antiracist* (London, England: Bodley Head, 2019).

10. Kenneth Jones and Tema Okun, *Dismantling Racism: A Workbook for Social Change Groups* (ChangeWork, 2001).

11. To protect their privacy, I have changed the names of the instructors and mentors who participated in the groups throughout the book.

12. To protect their privacy, I have changed the names of the girls who participated in the groups throughout the book.

CHAPTER 1

1. National Sexual Violence Resource Center, "Child Sexual Abuse Prevention Resources," accessed May 17, 2024, https://www.nsvrc.org/node/4737; US Department of Justice, "Sexual Assault," accessed May 17, 2024, https://www.justice.gov/archives/ovw/sexual-assault; M. C. Black, K. C. Basile, M. J. Breiding, et al., *The National Intimate Partner and Sexual Violence Survey: 2010 Summary Report*, National Center for Injury Prevention and Control, Centers for Disease Control and Prevention (2011), https://www.cdc.gov/violenceprevention/pdf/nisvs_report2010-a.pdf; RAINN, "Children and Teens," accessed May 17, 2024, https://www.rainn.org/children-and-teens; C. Hill and H. Kearl, *Crossing the Line: Sexual Harassment at School* (American Association of University Women, 2011); US Department of Education, Office for Civil Rights, *Sexual Violence Data Analysis* (2018), https://www2.ed.gov/about/offices/list/ocr/docs/sexual-violence.pdf.

2. Centers for Disease Control and Prevention, *Preventing Child Sexual Abuse* (2020), https://www.cdc.gov/violenceprevention/childabuseand-neglect/childsexualabuse.html.

3. S. G. Smith, X. Zhang, K. C. Basile, et al., *National Intimate Partner and Sexual Violence Survey: 2015 Data Brief—Updated Release* (Centers for Disease Control and Prevention, 2018), https://www.cdc.gov/violenceprevention/pdf/2015data-brief508.pdf.

4. B. Livingston, "United States: Hollaback! International Street Harassment Survey," slides (Hollaback!, 2015), https://www.ihollaback.org/cornell-international-survey-on-street-harassment/#us.

5. Black et al., *National Intimate Partner and Sexual Violence Survey: 2010 Summary Report*.

6. Rights4girls, *Sexual Violence among Native Women and Girls* (Rights4girls, 2019), https://rights4girls.org/wp/wp-content/uploads/r4g/2019/05/Native-women-and-girls-fact-sheet-May-2019-1.pd.

NOTES

7. Federal Bureau of Investigation, "FBI Releases 2020 Hate Crime Statistics," August 31, 2021, https://www.fbi.gov/news/press-releases/press-releases/fbi-releases-2020-hate-crime-statistics.

8. L. Kann et al. (2018, June 15), "Youth Risk Behavior Surveillance—United States, 2017." *Morbidity and Mortality Weekly Report Surveillance Summaries*, 67(8). https://www.cdc.gov/healthyyouth/data/yrbs/pdf/2017/ss6708.pdf.

9. M. M. Johns, R. Lowry, J. Andrzejewski, et al., "Transgender Identity and Experiences of Violence Victimization, Substance Use, Suicide Risk, and Sexual Risk Behaviors among High School Students—19 States and Large Urban School Districts, 2017," *Morbidity and Mortality Weekly Report* 68, no. 3 (2019): 67–71, http://dx.doi.org/10.15585/mmwr.mm6803a3.

10. Rape Abuse Incest National Network, State Law Database, https://www.rainn.org/types-sexual-violence.

11. Substance Abuse and Mental Health Services Administration, *Key Substance Use and Mental Health Indicators in the United States: Results from the 2019 National Survey on Drug Use and Health* (Substance Abuse and Mental Health Services Administration, 2020), https://www.samhsa.gov/data/sites/default/files/reports/rpt29393/2019NSDUHFFRPDFWHTML/2019NSDUHFFR090120.htm.

12. Jessica C. Harris, Christina Cheah, and Danielle Boatright, *College Students of Color and Mental Health: An Exploratory Study* (The Steve Fund, 2018), https://www.stevefund.org/wp-content/uploads/2021/03/HARRIS-FINAL.pdf.

13. Samuel J. Cash, Jodie L. Daquin, Ashley M. English, et al., "Race and Trends in Rates of Suicide Attempts among Elementary School-Aged Girls in the United States, 2009–2018," *JAMA Pediatrics* 175, no. 9 (2021): 915–23, https://doi.org/10.1001/jamapediatrics.2021.1763.

14. Ellen Yard et al., "Emergency Visits for Suspected Suicide Attempts among Persons Aged 12–25 Years before and during the COVID-19 Pandemic, United States, January 2019–May 2021," *Morbidity and Mortality Weekly Report* 70, no. 24 (2021): 888–94, https://doi.org/10.15585/mmwr.mm7024e1.

15. Candice L. Odgers and Michaeline R. Jensen, "Annual Research Review: Adolescent Mental Health in the Digital Age: Facts, Fears, and Future Directions," *Journal of Child Psychology and Psychiatry* 61, no. 3 (2020): 336–48.

16. AP-NORC Center, "The Hazards of New Technology for Adolescents in a Changing Digital World" (Associated Press-NORC Center for Public Affairs Research, 2022), https://apnorc.org/projects/the-hazards-of-new-technology-for-adolescents-in-a-changing-digital-world/.

17. Sarah M. Coyne, Adam A. Rogers, Jessica D. Tinsley, et al., "Associations among Social Media Use, Depressive Symptoms, Psychological Well-Being, and Suicidal Ideation in Young Adults," *JAMA Psychiatry* 77, no. 4 (2020): 420–22, https://doi.org/10.1001/jamapsychiatry.2019.4310.

18. Marika Tiggemann and Mia Zaccardo, "'Instagram Gave Me Orthorexia': The Portrayal of Healthy Eating on Instagram," *British Journal of Education, Society and Behavioural Science* 23, no. 2 (2018): 1–14, https://doi.org/10.9734/BJESBS/2018/39629.

19. US Department of Education, National Center for Education Statistics, "Education Statistics: Facts About American Schools," *Education Week*, January 30, 2019, https://www.edweek.org/leadership/education-statistics-facts-about-american-schools/2019/01.

20. Office for Civil Rights, *Civil Rights Data Collection Snapshot: College and Career Readiness* (United States Department of Education, 2014), http://www2.ed.gov/about/offices/list/ocr/docs/crdc-college-and-career-readiness-snapshot.pdf.

21. Institute for Women's Policy Research, *Analysis of American Community Survey Microdata*, accessed May 8, 2024, https://statusofwomendata.org/women-of-color/#spotlightpowoc.

22. National Women's Law Center and Poverty and Race Research Action Council, *Finishing Last: Girls of Color and School Sports Opportunities* (National Women's Law Center and Poverty and Race Research Action Council, 2015), http://nwlc.org/wp-content/uploads/2015/08/final_nwlc_girlsfinishinglast_report.pdf.

23. C. E. Jacobs, *Ready to Lead: Leadership Supports and Barriers for Black and Latinx Girls* (Girls Leadership, 2020), https://cdn.girlsleadership.org/app/uploads/2020/07/GirlsLeadership_ReadytoLeadReport.pdf.

24. Monique W. Morris, *Pushout: The Criminalization of Black Girls in Schools* (New York: The New Press, 2018); R. Epstein, J. Blake, and T. González, *Girlhood Interrupted: The Erasure of Black Girls' Childhood* (Georgetown Law Center on Poverty and Inequality, 2017), https://www.law.georgetown.edu/poverty-inequality-center/wp-content/uploads/sites/14/2017/08/girlhood-interrupted.pdf.

25. R. Epstein, E. Godfrey, T. González, and S. Javdani, *Data Snapshot: 2017–2018 National Data on School Discipline by Race and Gender* (Georgetown Law Center on Poverty and Inequality, 2020), https://genderjusticeandopportunity.georgetown.edu/wp-content/uploads/2020/12/National-Data-on-School-Discipline-by-Race-and-Gender.pdf.

26. Rana M. Halim, Claire A. Etkin, and Diane N. Ruble, "Girls' Declining Motivation to Pursue Leadership Roles from Age 6 to 10," *Journal of Abnormal Psychology* 131, no. 2 (2022): 197–208.

NOTES

27. Lin Bian, Sarah-Jane Leslie, and Andrei Cimpian, "The Roots of the Leadership Labyrinth: Gender, Culture, and the Origins of Leadership Stereotypes," *Developmental Review* 61 (2021): 101010.

28. Gabriela V. Yost, Constantina A. Stover, and Olga Jarrin, "Lost and Found: When Adolescent Girls Lose and Regain Their Confidence and Leadership Ambition" (International Girls Study Group, 2017).

29. Pew Research Center, "Young, Underemployed and Optimistic: Coming of Age, Slowly, in a Tough Economy," Pew Research Center, February 9, 2012, https://www.pewsocialtrends.org/2012/02/09/young-underemployed-and-optimistic/.

30. Catalyst, "Women in Science, Technology, Engineering, and Mathematics (STEM)," Catalyst, September 13, 2022, https://www.catalyst.org/research/women-in-science-technology-engineering-and-mathematics-stem/.

31. Payscale, *The State of the Gender Pay Gap in 2022*, Payscale, accessed May 20, 2024, https://www.payscale.com/data/gender-pay-gap.

32. Rutgers Eagleton Institute of Politics, "Current Numbers," Rutgers Eagleton Institute of Politics, accessed May 20, 2024, https://cawp.rutgers.edu/current-numbers.

33. National Conference of State Legislatures, "Women in State Legislatures for 2023," National Conference of State Legislatures, January 5, 2023, https://www.ncsl.org/legislators-staff/legislators/womens-legislative-network/women-in-state-legislatures-for-2023.aspx.

CHAPTER 2

1. The Youth Program Quality Assessment (YPQA) is a tool used to evaluate the quality of youth programs. Developed by the HighScope Educational Research Foundation, it involves trained observers visiting youth programs and rating various quality indicators across four areas: safe environment, supportive environment, interaction, and engagement. Observers use a rubric to assess these indicators, providing a comprehensive picture of program quality. Research studies have found the YPQA to be a reliable and consistent tool for evaluation. Programs with higher scores on the YPQA have been linked to better outcomes for youth, such as increased engagement, motivation, and social skills.

2. Ms. Foundation, *The New Girls' Movement: Implications for Youth Programs* (Ms. Foundation, 2001), http://www.cpn.org/topics/families/pdfs/New_Girls_Movement.pdf.

3. Charles Smith, Amanda C. Akiva, Deborah Lowe Vandell, and Roger Hart, "Introduction to the Youth Program Quality Assessment: History, Development, and Applications," in *Quality in Out-of-School Time:*

Tools and Techniques for Evaluating and Improving Programs, ed. Charles Smith and Amanda C. Akiva (Charlotte, NC: Information Age Publishing, Inc., 2016), 3–18.

4. Ann Muno, "And Girl Justice for All: Blending Girl-Specific and Youth Development Practices," *Afterschool Matters* 19 (2014): 28–35.

5. Lyn Mikel Brown and Carol Gilligan, *Meeting at the Crossroads: Women's Psychology and Girls' Development* (Harvard University Press, 1992); E. Debold, M. Wilson, and I. Malave, *Mother Daughter Revolution: From Betrayal to Power* (Addison-Wesley, 1993); Lyn Mikel Brown, *Girlfighting: Betrayal and Rejection among Girls* (New York University Press, 2003); N. Way, "'Can't You See the Courage, the Strength That I Have?' Listening to Urban Adolescent Girls Speak about Their Relationships," *Psychology of Women Quarterly* 19, no. 1 (1995): 107–28.

6. Ms. Foundation for Women, *The New Girls' Movement: Charting the Path*, Collaborative Fund for Healthy Girls/Healthy Women (New York: Ms. Foundation for Women, 2000); Nicole Archard, "Adolescent Girls and Leadership: The Impact of Confidence, Competition, and Gender Norms," *International Journal of Adolescence and Youth* 25, no. 1 (2020): 862–79; C. E. Jacobs, *Ready to Lead: Leadership Supports and Barriers for Black and Latinx Girls* (Girls Leadership, 2020), https://cdn.girlsleadership.org/app/uploads/2020/07/GirlsLeadership_ReadytoLeadReport.pdf; Jill Denner, "Voices of Adolescent Girls and Leadership: Exploring the Narratives of Latina, Black, and Multiracial Girls," *Journal of Research on Adolescence* 30, no. 1 (2020): 186–203.

7. Debold, Wilson, and Malave, *Mother Daughter Revolution*; John Bell, *Understanding Adultism: A Major Obstacle to Developing Positive Youth-Adult Relationships* (YouthBuild USA, Sacramento County Office of Education, March 1995), https://www.saclink.com/pdfs/understanding-adultism.pdf; L. Phillips, *Speak for Yourself: What Girls Say about What Girls Need* (Girls Best Friend Foundation. 2002).

8. L. M. Brown, *Raising Their Voices: The Politics of Girls' Anger* (Harvard University Press, 1998); D. L. Tolman, *Dilemmas of Desire: Teenage Girls Talk about Sexuality* (Harvard University Press, 2002); M. M. Linehan, "Validation and Psychotherapy," in *Empathy Reconsidered: New Directions in Psychotherapy*, ed. A. Bohart and L. Greenberg (American Psychological Association, 1997), 353–92, https://doi.org/10.1037/10226-016.

9. Phillips, *Speak for Yourself*.

Chapter 3

1. L. M. Brown, *Girlfighting: Betrayal and Rejection among Girls* (New York University Press, 2003).

NOTES

2. Tracy Vaillancourt and Dorothy L. Espelage, "Peer Victimization and Relational Aggression: Vulnerable Periods, Processes, and Protective Factors," in *The Development of Relational Aggression*, ed. Sarah M. Coyne and Jamie M. Ostrov (New York: Oxford University Press, 2018), 127–50.

3. Pew Research Center, "Teens and Their Experiences on Social Media," Pew Research Center, March 16, 2022, https://www.pewresearch.org/internet/2022/03/16/teens-and-their-experiences-on-social-media/.

4. US Government Accountability Office, *K–12 Education: Student Population Has Significantly Diversified, But Many Schools Remain Highly Segregated by Race and Ethnicity*, GAO-22-104737 (2022), https://www.gao.gov/products/gao-22-104737.

5. James Moody, "Peer Persistence: A Longitudinal Look at Student Integration in a Desegregated High School," in *Desegregating the City: Ghettos, Enclaves, and Inequality*, ed. David P. Varady (Albany: State University of New York Press, 2005), 103–28.

6. L. M. Brown and Carol Gilligan, *Meeting at the Crossroads: Women's Psychology and Girls' Development* (Cambridge, MA: Harvard University Press, 1992); Brown, *Girlfighting*; American Psychological Association, *A New Look at Adolescent Girls* (American Psychological Association, 2008), accessed May 15, 2024, https://www.apa.org/pi/families/resources/adolescent-girls.

7. Patricia K. Kerig, "For Better or Worse: Intimate Relationships as Sources of Risk or Resilience for Girls' Delinquency," *Journal of Research on Adolescence* 24, no. 1 (2014): 1–11, 1–2.

8. Kathryn C. Monahan, Julia Dmitrieva, and Elizabeth Cauffman, "Bad Romance: Sex Differences in the Longitudinal Association between Romantic Relationships and Deviant Behavior," *Journal of Research on Adolescence* 24, no. 1 (2014): 12–26.

9. Lucia E. Klencakova, Maria Pentaraki, and Carolyn McManus. "The Impact of Intimate Partner Violence on Young Women's Educational Well-Being: A Systematic Review of Literature," *Trauma, Violence, & Abuse* 24, no. 2 (April 2023): 1172–87, https://doi.org/10.1177/15248380211052244.

10. Elena Agular's 2021 book *The Art of Coaching: Effective Strategies for School Transformation* is an excellent recent guide to coaching and practical resource. The book uses a student-centered focus, with a spotlight on addressing equity issues in schools.

11. In 2008, Duane Bidwell, an associate professor of practical theology at Claremont School of Theology in California, who studied hope among children suffering from chronic illness, and his colleague Dr. Donald Batisky, a pediatric nephrologist at Emory University School of Medicine in Atlanta, analyzed mass amounts of data from a diverse group of children suffering from various end-stage illnesses.

CHAPTER 4

1. Lyn Mikel Brown, *The Politics of Girls' Anger* (Cambridge, MA: Harvard Education Press, 2018), 14.

2. Amanda E. Ruble et al., "The Role of Gender Constancy in Early Stigmatization of Anger Expression," *Child Development* 89, no. 2 (2018): 372–86.

3. Campbell Leaper et al., "Angels or Angels: Associations of Adolescents' Gender Typicality with Anger and Depression," *Sex Roles* 80, nos. 3–4 (2019): 97–112.

4. Rachel Simmons, *Odd Girl Out: The Hidden Culture of Aggression in Girls* (Boston: Mariner Books, 2003), 21–35.

5. Brown, *Girlfighting*, 78–92.

6. National Crittenton Foundation, *Beyond ACE: Promoting Resilience and Sustaining Progress* (National Crittenton Foundation, accessed May 20, 2024), https://nationalcrittenton.org/portfolio/publications-beyond-ace-2016/.

7. Anita Arora and Lisa Thompson, "Skills for Resolving Adolescents' Conflicts (SRAC)," in *Evidence-Based School Counseling*, ed. Carey Dimmitt et al. (New York: Routledge, 2018), 157.

8. Anita Arora et al., "Effects of the SRAC (Students, Resources, and Conflict) Peer Mediation Program on School Conflict Resolution," *Journal of Primary Prevention* 39, no. 6 (2018): 539–51.

9. Judith G. Smetana et al., "Adolescent-Parent Conflict in Middle Class African American Families," *Child Development* 67, no. 5 (1996): 2245–65.

10. Dana Coman Tanner, "Navigating the Storms of Conflict at Work," Society for Human Resource Management, April 28, 2014, https://www.shrm.org/resourcesandtools/hr-topics/employee-relations/pages/navigating-storms-conflict-work.aspx.

11. School Resource Officers (SROs) are law-enforcement officers with arrest powers who work in a school setting. Nearly all SROs are armed, and most carry other restraints like handcuffs as well. The presence of police in public schools "has exploded since the mid-1990s," according to the Vera Institute of Justice, a national advocacy nonprofit that works to remove law enforcement from schools.

12. Bun Yamagata, Kou Murayama, Jessica M. Black, et al., "Female-Specific Intergenerational Transmission Patterns of the Human Corticolimbic Circuitry," *Journal of Neuroscience* 36, no. 4 (January 27, 2016): 1254–60, DOI: 10.1523/JNEUROSCI.4974-14.2016.

13. Elizabeth Debold, Lyn Mikel Brown, Deborah Tolman, and Christina Schulyer, "Reconstituting the Narrative of the Adolescent Mother-Daughter Relationship in Feminist Counseling," *Procedia: Social*

and Behavioral Sciences 79 (2013): 37–43, https://doi.org/10.1016/j.sbspro.2013.05.055; Judy Miller and Janet Surrey, "Mothers and Their Adult Daughters," *Psychology Today*, September 1983, https://www.psychologytoday.com/sites/default/files/attachments/115726/mothers-and-their-adult-daughters.pdf.

14. Margaret A. Zahn et al., "Violent Entries: Strategies in Youth Work Engaging Girls in the Justice System," *Journal of Institutional Child Abuse* 1, no. 1 (2020): 174–88, https://doi.org/10.1080/26855024.2019.1705116.

15. National Crittenton Foundation, *Unintended Consequences: Addressing the Overcriminalization of Girls of Color* (National Crittenton Foundation, 2022), https://nationalcrittenton.org/wp-content/uploads/2022/02/5.31FINAL.Unintended-Consequences-SL.pdf.

16. The encouraging news is that advocates are expanding school programs across the United States dedicated to nurturing conflict resolution skills in small groups of girls. The Girls to Women program at Cincinnati Public Schools (CPS) concentrates on conflict resolution as part of empowering young women, particularly those facing poverty. "Girls face similar challenges everywhere," states Ife Bell, a CPS deputy, while also recognizing that those growing up in poverty may encounter additional, distinct experiences. By integrating elements of the Girls Leadership program with the Sister Accord empowerment curriculum, CPS adopts a nuanced approach that melds gender-specific social and emotional learning with an understanding that experiences can vary across different communities.

17. Joel Garfinkle, an executive coach and author of *Difficult Conversations*, puts it this way: "While it's natural to want to be liked, that's not always the most important thing." Garfinkle says that instead of increasing your likability, focus on respect—giving it and earning it. Given that girls are typically socialized to be agreeable and liked, shifting the norms of engaging in conflict to emphasizing "respect" instead of "likability" is another important tool for renorming conflict.

18. The Centers for Disease Control suggests that strategies for preventing violence at the individual level should include conflict resolution and life skills training, social-emotional learning, and safe dating and healthy relationship skills programs.

CHAPTER 5

1. A well-regarded online educational resource called the "Antiracist 30-Day Challenge" provides you with opportunities to cultivate mindfulness and daily practices centered around equality, justice, and humanity as you integrate, and offer girls the opportunity to integrate, the Antiracist Table Core Principles into your life. Find out more at theantiracisttable.com.

2. US Department of Education, National Center for Education Statistics, "Education Statistics: Facts about American Schools," *Education Week*, January 30, 2019, https://www.edweek.org/leadership/education-statistics-facts-about-american-schools/2019/01.

3. Office for Civil Rights, *Civil Rights Data Collection Snapshot: College and Career Readiness* (United States Department of Education, 2014), http://www2.ed.gov/about/offices/list/ocr/docs/crdc-college-and-career-readiness-snapshot.pdf.

4. National Science Board, *Science and Engineering Indicators 2016* (National Science Foundation, 2016), https://www.nsf.gov/statistics/2016/nsb20161/uploads/1/14/at01-15.pdf.

5. National Women's Law Center and Poverty and Race Research Action Council, *Finishing Last: Girls of Color and School Sports Opportunities* (National Women's Law Center, 2015), http://nwlc.org/wp-content/uploads/2015/08/final_nwlc_ girlsfinishinglast_report.pdf.

6. C. E. Jacobs, *Ready to Lead: Leadership Supports and Barriers for Black and Latinx Girls* (Girls Leadership, 2020), https://cdn.girlsleadership.org/app/uploads/2020/07/GirlsLeadership_ ReadytoLeadReport.pdf

7. Monique W. Morris, *Pushout: The Criminalization of Black Girls in Schools* (New York: The New Press, 2018); R. Epstein, J. Blake, and T. González, *Girlhood Interrupted: The Erasure of Black Girls' Childhood* (Georgetown Law Center on Poverty and Inequality, 2017), https://www.law.georgetown.edu/poverty-inequality-center/wp-content/uploads/sites/14/2017/08/girlhood-interrupted.pdf.

8. R. Epstein, E. Godfrey, T. González, and S. Javdani, *Data Snapshot: 2017–2018 National Data on School Discipline by Race and Gender* (Georgetown Law Center on Poverty and Inequality, 2020), https://genderjusticeandopportunity.georgetown.edu/wp-content/uploads/2020/12/National-Data-on-School-Discipline-by-Race-and-Gender.pdf.

9. Institute for Women's Policy Research, *Analysis of American Community Survey Microdata* (Institute for Women's Policy Research, accessed May 8, 2024), https://statusofwomendata.org/women-of-color/#spotlightpowoc.

10. Seattle Children's Hospital, *The Traumatic Impact of Racism and Discrimination on Young People and How to Talk about It* (Seattle Children's Hospital, accessed May 8, 2024), https://www.seattlechildrens.org/globalassets/documents/clinics/diversity/the-traumatic-impact-of-racism-and-discrimination-on-young-people-and-how-to-talk-about-it.pdf.

11. Management Center, "SMARTIE Goals Worksheet" (Management Center, accessed May 26, 2024), https://www.managementcenter.org/resources/smartie-goals-worksheet.

12. Georgetown Law Center on Gender Justice and Opportunity, "Adultification Bias" (Georgetown Law Center on Gender Justice and Opportunity, accessed June 2, 2024), genderjusticeandopportunity.georgetown.edu/adultification-bias/.

13. K. E. Edwards, "Aspiring Social Justice Ally Identity Development," *NASPA Journal* 43, no. 4 (2006): 39–60.

Chapter 6

1. A. Bandura, *Self-Efficacy: The Exercise of Control* (New York: Freeman, 1997).

2. Sandra K. M. Tsang, Eadaoin K. P. Hui, Bella C. M. Law, "Self-Efficacy as a Positive Youth Development Construct: A Conceptual Review," *The Scientific World Journal* 2012, Article ID 452327, https://doi.org/10.1100/2012/452327.

3. K. Kay and C. Shipman, *The Confidence Code: The Science and Art of Self-Assurance—What Women Should Know* (HarperBusiness, 2014).

4. US Department of Health and Human Services, Office of Disease Prevention and Health Promotion, *Healthy People 2030*, https://health.gov/healthypeople/objectives-and-data/social-determinants-health.

5. Rape Abuse Incest National Network, State Law Database, https://www.rainn.org/types-sexual-violence.

6. Understanding how adverse childhood experiences (ACEs) impact a girl is incredibly important, and the stakes incredibly high. ACEs can portend *long-term* physical, mental, and behavioral health effects. Research also shows that girls face a greater risk of experiencing *more forms* of ACEs, at higher prevalence rates, and that they are more likely to experience mental health disorders as a result of these traumatic incidents. For girls in families with low incomes, the ACEs risk goes up: 62 percent of these children had experienced one or more ACEs. Youth of color are also at particularly high risk of experiencing ACEs: 51 percent of Latinx children and almost 64 percent of Black children had experienced one or more ACEs. Though there is a lack of information on American Indian/Alaskan Native children and ACEs, available data strongly suggests that they are also at increased risk of experiencing ACEs.

Chapter 7

1. Chimamanda Ngozi Adichie, *We Should All Be Feminists* (Fourth Estate, 2014).

2. Peggy Orenstein, *Don't Call Me Princess: Essays on Girls, Women, Sex, and Life* (Harper, 2018).

3. Centers for Disease Control and Prevention, "*Youth Risk Behavior Surveillance Data Summary & Trends Report: 2009–2019* (US Department of Health and Human Services, 2022), https://www.cdc.gov/nchhstp/dear_colleague/2020/dcl-102320-YRBS-2009-2019-report.html.

4. Lauren Leatherby and Rebecca Halleck, "Facebook Knows Instagram Is Toxic for Teen Girls, Company Documents Show," *Wall Street Journal*, September 14, 2021, https://www.wsj.com/articles/facebook-knows-instagram-is-toxic-for-teen-girls-company-documents-show-11631620739.

5. S. Grabe, J. S. Hyde, and S. M. Lindberg, "Body Objectification and Depression in Adolescent Girls: The Role of Gender, Shame, and Rumination," *Psychology of Women Quarterly* 31, no. 2 (2007): 164–75.

6. D. L. Tolman, C. P. Bowman, and B. Fahs, "Sexuality and Embodied Selfhood: Theoretical Considerations and Sexual Health for Adolescent Girls," in *Sexual Development* (Springer, Cham, 2014), 77–94.

7. Jacobs, Hasson, and Bogolub, "Embodied Respect in the Treatment of Adolescent Girls," *Journal of Feminist Family Therapy* 25, no. 1 (2013): 23–40.

8. Bessel A. Van der Kolk, *The Body Keeps the Score: Brain, Mind, and Body in the Healing of Trauma* (New York: Viking, 2014).

9. Daniel J. Siegel, *Brainstorm: The Power and Purpose of the Teenage Brain* (New York: Penguin, 2014).

10. Amy Banks, "Wired to Connect: The Lasting Effects of Relational Health," presented at the Jean Baker Miller Training Institute, Wellesley Centers for Women, Wellesley College, March 2018; Sharon Lamb and Joni Roberts, "An Introduction to the Harvard Model of Human Development," in *Applying the Harvard Model* (Cambridge, MA: Harvard University Press, 2014), 3–18. This chapter discusses the Harvard model, which emphasizes how relationships/connections shape human development, contrasting with limited individualistic models. Deborah Tolman, "Adolescent Girls' Struggles for/with Sexuality: Exploring the Cultural Landscape," in *Sexual Development through the Life Course*, ed. Laura M. Carpenter and John DeLamater (Boston: Springer, 2012), 191–207.

11. In Francis T. Sherman and Annie Black's 2015 report *Gender Injustice*, they write: "Trauma from abusive and unhealthy family and peer relationships, unhealthy and dangerous living conditions, and failed structural support mold girls' development and can push a girl into juvenile justice involvement."

12. Malika Saada Saar et al., *The Sexual Abuse to Prison Pipeline: The Girls' Story* (Human Rights Project for Girls, 2015), https://rights4girls.org/wp-content/uploads/r4g/2015/02/2015_COP_sexual-abuse_layout_web-pdf.pdf.

Notes

13. Barbara Fedders, *Clinic Study on Commercial Sexual Exploitation of Girls in the United States* (University of North Carolina School of Law, 2014).

14. RAINN, "What Is Consent?" accessed May 25, 2024, https://www.rainn.org/articles/what-is-consent.

15. Additional note on disclosure: These conversations can lead to disclosing a history or specific incidence of violence. You need to remind girls that you are a mandatory reporter. If they disclose that someone is/has hurt them, or that they are considering hurting themselves, you are required by law to report this to your local Child Protective Services. Notify girls that if you did need to make a CPS report, you would have a conversation with the girl first and let her guide the process as much as possible—i.e., do they want to make the call, do they want you to make the call, are there family members they'd prefer to stay with, etc.

16. *Sexual Assault Experiences and Perceptions of Community Response to Sexual Assault: A Study of Washington State Women, 2001* (Office of Crimes Victims Advocacy, 2001).

17. Parents and guardians do have choice in the involvement of their student. They must be notified at least one month in advance of planned instruction, must be able to review all CSHE instructional materials, and must be given the opportunity to opt their child out of CSHE instruction. Parents and guardians do not need to review instructional materials to opt their child out of CSHE instruction. However, if parents/guardians wish to opt their child out of HIV/AIDS prevention instruction specifically, they are required by the AIDS Omnibus Act to preview those instructional materials prior to opting their child out of HIV/AIDS prevention instruction. After the 2022–2023 school year, all districts must report annually to the Office of the Superintendent of Public Instruction (OSPI), and OSPI must report annually to the legislature. OSPI has provided extraordinary guidance and resources for implementation for staff and parents.

Chapter 8

1. Jose Sisneros, Catherine Stakeman, Mildred C. Joyner, and Catheryne E. Schmitz, *Critical Multicultural Social Work* (Lyceum, 2008), 81.

2. J. B. Miller, *Toward a New Psychology of Women* (Boston: Beacon Press, 1976).

3. Carol Gilligan, *In a Different Voice* (Cambridge, MA: Harvard University Press, 1982).

4. Michelle Fine and Lois Weis, "Feminist Praxis and the Voices of Adolescent Girls," in *Beyond Silenced Voices: Class, Race, and Gender in*

United States Schools, rev. ed. (Albany: State University of New York Press, 2005), 59–86.

5. Kimberlé Crenshaw, "Demarginalizing the Intersection of Race and Sex: A Black Feminist Critique of Antidiscrimination Doctrine, Feminist Theory and Antiracist Politics," *The University of Chicago Legal Forum* 140 (1989): 139–67, http://philpapers.org/archive/CREDTI.pdf.

6. Maureen Walker and Wendy B. Rosen, eds., *How Connections Heal: Stories from Relational-Cultural Therapy*, illustrated ed. (New York: Guilford Press, 2004); Laura L. Frey, "Relational-Cultural Theory and Anti-Oppression Values in Women's Development: A Qualitative Study of Girls' Perspectives," *International Journal of Smart Education and Urban Society* 5, no. 1 (2021): 1–11.

7. Linda Charmaraman and Amanda M. Richer. "Social Media Reflective of Self or Filtering of Self? Links between Positive Self-Concept and Social Media Engagement among Adolescents," *Cyberpsychology* 13, no. 2 (2019), https://doi.org/10.5817/CP2019-2-2; Lisa Damour, *Untangled: Guiding Teenage Girls through the Seven Transitions into Adulthood* (Ballantine Books, 2016).

8. Claude M. Steele, "A Threat in the Air: How Stereotypes Shape Intellectual Identity and Performance," *American Psychologist* 52, no. 6 (1997): 613–29.

9. Pauline R. Clance and Suzanne A. Imes, "The Imposter Phenomenon in High Achieving Women: Dynamics and Therapeutic Intervention," *Psychotherapy Theory, Research and Practice* 15, no. 3 (1978): 241–47.

10. Kevin Cokley et al., "Impostor Feelings as a Moderator and Mediator of the Relationship between Perceived Discrimination and Mental Health among Racial/Ethnic Minority College Students," *Journal of Counseling Psychology* 64, no. 2 (2017): 141–54.

11. Samarpita Mullangi and Nicola T. Jagsi. "Impostor Phenomenon and Burnout in General Surgery and Surgery Subspecialties in the United States," *Journal of Surgical Education* 76, no. 1 (2019): 99–109.

12. Janis V. Sanchez-Hucles and Donald D. Davis, "The Culturally Responsive Instructor: Examining the Origins of Cultural Differences," *Academia* (2010), https://www.academia.edu/5569962/The_Culturally_Responsive_Instructor_Examining_the_Origins_of_Cultural_Differences.

CHAPTER 9

1. Mikki Kendall, *Hood Feminism* (London, England: Bloomsbury Publishing PLC, 2021).

2. Lisa Delpit, "The Silenced Dialogue: Power and Pedagogy in Educating Other People's Children," *Harvard Educational Review* 58, no. 3 (1988): 280–98, https://doi.org/10.17763/haer.58.3.c43481778r528qw4.

3. Isma'il Küçük Handley, Elizabeth R. Brown, Christy Buchanan, and Diana Mutz, "Speaking While Female: Femininity Norms and Backlash toward Vocal Women," unpublished manuscript, University of Pennsylvania, 2021.

4. Adrienne B. Hancock and Benjamin A. Rubin, "Influence of Communication Partner's Gender on Language," *Journal of Language and Social Psychology* 34, no. 1 (2015): 46–64, https://doi.org/10.1177/0261927X14533197.

5. Richard Wilkinson and Kate Pickett, *The Spirit Level: Why Greater Equality Makes Societies Stronger* (Bloomsbury Press, 2009).

6. Here is a helpful TED talk (by Reshma Saujani) to this point: https://www.ted.com/talks/reshma_saujani_teach_girls_bravery_not_perfection.

CHAPTER 10

1. Ms. Foundation for Women, *The New Girls' Movement: Charting the Path* (New York: Ms. Foundation for Women, 2000).

2. Girl Scouts Research Institute, *Change It Up! What Girls Say about Redefining Leadership* (New York: Girl Scouts of the USA, 2008).

3. Adrienne Brown, *Emergent Strategy* (Edinburgh, Scotland: AK Press, 2017).

4. K. E. Edwards, "Aspiring Social Justice Ally Identity Development," *NASPA Journal* 43, no. 4 (2006), 39–60.

5. Robin J. Ely and Irene Padavic. "What's Really Holding Women Back?" *Harvard Business Review* 98, no. 2 (March–April 2020): 58–67.

6. Crystal L. Hoyt and Susan E. Murphy, "Managing to Clear the Air: Stereotype Threat, Women, and Leadership," *The Leadership Quarterly* 27, no. 3 (2016): 387–99, https://doi.org/10.1016/j.leaqua.2015.11.002.

7. Antoine Cilluffo and Richard Fry, "An Early Look at the 2020 Electorate," Pew Research Center, January 30, 2019, https://www.pewsocialtrends.org/essay/an-early-look-at-the-2020-electorate/; Alec Tyson and Shiva Maniam, "Behind Trump's Victory: Divisions by Race, Gender, Education," Pew Research Center, November 9, 2016, https://www.pewresearch.org/fact-tank/2016/11/09/behind-trumps-victory-divisions-by-race-gender-education/.

8. American Association of University Women, "Women and Girls in STEM" (AAUW, 2023), https://www.aauw.org/resources/respected-partners/.

9. McKinsey and Company, "It's a New Era for Corporate Leaders," May 2, 2022, https://www.mckinsey.com/capabilities/people-and-organizational-performance/our-insights/its-a-new-era-for-corporate-leaders.

10. John Bell, *Understanding Adultism: A Major Obstacle to Developing Positive Youth-Adult Relationships* (YouthBuild USA via Sacramento County Office of Education, March 1995).

11. Adam Fletcher, "Adultism" (Freechild Institute, archived from the original on January 24, 2021).

12. A. Fletcher, *Washington Youth Voice Handbook: The What, Who, Why, Where, When, and How Youth Voice Happens* (Olympia, WA: CommonAction, 2006).

13. Tara N. Brannon, Christina N. Lacayo, and David Wetts, "Girl Power: The Role of Experience and Exposure in Changing Gender Stereotypes and Increasing Ambition among Girls," *Journal of Women, Politics and Policy* 41, no. 3 (2020): 332–56, https://doi.org/10.1080/1554477X.2020.1787030.

14. Kacey Elsesser, "How to Get Girls to Become Leaders," *Forbes*, April 8, 2019, https://www.forbes.com/sites/kelseybrooksolutions/2019/04/08/how-to-get-girls-to-become-leaders/.

15. Eleith N. Powell, Leslie A. Schwindt-Bayer, and Gisela Sin, "Women in Legislative Studies: Improving Gender Equality," *PS: Political Science and Politics* 56, no. 4 (2023): 591–97, https://doi.org/10.1017/S1049096523000306.

Bibliography

Adichie, Chimamanda Ngozi. *We Should All Be Feminists*. New York: Fourth Estate, 2014.

American Association of University Women. *Shortchanging Girls, Shortchanging America*. American Association of University Women, 1991. http://www.aauw.org/files/2013/02/shortchanging-girls-shortchanging-america-executive-summary.pdf.

American Association of University Women. "Women and Girls in STEM." American Association of University Women, 2023. https://www.aauw.org/resources/respected-partners/.

American Psychological Association. *A New Look at Adolescent Girls*. Accessed May 15, 2024. https://www.apa.org/pi/families/resources/adolescent-girls.

AP-NORC Center. "The Hazards of New Technology for Adolescents in a Changing Digital World." Associated Press-NORC Center for Public Affairs Research, 2022. https://apnorc.org/projects/the-hazards-of-new-technology-for-adolescents-in-a-changing-digital-world/.

Arora, Anita, and Lisa Thompson. "Skills for Resolving Adolescents' Conflicts (SRAC)." In *Evidence-Based School Counseling*, edited by Carey Dimmitt et al., 157. New York: Routledge, 2018.

Arora, Anita, et al. "Effects of the SRAC (Students, Resources, and Conflict) Peer Mediation Program on School Conflict Resolution." *Journal of Primary Prevention* 39, no. 6 (2018): 539–51.

Bandura, A. *Self-Efficacy: The Exercise of Control*. New York: Freeman, 1997.

Banks, Amy. "Wired to Connect: The Lasting Effects of Relational Health." Presented at the Jean Baker Miller Training Institute, Wellesley Centers for Women, Wellesley College, March 2018.

Bell, John. *Understanding Adultism: A Major Obstacle to Developing Positive Youth-Adult Relationships*. YouthBuild USA, Sacramento County Office of Education, March 1995. https://www.saclink.com/pdfs/understanding-adultism.pdf.

Bian, Lin, Sarah-Jane Leslie, and Andrei Cimpian. "The Roots of the Leadership Labyrinth: Gender, Culture and the Origins of Leadership Stereotypes." *Developmental Review* 61 (2021): 101010.

Bidwell, Duane, and Donald Batisky. "Analysis of Data from a Diverse Group of Children Suffering from Various End-Stage Illnesses." Claremont School of Theology and Emory University School of Medicine, 2008.

Bibliography

Black, M. C., K. C. Basile, M. J. Breiding, S. G. Smith, M. L. Walters, M. T. Merrick, J. Chen, and M. R. Stevens. *The National Intimate Partner and Sexual Violence Survey: 2010 Summary Report*. National Center for Injury Prevention and Control, Centers for Disease Control and Prevention, 2011.

Brannon, Tara N., Christina N. Lacayo, and David Wetts. "Girl Power: The Role of Experience and Exposure in Changing Gender Stereotypes and Increasing Ambition among Girls." *Journal of Women, Politics and Policy* 41, no. 3 (2020): 332–56. https://doi.org/10.1080/1554477X.2020.1787030.

Brown, Adrienne. *Emergent Strategy*. Edinburgh, Scotland: AK Press, 2017.

Brown, L. M. *Girlfighting: Betrayal and Rejection among Girls*. New York University Press, 2003.

Brown, L. M. *Raising Their Voices: The Politics of Girls' Anger*. Cambridge, MA: Harvard University Press, 1998.

Brown, L. M., and Carol Gilligan. *Meeting at the Crossroads: Women's Psychology and Girls' Development*. Cambridge, MA: Harvard University Press, 1992.

Brown, Lyn Mikel. *The Politics of Girls' Anger*. Cambridge, MA: Harvard Education Press, 2018.

Catalyst. "Women in Science, Technology, Engineering, and Mathematics (STEM)." September 13, 2022. https://www.catalyst.org/research/women-in-science-technology-engineering-and-mathematics-stem/.

Centers for Disease Control and Prevention. "Preventing Child Sexual Abuse." Centers for Disease Control and Prevention, March 20, 2020. https://www.cdc.gov/violenceprevention/childabuseand-neglect/childsexualabuse.html.

Centers for Disease Control and Prevention. "Youth Risk Behavior Surveillance Data Summary and Trends Report: 2009–2019." US Department of Health and Human Services, 2022. https://www.cdc.gov/nchhstp/dear_colleague/2020/dcl-102320-YRBS-2009-2019-report.html.

Centers for Disease Control and Prevention. *Key Substance Use and Mental Health Indicators in the United States: Results from the 2019 National Survey on Drug Use and Health*. Centers for Disease Control and Prevention, 2020. https://www.samhsa.gov/data/sites/default/files/reports/rpt29393/2019NSDUHFFRPDFWHTML/2019NSDUHFFR090120.htm.

Charmaraman, Linda, and Amanda M. Richer. "Social Media Reflective of Self or Filtering of Self? Links between Positive Self-Concept and Social Media Engagement among Adolescents." *Cyberpsychology* 13, no. 2 (2019). https://doi.org/10.5817/CP2019-2-2.

Cilluffo, Antoine, and Richard Fry. "An Early Look at the 2020 Electorate." Pew Research Center, January 30, 2019. https://www.pewresearch.org/fact-tank/2016/11/09/behind-trumps-victory-divisions-by-race-gender-education/.

Clance, Pauline R., and Suzanne A. Imes. "The Imposter Phenomenon in High Achieving Women: Dynamics and Therapeutic Intervention." *Psychotherapy Theory, Research and Practice* 15, no. 3 (1978): 241–47.

Cokley, Kevin, et al. "Impostor Feelings as a Moderator and Mediator of the Relationship between Perceived Discrimination and Mental Health among Racial/Ethnic Minority College Students." *Journal of Counseling Psychology* 64, no. 2 (2017): 141–54.

Coyne, Sarah M., et al. "Associations among Social Media Use, Depressive Symptoms, Psychological Well-Being, and Suicidal Ideation in Young Adults." *JAMA Psychiatry* 77, no. 4 (2020): 420–22. https://doi.org/10.1001/jamapsychiatry.2019.4310.

Crenshaw, Kimberlé. "Demarginalizing the Intersection of Race and Sex: A Black Feminist Critique of Antidiscrimination Doctrine, Feminist Theory and Antiracist Politics." *The University of Chicago Legal Forum* 140 (1989): 139–67. http://philpapers.org/archive/CREDTI.pdf.

Damour, Lisa. *Untangled: Guiding Teenage Girls through the Seven Transitions into Adulthood.* New York: Ballantine Books, 2016.

Debold, Elizabeth, Lyn Mikel Brown, Deborah Tolman, and Christina Schulyer. "Reconstituting the Narrative of the Adolescent Mother-Daughter Relationship in Feminist Counseling." *Procedia: Social and Behavioral Sciences* 79 (2013): 37–43. https://doi.org/10.1016/j.sbspro.2013.05.055.

Debold, E., M. Wilson, and I. Malave. *Mother Daughter Revolution: From Betrayal to Power.* Addison-Wesley, 1993.

Delpit, Lisa. "The Silenced Dialogue: Power and Pedagogy in Educating Other People's Children." *Harvard Educational Review* 58, no. 3 (1988): 280–98. https://doi.org/10.17763/haer.58.3.c43481778r528qw4.

Denner, Jill. "Voices of Adolescent Girls and Leadership: Exploring the Narratives of Latina, Black, and Multiracial Girls." *Journal of Research on Adolescence* 30, no. 1 (2020): 186–203.

Edwards, K. E. "Aspiring Social Justice Ally Identity Development." *NASPA Journal* 43, no. 4 (2006): 39–60.

Elsesser, Kacey. "How to Get Girls to Become Leaders." *Forbes*, April 8, 2019. https://www.forbes.com/sites/kelseybrooksolutions/2019/04/08/how-to-get-girls-to-become-leaders/.

Ely, Robin J., and Irene Padavic. "What's Really Holding Women Back?" *Harvard Business Review* 98, no. 2 (March–April 2020): 58–67.

Epstein, R., J. Blake, and T. González. *Girlhood Interrupted: The Erasure of Black Girls' Childhood.* Georgetown Law Center on Poverty and Inequality, 2017. https://www.law.georgetown.edu/poverty-inequality-center/wp-content/uploads/sites/14/2017/08/girlhood-interrupted.pdf.

Epstein, R., E. Godfrey, T. González, and S. Javdani. *Data Snapshot: 2017–2018 National Data on School Discipline by Race and Gender.* Georgetown Law Center on Poverty and Inequality, 2020.

Fedders, Barbara. "Clinic Study on Commercial Sexual Exploitation of Girls in the United States." University of North Carolina School of Law, 2014.

Bibliography

Federal Bureau of Investigation. "FBI Releases 2020 Hate Crime Statistics." Federal Bureau of Investigation, August 20, 2021. https://www.fbi.gov/news/press-releases/press-releases/fbi-releases-2020-hate-crime-statistics.

Fine, Michelle. "Sexuality, Schooling, and Adolescent Females: The Missing Discourse of Desire." *Harvard Educational Review* 58, no. 1 (1988): 29–53.

Fine, Michelle, and Lois Weis. "Feminist Praxis and the Voices of Adolescent Girls." In *Beyond Silenced Voices: Class, Race, and Gender in United States Schools*, rev. ed., 59–86. Albany: State University of New York Press, 2005.

Fletcher, A. "Washington Youth Voice Handbook: The What, Who, Why, Where, When, and How Youth Voice Happens." Olympia, WA: CommonAction, 2006.

Fletcher, Adam. "Adultism." Freechild Institute. Archived from the original on January 24, 2021. https://web.archive.org/web/20210124171923/https://freechild.org/adultism/.

Frey, Laura L. "Relational-Cultural Theory and Anti-Oppression Values in Women's Development: A Qualitative Study of Girls' Perspectives." *International Journal of Smart Education and Urban Society* 5, no. 1 (2021): 1–11.

Georgetown Law Center on Gender Justice and Opportunity. "Adultification Bias." Georgetown Law Center on Gender Justice and Opportunity. Accessed June 2, 2024. https://genderjusticeandopportunity.georgetown.edu/adultification-bias/.

Girl Scouts Research Institute. *Change It Up! What Girls Say about Redefining Leadership*. New York: Girl Scouts of the USA, 2008.

Gilligan, Carol. *In a Different Voice*. Cambridge, MA: Harvard University Press, 1982.

Grabe, S., J. S. Hyde, and S. M. Lindberg. "Body Objectification and Depression in Adolescent Girls: The Role of Gender, Shame, and Rumination." *Psychology of Women Quarterly* 31, no. 2 (2007): 164–75.

Halim, Rana M., Claire A. Etkin, and Diane N. Ruble. "Girls' Declining Motivation to Pursue Leadership Roles from Age 6 to 10." *Journal of Abnormal Psychology* 131, no. 2 (2022): 197–208.

Hancock, Adrienne B., and Benjamin A. Rubin. "Influence of Communication Partner's Gender on Language." *Journal of Language and Social Psychology* 34, no. 1 (2015): 46–64. https://doi.org/10.1177/0261927X14533197.

Handley, Isma'il Küçük, Elizabeth R. Brown, Christy Buchanan, and Diana Mutz. "Speaking While Female: Femininity Norms and Backlash toward Vocal Women." Unpublished manuscript, University of Pennsylvania, 2021.

Harris, Jessica C., Christina Cheah, and Danielle Boatright. *College Students of Color and Mental Health: An Exploratory Study*. The Steve Fund, 2018. https://www.stevefund.org/wp-content/uploads/2021/03/HARRIS-FINAL.pdf.

Hill, C., and H. Kearl. *Crossing the Line: Sexual Harassment at School*. American Association of University Women, 2011.

Bibliography

Hoyt, Crystal L., and Susan E. Murphy. "Managing to Clear the Air: Stereotype Threat, Women, and Leadership." *The Leadership Quarterly* 27, no. 3 (2016): 387–99. https://doi.org/10.1016/j.leaqua.2015.11.002.

Institute for Women's Policy Research. *Analysis of American Community Survey Microdata*. Institute for Women's Policy Research, accessed May 8, 2024. https://statusofwomendata.org/women-of-color/#spotlightpowoc.

Jacobs, C. E. *Ready to Lead: Leadership Supports and Barriers for Black and Latinx Girls*. Girls Leadership, 2020. https://cdn.girlsleadership.org/app/uploads/2020/07/GirlsLeadership_ReadytoLeadReport.pdf.

Jacobs, Hasson, and Bogolub. "Embodied Respect in the Treatment of Adolescent Girls." *Journal of Feminist Family Therapy* 25, no. 1 (2013): 23–40.

Johns, M. M., R. Lowry, J. Andrzejewski, L. C. Barrios, Z. Demissie, T. McManus, and J. M. Underwood. "Transgender Identity and Experiences of Violence Victimization, Substance Use, Suicide Risk, and Sexual Risk Behaviors among High School Students—19 States and Large Urban School Districts, 2017." *Morbidity and Mortality Weekly Report* 68, no. 3 (2019): 67–71. http://dx.doi.org/10.15585/mmwr.mm6803a3.

Jones, Kenneth, and Tema Okun. *Dismantling Racism: A Workbook for Social Change Groups*. ChangeWork, 2001.

Kann, L. et al., "Youth Risk Behavior Surveillance: United States, 2017." *Morbidity and Mortality Weekly Report Surveillance Summaries* 67, no. 8 (June 15, 2018). https://www.cdc.gov/healthyyouth/data/yrbs/pdf/2017/ss6708.pdf.

Kay, Katty, and Claire Shipman. *The Confidence Code: The Science and Art of Self-Assurance—What Women Should Know*. New York: HarperBusiness, an imprint of HarperCollinsPublishers, 2014.

Kendall, Mikki. *Hood Feminism*. London: Bloomsbury Publishing PLC, 2021.

Kendi, Ibram X. *How to Be an Antiracist*. London: Bodley Head, 2019.

Kerig, Patricia K. "For Better or Worse: Intimate Relationships as Sources of Risk or Resilience for Girls' Delinquency." *Journal of Research on Adolescence* 24, no. 1 (2014): 1–11.

Klencakova, Lucia E., Maria Pentaraki, and Carolyn McManus. "The Impact of Intimate Partner Violence on Young Women's Educational Well-Being: A Systematic Review of Literature." *Trauma, Violence, & Abuse* 24, no. 2 (April 2023): 1172–87. https://doi.org/10.1177/15248380211052244.

Lamb, Sharon, and Joni Roberts. "An Introduction to the Harvard Model of Human Development." In *Applying the Harvard Model*, 3–18. Cambridge, MA: Harvard University Press, 2014.

Leaper, Campbell, et al. "Angels or Angels: Associations of Adolescents' Gender Typicality with Anger and Depression." *Sex Roles* 80, no. 3–4 (2019): 97–112.

Leatherby, Lauren, and Rebecca Halleck. "Facebook Knows Instagram Is Toxic for Teen Girls, Company Documents Show." *Wall Street Journal*, September

14, 2021. https://www.wsj.com/articles/facebook-knows-instagram-is-toxic-for-teen-girls-company-documents-show-11631620739.

Linehan, M. M. "Validation and Psychotherapy." In *Empathy Reconsidered: New Directions in Psychotherapy*, edited by A. Bohart and L. Greenberg, 353–92. American Psychological Association, 1997. https://doi.org/10.1037/10226-016.

Livingston, B. "United States: Hollaback! International Street Harassment Survey." Hollaback!, 2015. https://www.ihollaback.org/cornell-international-survey-on-street-harassment/#us.

Management Center. "SMARTIE Goals Worksheet." Management Center, accessed May 26, 2024. https://www.managementcenter.org/resources/smartie-goals-worksheet.

McKinsey and Company. "It's a New Era for Corporate Leaders." McKinsey and Company, May 2, 2022. https://www.mckinsey.com/capabilities/people-and-organizational-performance/our-insights/its-a-new-era-for-corporate-leaders.

Miller, J. B. *Toward a New Psychology of Women*. Boston: Beacon Press, 1976.

Miller, Judy, and Janet Surrey. "Mothers and Their Adult Daughters." *Psychology Today*, September 1983. https://www.psychologytoday.com/sites/default/files/attachments/115726/mothers-and-their-adult-daughters.pdf.

Monahan, Kathryn C., Julia Dmitrieva, and Elizabeth Cauffman. "Bad Romance: Sex Differences in the Longitudinal Association between Romantic Relationships and Deviant Behavior." *Journal of Research on Adolescence* 24, no. 1 (2014): 12–26.

Moody, James. "Peer Persistence: A Longitudinal Look at Student Integration in a Desegregated High School." In *Desegregating the City: Ghettos, Enclaves, and Inequality*, edited by David P. Varady, 103–28. Albany: State University of New York Press, 2005.

Morris, Monique W. *Pushout: The Criminalization of Black Girls in Schools*. New York: The New Press, 2018.

Ms. Foundation. *The New Girls' Movement: Implications for Youth Programs*. Ms. Foundation, 2001. http://www.cpn.org/topics/families/pdfs/New_Girls_Movement.pdf.

Ms. Foundation for Women. *The New Girls' Movement: Charting the Path*. Collaborative Fund for Healthy Girls/Healthy Women. New York: Ms. Foundation for Women, 2000.

Mullangi, Samarpita, and Nicola T. Jags. "Impostor Phenomenon and Burnout in General Surgery and Surgery Subspecialties in the United States." *Journal of Surgical Education* 76, no. 1 (2019): 99–109.

Muno, Ann. "And Girl Justice for All: Blending Girl-Specific and Youth Development Practices." *Afterschool Matters* 19 (2014): 28–35.

National Conference of State Legislatures. "Women in State Legislatures for 2023." National Conference of State Legislatures, January 5, 2023.

https://www.ncsl.org/legislators-staff/legislators/womens-legislative-network/women-in-state-legislatures-for-2023.aspx.

National Crittenton Foundation. *Beyond ACEs: Study of Student Resilience*. National Crittenton Foundation, accessed May 8, 2024. https://nationalcrittenton.org/portfolio/publications-beyond-ace-2016/.

National Crittenton Foundation. *Unintended Consequences: Addressing the Overcriminalization of Girls of Color*. National Crittenton Foundation, 2022. https://nationalcrittenton.org/wp-content/uploads/2022/02/5.31FINAL.Unintended-Consequences-SL.pdf.

National Sexual Violence Resource Center. "Child Sexual Abuse Prevention Resources." National Sexual Violence Resource Center, accessed May 17, 2024. https://www.nsvrc.org/node/4737.

National Science Board. *Science and Engineering Indicators 2016*. National Science Foundation, 2016. https://www.nsf.gov/statistics/2016/nsb20161/uploads/1/14/at01-15.pdf.

National Women's Law Center and Poverty and Race Research Action Council. *Finishing Last: Girls of Color and School Sports Opportunities*. National Women's Law Center and Poverty and Race Research Action Council, 2015. http://nwlc.org/wp-content/uploads/2015/08/final_nwlc_girlsfinishinglast_report.pdf.

Odgers, Candice L., and Michaeline R. Jensen. "Annual Research Review: Adolescent Mental Health in the Digital Age: Facts, Fears, and Future Directions." *Journal of Child Psychology and Psychiatry* 61, no. 3 (2020): 336–48.

Office for Civil Rights. *Civil Rights Data Collection Snapshot: College and Career Readiness*. United States Department of Education, 2014. http://www2.ed.gov/about/offices/list/ocr/docs/crdc-college-and-career-readiness-snapshot.pdf.

Orenstein, Peggy. *Don't Call Me Princess: Essays on Girls, Women, Sex, and Life*. New York: Harper, 2018.

Orenstein, Peggy. *Schoolgirls: Young Women, Self-Esteem, and the Confidence Gap*. New York: Anchor, 1995.

Pew Research Center. "Teens and Their Experiences on Social Media." Pew Research Center, March 16, 2022. https://www.pewresearch.org/internet/2022/03/16/teens-and-their-experiences-on-social-media/.

Pew Research Center. "Young, Underemployed and Optimistic: Coming of Age, Slowly, in a Tough Economy." February 9, 2012.

Payscale. *The State of the Gender Pay Gap in 2022*. Payscale, accessed May 20, 2024. https://www.payscale.com/data/gender-pay-gap.

Phillips, L. *Speak for Yourself: What Girls Say about What Girls Need*. Girls Best Friend Foundation, 2002.

Pipher, Mary. *Reviving Ophelia: Saving the Selves of Adolescent Girls*. New York: Putnam, 1994.

BIBLIOGRAPHY

Rape Abuse Incest National Network. "Children and Teens." Rape Abuse Incest National Network, accessed May 17, 2024. https://www.rainn.org/children-and-teens.

Rape Abuse Incest National Network. State Law Database. https://www.rainn.org/types-sexual-violence.

Rape Abuse Incest National Network. "What Is Consent?" Rape Abuse Incest National Network, accessed May 25, 2024. https://www.rainn.org/articles/what-is-consent.

Rights4girls. *Sexual Violence among Native Women and Girls.* Rights4girls, 2019. https://rights4girls.org/wp/wp-content/uploads/r4g/2019/05/Native-women-and-girls-fact-sheet-May-2019-1.pdf.

Ruble, Amanda E., et al. "The Role of Gender Constancy in Early Stigmatization of Anger Expression." *Child Development* 89, no. 2 (2018): 372–86.

Rutgers Eagleton Institute of Politics. "Current Numbers." Rutgers Eagleton Institute of Politics, accessed May 20, 2024. https://cawp.rutgers.edu/current-numbers.

Saar, Malika Saada, et al. *The Sexual Abuse to Prison Pipeline: The Girls' Story.* Human Rights Project for Girls, 2015. https://rights4girls.org/wp-content/uploads/r4g/2015/02/2015_COP_sexual-abuse_layout_web-pdf.pdf.

Saujani, Reshma. "Teach Girls Bravery, Not Perfection." TED video, 14:25. April 2016. https://www.ted.com/talks/reshma_saujani_teach_girls_bravery_not_perfection.

Sanchez-Hucles, Janis V., and Donald D. Davis. "The Culturally Responsive Instructor: Examining the Origins of Cultural Differences." *Academia*, 2010. https://www.academia.edu/5569962/The_Culturally_Responsive_Instructor_Examining_the_Origins_of_Cultural_Differences.

Seattle Children's Hospital. *The Traumatic Impact of Racism and Discrimination on Young People and How to Talk about It.* Seattle Children's Hospital, accessed May 8, 2024. https://www.seattlechildrens.org/globalassets/documents/clinics/diversity/the-traumatic-impact-of-racism-and-discrimination-on-young-people-and-how-to-talk-about-it.pdf.

Sherman, Francis T., and Annie Black. *Gender Injustice.* 2015.

Siegel, Daniel J. *Brainstorm: The Power and Purpose of the Teenage Brain.* New York: Penguin, 2014.

Simmons, Rachel. *Odd Girl Out: The Hidden Culture of Aggression in Girls.* Boston: Mariner Books, 2003.

Sisneros, Jose, Catherine Stakeman, Mildred C. Joyner, and Catheryne E. Schmitz. *Critical Multicultural Social Work.* Lyceum, 2008.

Smetana, Judith G., et al. "Adolescent-Parent Conflict in Middle Class African American Families." *Child Development* 67, no. 5 (1996): 2245–65.

Smith, Charles, Amanda C. Akiva, Deborah Lowe Vandell, and Roger Hart. "Introduction to the Youth Program Quality Assessment: History, Development, and Applications." In *Quality in Out-of-School Time: Tools and Techniques for Evaluating and Improving Programs*, edited by Charles Smith and Amanda C. Akiva, 3–18. Charlotte, NC: Information Age Publishing, Inc., 2016.

Smith, S. G., X. Zhang, K. C. Basile, M. T. Merrick, J. Wang, M. Kresnow, and J. Chen. "National Intimate Partner and Sexual Violence Survey: 2015 Data Brief—Updated Release." Centers for Disease Control and Prevention, 2018. https://www.cdc.gov/violenceprevention/pdf/2015data-brief508.pdf.

Steele, Claude M. "A Threat in the Air: How Stereotypes Shape Intellectual Identity and Performance." *American Psychologist* 52, no. 6 (1997): 613–29.

Substance Abuse and Mental Health Services Administration. *Key Substance Use and Mental Health Indicators in the United States: Results from the 2019 National Survey on Drug Use and Health*. Substance Abuse and Mental Health Services Administration, 2020. https://www.samhsa.gov/data/sites/default/files/reports/rpt29393/2019NSDUHFFRPDFWHTML/2019NSDUHFFR090120.htm.

Tanner, Dana Coman. "Navigating the Storms of Conflict at Work." Society for Human Resource Management, April 28, 2014. https://www.shrm.org/resourcesandtools/hr-topics/employee-relations/pages/navigating-storms-conflict-work.aspx.

Tiggemann, Marika, and Mia Zaccardo. "'Instagram Gave Me Orthorexia': The Portrayal of Healthy Eating on Instagram." *British Journal of Education, Society & Behavioural Science* 23, no. 2 (2018): 1–14. https://doi.org/10.9734/BJESBS/2018/39629.

Tolman, D. L. *Dilemmas of Desire: Teenage Girls Talk about Sexuality*. Cambridge, MA: Harvard University Press, 2002.

Tolman, D. L., C. P. Bowman, and B. Fahs. "Sexuality and Embodied Selfhood: Theoretical Considerations and Sexual Health for Adolescent Girls." In *Sexual Development*, 77–94. Boston: Springer, Cham, 2014.

Tolman, Deborah. "Adolescent Girls' Struggles for/with Sexuality: Exploring the Cultural Landscape." In *Sexual Development through the Life Course*, edited by Laura M. Carpenter and John DeLamater, 191–207. Boston: Springer, 2012.

Tolman, Deborah L. "Female Adolescent Sexuality in Relational Contexts: Beyond Sexual Decision Making." In *Beyond Appearance: A New Look at Adolescent Girls*, edited by Norine G. Johnson, Michael C. Roberts, and Judith Worell. Washington, DC: American Psychological Association, 1999.

Tsang, Sandra K. M., Eadaoin K. P. Hui, and Bella C. M. Law. "Self-Efficacy as a Positive Youth Development Construct: A Conceptual Review." *The Scientific World Journal*, vol. 2012, Article ID 452327, 7 pages. https://doi.org/10.1100/2012/452327.

Tyson, Alec, and Shiva Maniam. "Behind Trump's Victory: Divisions by Race, Gender, Education." Pew Research Center, November 9, 2016. https://www.pewresearch.org/fact-tank/2016/11/09/behind-trumps-victory-divisions-by-race-gender-education/.

US Department of Education, National Center for Education Statistics. "Education Statistics: Facts about American Schools." *Education Week*, January 30, 2019. https://www.edweek.org/leadership/education-statistics-facts-about-american-schools/2019/01.

US Department of Education, Office for Civil Rights. *Sexual Violence Data Analysis* (2018). US Department of Education, accessed May 17, 2024. https://www2.ed.gov/about/offices/list/ocr/docs/sexual-violence.pdf.

US Department of Health and Human Services, Office of Disease Prevention and Health Promotion. Healthy People 2030. "Society Determinants of Health" graphic. US Department of Health and Human Services, Office of Disease Prevention and Health Promotion. https://health.gov/healthypeople/objectives-and-data/social-determinants-health.

US Department of Justice. "Sexual Assault." US Department of Justice, accessed May 17, 2024. https://www.justice.gov/archives/ovw/sexual-assault.

US Government Accountability Office. *K–12 Education: Student Population Has Significantly Diversified, But Many Schools Remain Highly Segregated by Race and Ethnicity*. GAO-22-104737, Washington, DC, 2022. https://www.gao.gov/products/gao-22-104737.

Vaillancourt, Tracy, and Dorothy L. Espelage. "Peer Victimization and Relational Aggression: Vulnerable Periods, Processes, and Protective Factors." In *The Development of Relational Aggression*, edited by Sarah M. Coyne and Jamie M. Ostrov, 127–50. New York: Oxford University Press, 2018.

Van der Kolk, Bessel A. *The Body Keeps the Score: Brain, Mind, and Body in the Healing of Trauma*. New York: Viking, 2014.

Walker, Maureen, and Wendy B. Rosen, eds. *How Connections Heal: Stories from Relational-Cultural Therapy*. Illustrated ed. Foreword by Jean Baker Miller. New York: Guilford Press, 2004.

Way, N. "'Can't You See the Courage, the Strength That I Have?' Listening to Urban Adolescent Girls Speak about Their Relationships." *Psychology of Women Quarterly* 19, no. 1 (1995): 107–28.

Wilkinson, Richard, and Kate Pickett. *The Spirit Level: Why Greater Equality Makes Societies Stronger*. New York: Bloomsbury Press, 2009.

Wiseman, Rosalind. *Queen Bees and Wannabes: Helping Your Daughter Survive Cliques, Gossip, Boyfriends, and the New Realities of Girl World*. New York: Harmony, 2009.

Yamagata, Bun, et al. "Female-Specific Intergenerational Transmission Patterns of the Human Corticolimbic Circuitry." *Journal of Neuroscience* 36, no. 4 (2016): 1254–60. https://doi.org/10.1523/JNEUROSCI.4974-14.2016.

Yard, Ellen, et al. "Emergency Visits for Suspected Suicide Attempts among Persons Aged 12–25 Years before and during the COVID-19 Pandemic, United States, January 2019–May 2021." *Morbidity and Mortality Weekly Report* 70, no. 24 (2021): 888–94. https://doi.org/10.15585/mmwr.mm7024e1.

BIBLIOGRAPHY

Yost, Gabriela V., Constantina A. Stover, and Olga Jarrin. "Lost and Found: When Adolescent Girls Lose and Regain Their Confidence and Leadership Ambition." Report, International Girls Study Group, 2017.

Zahn, Margaret A., et al. "Violent Entries: Strategies in Youth Work Engaging Girls in the Justice System." *Journal of Institutional Child Abuse* 1, no. 1 (2020): 174–88. https://doi.org/10.1080/26855024.2019.1705116.

INDEX

AAUW. *See* American Association of University Women
abuse: adverse childhood experiences (ACEs), 111–12; child abuse prevention, 22–25; sexual abuse prevention, 25–28. *See also* trauma; violence
ACES. See adverse childhood experiences
activism: girls' organizing and, 231–32, 243–45; racial justice organizing, 90–92. *See also* advocacy; leadership
Adanech (girls' group participant, daughter), xxiv- xxv, 215–20, 233–36
Adichie, Chimamanda Ngozi, 125
adultification bias, 94
adultism, 17–18, 230–31
adverse childhood experiences, 111–12. *See also* violence
advocacy, 90–92, 117–21,144–45, 174–75, 231–32, 243–45
African Americans, 3, 6, 53, 74, 76–79, 80–84, 90–93, 107–8, 130, 217–20. *See also* Black
African immigrants, 50–56, 153–60, 184–88, 200–203, 215, 215–20, 216–20, 233–236
aggression 23–24
Alexander, Kevin (spouse), 228–30
Alicia (girls' group participant), 48–49, 53–56, 64–66
ally identity development, 96

American Association of University Women, xvii, 222
Amina (girls' group instructor), 50–56, 153–60
Angela (girls' group instructor), 184–94
anger, 46–47, 57–58
Asian Americans, 3, 106–8

Bandura, Albert, 100–101
Banks, Amy, 127
Batisky, Donald, 42
Beijing UN Women's Conference (1995), xvi–xvii, 110–11
Bell, John, 231
Bella (girls' group participant, daughter), xxiv–xxv, 223–26, 234, 236–38
Betelhem (girls' group participant, daughter), xxiv–xxv,184–88, 200–203, 215
Beyoncé, 170
BIPOC. *See* Black, Indigenous, and people of color
Bian, Lin, 223–25
Bidwell, Duane, 42
biracial Americans: biracial, 30–32, 74, 80–84, 102–5, 153, 168–69,184–94; Black and Filipina, 160–63; Black and Japanese, 151–53, 168–69; Black and White, 101–5, 114–17
Black Americans, 3, 6, 53, 74, 76–79, 80–84, 90–93, 107–8, 130, 217–20

INDEX

Black, Indigenous, and people of color, xxviii, xxvi–xxvii, 2–5, 72–75, 144, 180
body autonomy, 126–32. *See also* consent; sexual health education
body image, 4, 126–27, 145–46. *See also* media influence; self-care
Brea (girls' group participant), 53
Brown, Adrienne Mari, 211
Brown, Lyn Mikel, 21–26, 46, 148–49. *See also* conflict; relationships
Brumberg, Joan Jacobs, 142–43
bullying research, 22

Center for American Women in Politics, 239
Centers for Disease Control and Prevention, 217, 219–20
Charmaraman, Linda, 149
choice and consent: comprehensive sex education, 143–45; decision-making, 127–28; media literacy class, 106–9; paper bag fashion show activity, 132–34; policy development, 144; sexual health and education class, 129–32; values class, 102–5. *See also* body autonomy; sexual health education
Chris (girls' group instructor), 76–79
Cisneros, Jose, 148
Clance, Pauline R., 150
Claire (mentor), 35–38
cliques, 23–24
code switching: code switching workshop, 184–88; cultural navigation, 179–82; definition and practice, 182–83; in education, 180; leadership authenticity, 188–90; workplace dynamics, 181–82
Common Ground activity, 27–28
Cole (girls' group instructor), 30–32, 102–5

comprehensive sexual health education (CSHE), 143–45. *See also* sexual health education
confidence, 5–7, 100–101, 209
conflict: conflict skills workshop, 50–54; gender norms and patterns, 45–48; healthy vs. unhealthy, 45–47; impact of developing conflict resolution skills, 47–48; one-on-one conflict skill power building activity, 54–57; PLOW method, 53–54; research on, 21–22; resolution skills, 47–48
Congress on Racial Equity, 80–81, 185
corporate leadership barriers, 6, 211–13, 222
COVID-19 pandemic, mental health impacts of, 3–4
Crenshaw, Kimberlé, 149
criminalization of girls, 94, 121, 129–32

Damour, Lisa, 148
de Beauvoir, Simone, xvi, 166
Debold, Elizabeth, 149
Delores Barr Weaver Policy Center, 174
Delpit, Lisa, 73–75, 180
Delta Gamma Sorority, 165–66
DigiGirlz, 221
Divine Nine, 167
Dominique (girls' group participant), 101–5, 114–17
discrimination: educational impacts, 180–81; institutional racism, 73–75; racial bias, 74–75; workplace barriers, 181–82. *See also* racial dynamics; racism
Dylan (girls' group instructor), 80–84

educational equity: academic achievement gap, 72; cultural

competency training, 174; dropout rate, disproportionality in, 73; gender barriers in STEM, 223–25; LGBTQIA+ protections, 174–75; menstrual equity, 174; racial bias in school discipline, 73, 81–83; racial segregation, 80–83; school pushout of Black girls, 72; sports access for girls of color, 72; systemic barriers, 81–83; women in STEM, 223–25, 240

Edwards, Keith, 96

Eight Powers, definitions and foundations: celebrating identity not image, 147–53; creating healthy culture, 21–26; deciphering the codes of dominant culture, 179–84; developing race consciousness and confronting racism, 71–75; embracing horizontal leadership, 209–15; shifting conflict norms among girls, 45–50; trusting her instincts voicing consent, 125–29; using choice not chance, 99–102

Emily (girls' group participant), 133–34, 140–43

emotional development: anger expression, 46–47, 57–58; conflict management, 47–48; self-care, 214; validation theory, 18. *See also* female adolescent development

empowerment, 13–14. *See also* leadership

erosion of reproductive rights, 6

Espelage, Dorothy, 22

Evison, Jonathan, 173

family dynamics: gender roles, 230; marriage partnerships, 228–30; mother daughter relationships, 62–68; power sharing, 230, 234–35; sibling relationships, 234–39

female adolescent development, theories of, xvii–xviii, 46–47, 58–68; 126–27, 147–50, 210–11

feminism: Hood Feminism, 180; Intersectionality theory, 149; White feminism, xviii

Fine, Michelle, 149

Fletcher, Adam, 231

Florida education policies: book banning, 173–74; "Don't Say Gay" law, 173–74

Gay, Roxane, 100

Girls Advocacy and Impact Network (GAIN), 231–32

Gilligan, Carol, 62–65, 148–49

girl culture: Common Ground exercise, 27–28; community building, 25; definition, 23–26; group dynamics, 27; healthy development, 26–30; healthy girl culture class, 27–30; healthy relationships class, 30–32; media influence, 23; negative impacts of competition, 24; positive changes through, 26; racial dynamics in, 23–24; research on relationships, 25; social toxins in, 25; teaching practices, 25

girls' groups, 27–32

Girlvolution conference, 243–45

Girl Scouts Research Institute, 210–11

Grabe, 126

grief, 36–37

group facilitation, 27–28

Girlvolution conference, 243–45

Hana (girls' group instructor), 30–32

HBCU. *See* historically Black colleges and universities

health education: comprehensive approach, 57, 107–9, 127–28, 142, 143–45; sexual health curriculum,

137–39. *See also* sexual health education
healthy relationships, development and characteristics, 25–26, 31–32
historically Black colleges and universities, 91
hope research, 42
horizontal leadership: defining characteristics, 233–34; family applications, 228–30; historical context, 232; power distribution, 230–32

identity: authenticity vs. code-switching, 181–82; community mapping, 158–60; cultural navigation, 179–82; development theories, 148–50; gender identity and sexual orientation workshop, 160–63; identity and community class, 153–60; intersectionality, 149; LGBTQIA+ youth, 173–75; shame and stereotypes, 150–51
Iman (girls' group facilitator), 216–20
Indigenous girls, 2, 72, 113, 139
Instagram, mental health impacts, 4. *See also* social media
Intersectionality theory, 149
intimate partner violence, 25; academic impacts, 25; adolescent risk factors, 25; mental health effects, 25; research findings, 25. *See also* abuse and trauma
Iranian Americans, 48–49, 53–56, 64–66

Jacobs, 126
Jean (girls' group participant), 151–53, 170–72
Jenna (girls' group instructor), 153, 168–69
Jill (girls' group instructor), 132–34, 141
Jody (girls' group facilitator), 130

Jones, Kenneth, xviii–xix
Justice for Girls Coalition, 94, 277

Kay, Katty, 100–101
Kendall, Mikki, 180
Kendi, Ibram X., xviii
Kobabe, Maia, 173
Kunjufu, Jawanza, 1

Latina/Hispanic Americans, 24–25, 30, 33, 39–42
Lara (girls' group participant), 74, 90–93
leadership: advocacy programs, 231, 188–92; authenticity workshops, 188–94; barriers for women, 226; development in girls, 45–48; diminishing ambitions, 5–6; gender barriers, 226; girls' perspectives, 210–11; power dynamics, 211–12; STEM initiatives for girls, 223–25; styles and types, 210–11; sustainable practices, 227; voice and self-preservation workshops, 215–20. *See also* empowerment; power
Lena (girls' group participant, daughter), xxiv–xxv, 188–93, 203–5
LGBTQIA+/LBQ, xxvii, 3, 22, 51, 144, 172–75
Linehan, Marsha, 18
Long Winter (Ingalls Wilder), 35
Lopez, Shane, 42
Lorde, Audra, 214
Lyon, George Ella, 176
Lynn (girls' group instructor), 120–21, 130–32, 245

Madonna, 165
Magic 8 Ball activity, 104–5
marriage: partnerships, 228–30; power sharing, 230
Maria (girls' group instructor), 106–8

Index

Maya (girls' group instructor), 80–84
media literacy, 23–24, 106–8. *See also* social media
media: body image effects, 145–46; commercials and advertising, 40; gender stereotypes in, 40; magazine portrayals, 40; representation in, 38. *See also* social media
Meg (girls' group instructor), 243–45
mental health, 3–4,10, 22, 46–48,189; COVID-19 impacts, 3–4, 172–75; imposter syndrome, 150; racial disparities, 3; 73–75,104; substance abuse 3, 74, 90–93; suicide rates, 3–4; trauma impacts, 36–42, 66, 92; youth indicators, 15–18, 25. *See also* health; trauma
mentorship, 14–20, 223–25. *See also* power tools for parents/mentors
Mexican American, 24–25, 30, 33, 39–42
Miller, Jean Baker, 148–49
mother-daughter relationships, research on, 62–68. *See also* family dynamics; relationships
Ms. Foundation, 210
Muno, Kim, xii–xv, 245–47

Nat (girls' group instructor), 27–29
National Association of Community and Restorative Justice, 96
Nike Foundation Girl Effect Video, 118–19
neuroplasticity, 127

Okun, Tema, xviii–xix
Orenstein, Peggy; xvii, 126

peer relationships, 22–26, 47–48. *See also* relationships
Pew Research Center, 6, 23
Pickett, Kate, 181

pilgrimage, Via Francigena, 229, 234, 236–37
power: adultism concept, 230–31; creating healthy girl culture, 42–45; distribution in families, 234–39; distribution in organizations, 231–32; Eight Powers framework, 9–10; embracing horizontal leadership activity, 241–42; in abusive relationships, 40–41; in female relationships, 41–42; institutional systems, 79–82; media influence on, 40; personal safety and, 40–41; sharing in marriage, 230; sharing models, 230–32; types (over, under, with), 242; youth voice development, 231. *See also* leadership
power tools for parents/mentors: creating healthy culture, 34–35, 39, 42–44; celebrating identity not image, 163–64, 168, 175–76; developing race consciousness and confronting racism, 84–85, 89–90, 97–98; deciphering the codes of dominant culture tips, 194–96, 199–200, 206–7; embracing horizontal leadership, 226–27, 232–33, 241–42; shifting conflict norms among girls, 57–59, 63, 69–70; trusting her instincts voicing consent, 135–36, 140, 145–46; using choice not chance, 109–10, 113–14, 122–23
Powerful Voices, xvii–xxiii

race consciousness: development activities, 75–79; systemic understanding, 73–75; White privilege awareness, 73
racial awareness: internalized oppression, 38; personal examination of bias, 38;

stereotypes and discrimination, 38. *See also* discrimination
racial dynamics: academic segregation, 23–24; second-generation segregation, 24; social identity formation, 24. *See also* discrimination
racial justice: activism development, 90–92; community agreements activity, 76–79; educational equity research, 80–83; systemic racism power analysis activity, 79–84. *See also* discrimination; power
racial segregation: educational research, 23; second-generation segregation studies, 24; self-segregation patterns, 23–24; social identity formation research, 24
Rae (girls' group participant), 151–53, 168–69
relationships, 25, 30–32, 40–44. *See also* family dynamics; peer relationships
Relational-Cultural Theory, 148–49
Rhea (girls' group participant), 74
Robert Wood Johnson Foundation Interdisciplinary Leadership Program, 232
Rogers, Annie, 149
Rose (girls' group instructor), 160–63
Ruby (girls' group participant), 24–25, 30, 33, 39–42

safety: boundary setting, 40; in relationships, 40–41; personal empowerment and, 40–41
Sandra (girls' group instructor), 76–79
Sara (girls' group participant), 74
Sax, Leonard, 1
school culture: racial segregation, 23–24; self-segregation patterns, 24. *See also* education
School Resource Officers (SROs), 54

self-care, 214, 227
self-efficacy, 100–101
sexual health education: comprehensive approach, 143–45; consent education, 127–32; curriculum development, 137–39; Washington state policy studies, 144–45
Shanda (girls' group instructor), 107–8
Shipman, 100–101
Siegel, Daniel J., 58–62
Simmons, Rachel, 23–24
social media, 23
speaking while female, 181, 212, 217
STEM education: Exploration Day, 223; gender barriers, 223–25; women's participation data, 223–25. *See also* education
stereotype threat, 150
Steele, Claude, 150
systemic racism: educational impact, 80–83; institutional analysis, 79–82; power dynamics, 79–82. *See also* discrimination; racial justice

Tanisha (girls' group facilitator), 217–20
Tasha (girls' group participant), 130
Taylor, Sonya Renee, 219
teaching practices: community norms, 15; critical consciousness, 16; emotional validation, 18–19; healthy girl culture code, 15–16; leadership development, 16–17; microaggressions awareness, 15
teenage brain research, 58–62
Thomas, Jonathan, 173
Tolman, Deborah, 68–72, 126
trauma: adverse childhood experiences (ACEs), 111–12; healing approaches, 126–27; racial impact studies, 73; sexual violence

correlations, 129. *See also* abuse, mental health
trust: building through activities, 27–28; earning versus building, 28; in girl groups, 25; program development of, 25
Ty (girls' group instructor), 50–56, 153–60

undocumented status, educational impact of, 24–25

validation: cultural identity, 19; emotional expression, 18; feelings and choices, 18–19; navigating stereotypes, 19; of experiences, 18
Vaillancourt, Tracy, 22
van der Kolk, Bessel, 126
values development: activities research, 51–52, 103–5; conflict relationship studies, 51–52; one-on-one values exploration visit, 32–34; relationship impact, 32–33; values class, 102–5
violence, 25, 112; bullying, 22–23, 54–55, 65, 72; consent education, 30–35; experiences of intimate partner violence (IPV), 25, 40–41; experiences of sexual violence, 2–3, 30–35, 94, 101, 120, 129–46; LGBTQIA+ youth, 3; prevalence, 2–3, 94, 101, 120, 129; prevention, 30–35, 129–46; school settings, 3, 22–23, 54–55, 65, 72, 103; studies, 2–3, 47, 120, 129
Vivan (girls' group instructor); 27–29

Walker, Maureen, 149
Washington state: CSHE law, 144–45; cultural competency requirements, 174; LGBTQIA+ protections, 175; menstrual equity laws, 174; sexual health policy, 144–45
Way, Niobe, 24–25, 149
White Americans, 27–29, 50–56, 76–79, 120–21, 130–32, 132–34, 140–43, 151–60, 170–72, 188, 193, 203–5, 217–20, 223–26, 234, 236–38, 243–45
White privilege: awareness development, 73; confronting racism, 87–89. *See also* racial justice
White supremacy culture, xviii
Wilder, Laura Ingalls, 35
Wilkinson, Richard, 181
Wilson, Claire (state senator), 145
Wiseman, Rosalind, 23–24
women's movement: Beijing Conference, xvi–xvii; historical context, xvi–xvii

Young Women Empowered (Y-WE), 234–35
Y-Scholars, 235
youth advocacy, 80–83, 174–75, 231–32. *See also* activism; leadership
youth development, 12–13, 16–19

About the Author

Ann Muno's life changed forever when she attended the 1995 UN Women's Conference in Beijing, encountering a global sisterhood of advocates that inspired her life's mission. Returning home, she cofounded an organization dedicated to girl justice and began working to understand approaches that shift the girlhood narrative from powerlessness to power, and from toxic rivalry to the creation of a healthy culture. Now directing Justice for Girls, a statewide policy nonprofit in Seattle, Ann combines her professional expertise with the personal experience of raising four daughters—two biological and two adopted from Ethiopia—to forge a powerful voice for girl-related issues.